STARTING A SUCCESSFUL BUSINESS
IN CANADA KIT

STARTING A SUCCESSFUL BUSINESS IN CANADA KIT

Jack D. James, MBA, LLB

Self-Counsel Press
(a division of)
International Self-Counsel Press Ltd.
Canada   USA

Self-Counsel Press acknowledges the financial support of the Government of Canada through the Canada Book Fund (CBF) for our publishing activities.

Printed in Canada.

First edition: 1973
Tenth edition: 1989; Reprinted: 1990
Eleventh edition: 1991
Twelfth edition: 1992; Reprinted: 1993; 1994 (twice)
Thirteenth edition: 1995; Reprinted: 1996; 1997
Fourteenth edition: 1998; Reprinted: 1998; 1999
Fifteenth edition: 1999; Reprinted: 2000
Sixteenth edition: 2004
Seventeenth edition: 2007
Eighteenth edition: 2010; Reprinted: 2011; 2012

Library and Archives Canada Cataloguing in Publication

James, J. D. (Jack Douglas), 1943–

    Starting a successful business in Canada / Jack D. James. — 18th ed.

 ISBN 978-1-55180-861-1

    1. New business enterprises — Canada. 2. Small business — Canada — Management. 3. New business enterprises — Finance. I. Title.

HD62.7.J34 2009   658.1'10971   C2009-903137-X

Self-Counsel Press
(a division of)
International Self-Counsel Press Ltd.

North Vancouver, BC   Bellingham, WA
Canada   USA

MIX
Paper from
responsible sources
FSC® C004071

CONTENTS

5 FINANCIAL FORECASTING FOR A NEW BUSINESS

SAMPLES

TABLES

PREFACE

So you don't like bosses, rush hour traffic, large, impersonal buildings, and office politics. In other words, you hate the nine-to-five grind and working for anyone other than yourself. You want to be independent.

Excellent. This book is for those of you who sincerely want to be your own bosses. No doubt, you've probably had a dream about running your own business for years. It may only be a fleeting daydream that comes once in a blue moon or when the boss gives you a hard time. Maybe you have it refined to the point where you even know what kind of business you'd like it to be. Yet, somehow you've never dared to take the big jump. Well, maybe you're ready to start. Of course, *anyone* can start. The trick is to make a *success* of it.

This book contains a mixture of success tips and hard factual research to give you that "edge" over the competition. I've seen these techniques used many times, and they really do work! Follow them, and you, too, can be on the road to success.

Some small-business people seem to lack confidence, especially at the beginning of their business endeavours. As a potential entrepreneur, you are not a second-class citizen. Now, more than ever, the country depends on you to create the wealth and jobs needed to carry us through the uncertainty of the future.

Consider this: 98 percent of the businesses in Canada are small businesses with fewer than 100 employees. Small businesses are responsible for one-quarter of the total gross national product (GNP) and employ almost one-half of the working population. Small business is the single most important force in the creation of new jobs, and, consequently, for the future of this country.

Some of the obvious trends driving the growth of small business activity include the number of home-based businesses being established throughout the country, the increased willingness by large companies to "outsource" work to small companies, and the growing number of women who are joining the ranks of entrepreneurs by starting their own businesses.

All this means that small-business people don't have to take a back seat to anyone. The opportunities are there for all of us. This book will increase the chances of capitalizing on these opportunities.

ABOUT TAXES

Throughout this book, I make references to taxes and tax rates. Both federal and provincial taxes on small business have undergone significant changes in recent years, and I suspect more changes are coming with the drive toward harmonized sales taxes. For these reasons, please do not take the tax rates printed in this book as the exact rates you might pay! Check with your accountant, because the rates I describe may be higher than those available when you read this!

ABOUT THE NUMBERS

You will see numbers throughout this book. Numbers in balance sheet samples, numbers in estimates of office running costs, and numbers in break-even estimates. The numbers your business will generate will be different!

If you rent office space, for instance, in downtown Toronto or Vancouver, you will not be paying the $750 a month we show in one example, you will be paying a lot more. In many small towns and suburbs, $750 a month might rent you more office space than you need.

Our samples are just that — samples. They are there to help you understand the topic being discussed; they are not our estimate of what your business numbers will be!

ABOUT THE WORKBOOK

The *Starting a Successful Business in Canada Workbook*, previously sold separately, is now included with this book on a CD-ROM. It complements the information presented in this book, providing questions and worksheets for you to complete. These exercises are intended to reinforce what you have learned. There are no "wrong" answers!

NOTICE TO READERS

1
WHY GO INTO BUSINESS FOR YOURSELF?

Most people, when asked this question, will automatically answer: "To make profits." Well, "profits" sounds nice and rates a pass on any business exam you might take; however, in reality, "profits" is very far from the real reason why people go into business for themselves.

Some simply have to start a business because they can't hold a job anywhere else. Others are driven by some compulsion for power and feel that running a business is the most expedient way of obtaining that power. Still others have such a craving to be independent that they have to be free to make their own decisions in all aspects of their lives, including how they earn their livings. People with inherited money often need something simply to play around with. Some use

their businesses as a way to make them feel more secure or wanted by their employees, suppliers, creditors, or whomever. And the list goes on and on.

As a matter of fact, people who are truly successful at running their own businesses are those who profit from the things they enjoy doing most — because then profits and their ambitions and lifestyles go hand in hand. Work becomes play, or at least it does not become distasteful or boring like a lot of jobs that are available today. In this category are such people as skiing or sailing instructors, pilots, hobbyists who turn their hobbies into businesses, and so on.

"What enjoyment can I possibly get out of selling a hamburger?" you might ask. Well, perhaps there is not much intrinsic value in what you do, but there may be plenty of trade-offs that make the role of an independent business person worthwhile.

A big business is not necessarily a good business. The right size, from my point of view, means that it suits the needs of the people working within the organization. In fact, you can truly be called a successful business person if your business suits your lifestyle — not just if your business is large. I believe this could be true even if the business loses money, although because of the lack of profits you may have a dispute with the traditionalists on this point. But keep this in mind: If you are truly happy doing what you are doing, who can challenge the fact that you are successful?

The only problem with losing money is that over a period of time you will have to cease doing the activity you like so much because, no matter how much you enjoy something, there are certain other basic things you need, such as food and shelter. Therefore, over the long run, for a business to be truly successful, there has to be more money coming in than going out.

The point is, while you may be happy running a certain kind of business, regardless of its profit picture, sooner or later you must pay attention to the bottom line. Running a business for reasons that do not coincide with the financial health of a business will sooner or later lead to disaster. At this point you are far better off to step out of the picture and let someone else run the business. Both you and the business will be happier.

You must plan for success and follow your plan. The old adage "plan your work and work your plan" is even more true today. It is strange how most people spend more time planning

vacations than they do planning to pay for vacations! In other words, they put the cart before the horse. In business, you must have a horse (product, service, or skill) before you worry about the cart (capital, methods).

Furthermore, try to use your own skills and talents. You are a human being with special traits, skills, talents, experience, and life needs. Don't sell yourself short.

I remember a former air force pilot and glider enthusiast who was working in a warehouse. It bored him, and the pay was poor. Finally, he analyzed his situation, quit his job, formed a gliding club, charged reasonable membership fees and instruction rates, and is now rich, happy, and doing what he loves. He even designs and builds personalized gliders — and makes lots of money doing it! Can you see now how doing what you like best can pay off in profits?

Another friend of mine, an ex-naval officer, medically unfit for further service, couldn't forget the sea. Instead of crying in his beer, he bought, on a low-payment plan, a used fishing boat and now runs his own pleasure-fishing charter service. He's happy as his own boss and growing steadily richer. That's what I mean by turning your hobby or first love into a professional business.

Don't let these two stories fool you however. If you are in business for yourself, the hours are long and hard, and you are never really away from responsibility. You will know plenty of disappointments and failures. You must be able to make the final decision because the buck-passing stops at your desk. Failures cannot be explained away. The condition of the business is always there to destroy any illusions you may have.

Because of these problems, many (in fact, most) businesses do not make it. Naturally, the reason for any business failure is bad management. However, this does not really help you to understand why a business fails.

Management covers almost every aspect of human behaviour. Bad management can mean anything from not being honest with yourself to not being able to take a frank look at your strengths and weaknesses, needs and desires.

The most commonly pinpointed problem of a new business is that of undercapitalization. The owner typically overestimates the revenue and underestimates the costs and the length of time needed to get established. The business simply runs out of gas before it reaches the top of the hill and is able to coast, or it meets unexpected detours on the way and never gets back on the road to success.

The undercapitalization may be the result of lack of experience or knowledge, or because of one of the psychological reasons discussed above. All too often, a person with a little money and an idea jumps into a business opportunity only to become a mortality statistic by the end of the first year of operation.

To run a business successfully, you need the following five things:

(a) A product, service, or idea

(b) Some experience and knowledge in the area you are interested

(c) A battle plan or strategy

(d) Capital (money)

(e) A complete and honest assessment of your own character, which shows "you've got what it takes" to succeed

Now that you've got (or are putting together) the first four of these, there's the nagging question of the fifth qualification: Do you have the necessary personal qualities to run your own business? Some characteristics that are essential to business success are the following:

- **Drive:** That is, responsibility, vigour, initiative, persistence, and health. You must do more than dream; you must act. You waste no time blaming others. You take risks (although not wildly so) and can live comfortably with the uncertainties associated with these risks.

- **Thinking ability:** This includes original thinking, creative thinking, critical thinking, and analytical thinking. You are curious and have vision. You are never quite satisfied or content; there's always a better way.

- **Human relations ability:** This is comprised of emotional stability, sociability, cautiousness, consideration, cheerfulness, co-operation, and tact. You are persistent and keep trying. You don't make the same mistake twice but keep on trying until you hit the right combination.

- **Communications ability:** This is a combination of verbal and written communications. You must be persuasive and able to influence bankers to supply money, employees to work harder and better, suppliers to furnish materials at the lowest cost, and customers to buy.

- **Technical knowledge:** This means an all-encompassing knowledge of the business, your product or service, and your market.

Do these characteristics describe you? There are some people who are simply not cut out to be owners or managers of small businesses.

Let's face it: It's easy to say yes to all the above — and in your own mind the assessment is perfectly objective. However, if you plan to start a business, you have to be positive. Believe you are going to be successful and act like it every day you are working with it. A positive mental attitude does wonders for small businesses.

One word of caution, however: Do not let this attitude blind you to potential risks. Always keep one eye looking for potential liabilities and problems — because they *will* happen, and the ultimate success of your business depends on how you handle them.

But you are not alone. Remember, Canada has more than one million small businesses (defined as any firm that is "independently owned and operated").

Small businesses are important to the solution of Canada's unemployment problem. Politicians are finally waking up to the fact that it is the small business that is relatively labour intensive and provides employment opportunity and not the large (often foreign-owned) conglomerate. As a result, public purse strings are loosening up, and tax laws tend to favour small business.

Small businesses are also vitally important to the social health of this country. They contribute to the social fabric of what Canada is today and provide a vehicle for entrepreneurs.

Small-business people are hardworking, dynamic, innovative, progressive risk-takers — all qualities that we, as a country, desire.

2
SETTING YOUR MONEY GOAL AND ATTAINING IT

1. MONEY VERSUS YOUR PERSONAL LIFE

By now you've decided either that you can turn your main interest in life into a profit-making business or that you need to be your own boss — in other words you want to be independent.

To be independent you need to make a certain amount of money. You need to reach your "money goal" as fast as possible.

That approach to making money is the *only* way you can get the money you want to do the things you want to do before you are too old, too tired, and too disillusioned to care.

Let's dispel any misgivings about making money. Making money is not a mysterious, awesome secret meant only for a chosen few. Far

from it. Actually, making money is just about the easiest thing to do in this world — provided you have a money goal, skills, knowledge, and the drive to get what you want out of life.

Simple formula, isn't it? It is somewhat harder to put into practice, however, for in order to reach your money goal, you must have motivation, know-how, and a workable money plan with a time limit.

There are many interpretations of "need." People need houses, food, clothing, cars, vacations, love affairs, paintings, music, and books. For you, the big need is money: a certain amount of money within a certain period of time — in other words, *as soon as possible*.

You are no exception to the rule. You need all the things that most people need. All the ordinary needs mentioned are vital to everyday living, but to get them you need money.

"But," you argue, "some successful business people are millionaires many times over, yet seem to devote 24 hours a day to work. Really, they cannot enjoy that kind of grind day in and day out — or can they?"

The truth is, of course, that they truly do enjoy their work and the money is strictly a way of keeping score. (That's what can happen when you work at something you like.)

Now, perhaps this way of living is not to your liking; there is no doubt that people like this sacrifice other things in life, such as their family and friends. But no one is asking you to spend 24 hours a day at the job — and you don't have to in order to become successful. Almost anyone can start a business and run it with modest success, provided the business does not over-tax his or her abilities.

To fulfill your personal needs, you should make sure that you take care of all your life's responsibilities and yet leave enough creative energy to reach your financial goal. In other words, break life's needs down and handle them in order of their importance.

You should allot a sensible portion of the day to your leisure, as relaxation ultimately helps you to work harder. Also, you should be sure to get enough sleep; otherwise, you'll be too tired to work. Without good health, you can't do anything. Furthermore, you do have your family to think about. Don't neglect them.

I am sure you know or have heard of some very rich business people who devote their whole lives to making money and are millionaires because of it but have no home or family life. To me, the very reason for being in business is so that you have the time and money to enjoy the people and things you love.

2. ATTAINING YOUR FINANCIAL GOAL

You should write down the financial goal (say, per month) that you would like to attain at the end of a five-year period when your business is firmly established and you can afford to relax a bit. (Don't forget to make allowances for inflation.)

Next, list the amounts of money that you need just to get by. Be ruthless in listing only those things that are unavoidable expenses. After that, go through the list and see which of those you can cut without causing undue hardship. For example, suppose your car costs $600 a month for gas, maintenance, and insurance. Do you need such a big car? Do you fill up at discount stations? Can you do some of your own repairs? If not, do you have a mechanical friend who could do the repairs in exchange for something you can do?

Here is another example. You own a house and are paying off a rather large mortgage. Do you know that, by using part of the house for business purposes, you can write off part of those mortgage payments, not to mention part of the taxes, maintenance, and utilities payments?

Trivial you say? Not so. If you are paying off a mortgage now costing, say, $600 per month (most of which is interest) plus taxes, maintenance, and utilities of another $300 per month, for a total of $900, you actually need to earn about $1,400 at today's tax rates to pay that $900 mortgage and maintenance payment every month. By using, say, one-third of the house for business purposes, for storage, or for an office, you can write off approximately $300 per month, which saves you $100 per month in taxes. That's $1,200 per year — almost enough for a vacation (see Chapter 14 for details).

These are only a couple of examples. You would be amazed at the savings that can result from a little critical analysis of your spending habits.

"But," you say, "I'm not going into business to scrimp and save." That's not the point. The purpose of this whole exercise is to determine for yourself what you need to live on while establishing your business.

By doing this and adding on your other business costs — goods, advertising, other people's wages, rent, etc. — you can easily determine your break-even point or, in simpler terms, what you need to sell on a month-by-month basis to make it. And, don't forget, even if you are forced to spend less (temporarily), you have attained something that is priceless in the exchange: personal independence.

This is what we've established so far:

- You have a desire to do certain things.

- You have an idea about how to use that desire to make money.

- You know that your special skills and ability must be used professionally to get that money.

- You know that you need a certain amount of money to get by (while building your business).

- You know definitely that you will never get that amount of money by working for someone else; so, you will start your own one-person business in order to get that money.

Now, make a move. Get into action. Take the first steps right away.

A great number of people never succeed in becoming independent simply because they are afraid of failure. Some people, strange to say, are even afraid of success. Two-thirds of the things that people fear will happen can never happen.

So start now to be your own boss and make your own decisions. Put your money goal plan into action and start your own money-making business today!

3
WHAT KIND OF BUSINESS IS BEST FOR YOU?

Earlier, I mentioned that you should analyze your skills and experience to decide what type of business to go into. If that didn't give you any clear direction, don't be discouraged. There are literally thousands of very successful businesses in this country that require only a basic education and just good common sense to operate.

Obviously, you've got to be interested in whatever business you choose or you're not going to enjoy operating it. Those skills that you've developed over the years are more than likely the things you've enjoyed doing.

Most mechanics that I have met have always loved tinkering with cars from the time they first learned what a wrench was. The main thing to remember is that you are going to eat, sleep, and breathe this business. So, pick something you like.

Look at your hobbies. I've personally known several avid photography fans who have turned what was once a hobby into thriving photography businesses. Does anyone know a stamp dealer who didn't start out as a stamp collector? How many sporting goods shops are operated by someone who hasn't been a sports enthusiast since childhood?

Suppose you spent several years in the navy and you were born in Newfoundland or Nova Scotia. You might want to own and operate a boat rental marina. So, how would you assess your skills and interests? Well, living on an island, you spend a great part of your life on the water. You love the sea. You've built boats and you know a lot about engines. You've done boat repairs. You've successfully completed courses in seamanship and pilotage. Sounds like you're an expert sailor.

But what do you know about renting boats profitably? How would you get the boats to rent? Build them yourself or buy them? How are you going to finance your business? Where will you operate from? Shouldn't a boat rental business be near the sea or a large lake?

Too many questions? Just six questions so far. Let's hear your answers. You've worked for a boat rental firm. You'll buy boats (easier than building them yourself). You'll finance yourself by renting money from your local bank (see Chapter 6 for tips). You can lease a small chunk of land on a river that leads down to the sea or a lake.

Great. You are headed for success. You already own a boat? Better still. You can start renting it right away, can't you? And, you once worked as an insurance agent, so you know all about business insurance and how to protect yourself from breakage, theft, and depreciation. Terrific!

It looks as though your chances for immediate success are higher than most. So get started. Rent the boat you now have by placing a small classified advertisement in your local newspaper. Here's an example:

FOR RENT

19-ft. clinker-built runabout with 45-horse outboard, trailer included. Hourly, daily, and weekly rates. Phone ...

Warning: Before you rent your boat, make sure you are covered by insurance, and find out what you should charge by telephoning several commercial boat rental outfits. Keep your prices competitive, and you'll be pleasantly surprised.

Now, with a little money coming in from renting one boat, buy another boat on the time-payment plan and rent it. Then, when you are ready, rent out motors separately. A lot of people own boats but they don't have motors. Outboard motor rentals can be very profitable.

Get the picture now? Start small, have a growth plan, and keep to it.

Now let's take another look at your position:

- You own two boats and are making money renting them.

- You have several outboard motors of different sizes and you're renting them at a profit.

You have had inquiries about sailboats. What should you do? Hunt around for a good used sailboat that you can buy at a price you can afford. Buy or lease it, with option to buy, and rent it out the same way you rent out powerboats.

Let's size up how things stand now:

- You have two powerboats rented out almost all the time.

- You also have one sailboat that you rent regularly at a profit.

- You rent outboard motors separately.

Wait a minute. Aren't you missing out on another way to make money? You're an experienced sailor. You have papers to prove it. If ten people came to rent your sailboat, how many would you have to turn down because they didn't know a sailboat from a workhorse? Three? That means that at least 30 percent of the people who want to rent your sailboat cannot because they don't know how to sail it. Why don't you show them how to sail successfully? With your experience as a sailor, teaching sailing buffs how to sail should be easy — and profitable.

Again, getting started is a simple affair. Look in the Yellow Pages and hunt up the outfits that offer sailing and boating instruction. Get their prices (again, be competitive) and run a small classified advertisement, something like this:

WANT TO SAIL?

Professional sailor now accepting students in all phases of sailing. Boat and instruction at reasonable rates. Phone ...

See how every little bit helps?

Let's have a look and see how close you are to realizing your dream of owning your own business:

- You own and rent powerboats.
- You own and rent outboard motors.
- You own and rent a sailboat.
- You teach people how to sail.

Looks better all the time! How are you doing financially? Take a look at the facts and figures. The first week you netted a low $108 after expenses. The second week you made $140 after paying your bills; and the third week you cleared $164. Let's peek at the following weeks' profits:

Week 4	$260.00
Week 5	$332.00
Week 6	$390.20
Week 7	$439.80

It tells you, in no uncertain terms, that you are making more and more money each week. In other words, your business is starting to make money.

Should you dash to the bank now and scrounge money to buy more boats? No. Be careful. Look back over the past seven weeks. Where did most of your money come from? From renting boats and motors? Exactly. So, you see there's money in renting.

But, what did you do while your boats and motors were out on rental — sit and wait for the boats to come back home? Well, why sit and wait while your knowledge and skill with outboard motors remain idle?

There are thousands of outboard motors lying around, not in use because something went wrong and the owners don't have a clue about how to repair them or the money to pay to have them repaired. What does this suggest to you?

- You can repair outboard motors.
- You can buy used outboard motors, repair them yourself, and then rent them out at a profit.

Let's examine each idea in turn and see how you can develop it into a profit-making part of your new business.

First, pleasure boating is on the increase and sales of outboard motors are growing steadily. Each year there will be more motors needing repairs. You are an old hand at repairing motors. Why let your talent go to waste?

Repairing motors fits in with your business, anyway. So, again, you go to the Yellow Pages and get repair prices. Again you stay competitive. Now you run another small classified advertisement, like this one:

OUTBOARD MOTOR REPAIRS

Fast, expert service at reasonable rates. Jo's Boat Rentals, 191 Seaside Street. Phone ...

You have to repair your own motors. Why not make something extra fixing other motors? It will keep you busy while your rental boats are at sea. It will also advertise your business.

Second, you are already in the business of renting outboard motors and your business is growing. Naturally you want to increase your inventory of motors to make your rental profits grow.

Why buy brand new motors and lose money on depreciation and insurance costs? You'll be much further ahead financially if you purchase used motors, put them in perfect working condition, rent them out profitably, and, when you think they are almost on their last legs (or, in this case, propellers), sell them off cheaply and buy more used ones. Get the picture? A penny saved is a penny earned.

All right. You're on your way. Things are picking up. Give yourself a year or so and you'll be really successful, *provided you keep your fixed overhead down and your profits up.*

Let me point out now that it is your business, your dream, and your future. Do everything you possibly can yourself before you hire anyone, even part time.

The more you do yourself, the more you'll know about your business, and the more money you'll make. The old adage, "If you want something done right — do it yourself" is truer today than it ever was before!

One more thing: The most vital and important asset you have going for you is time. Use it well. Think business; eat business; sleep business. In other words, develop a one-track mind — always keep your financial goal in mind and work to achieve that goal!

4
HOW TO GET STARTED

At this point we have to back up a bit. After deciding what business you are getting into and what your short- and long-term financial goals are, you need to develop a plan of action to get yourself properly set up and operating. Now you need the answers to the following questions:

(a) What type of business structure should I choose?

(b) What licences or permits do I need?

(c) How much financing do I need and where do I get it? (This subject is so big and important that it takes an entire chapter — Chapter 6.)

1. WHAT TYPE OF BUSINESS STRUCTURE SHOULD YOU CHOOSE?

Businesses operating in Canada use one of the following forms of organization: proprietorship, partnership, or corporation.

1.1 A proprietorship

The simplest form of business organization is a proprietorship, which usually involves one person. It is the simplest form because, to get started, all you really need is a business licence and something to sell.

A sole proprietorship can be operated legally under the individual's name, even without registration, although registration protects the name of the business to a limited extent.

If you choose this form of organization, your personal assets and the assets of the business are commingled. Unsatisfied personal creditors can attach business assets and business creditors may look to your personal assets if you can't pay your business debts. If an employee of your business, acting in an official capacity, commits a tort (a civil wrong) against a customer, your personal fortune is jeopardized.

Also, in a proprietorship, the earnings of your business are the personal earnings of the owner. It does not matter what form these earnings take (cash, capital equipment, inventory, or accounts receivable). You pay income tax on the business's profits, regardless, at your personal tax rate. If your profits go into a new building with fancy equipment, you must pay the taxes in cash, even if you have to borrow to do so.

If you, the proprietor, die, your business dies with you and it has to be liquidated to pay capital gains taxes or to settle the claims of your creditors and heirs.

Your business is most likely to be a sole proprietorship if it is new. Tax consequences are not important when earnings are low, and the threat of personal liability is not felt very strongly anyway when all your assets are mortgaged to start the business.

Also, starting as a proprietor does have one important tax advantage, especially if you or your spouse are still working and bringing in outside income. If you operate a limited company instead of a proprietorship, any losses incurred can only be offset against future earnings of the company.

This ability to offset losses against outside income is a decided advantage to staying small. Don't forget that if your spouse is the one earning the income from another job, you will have to form a partnership in order to take advantage of this.

When the business grows and matures and you acquire assets and start your financial portfolio, you will probably take a closer look at the advantages of incorporating.

1.2 A partnership

A partnership is an intermediate form of business organization, more complex than an individual proprietorship but less complex than a limited company. It is governed by the *Partnership Act* of each province.

A partnership is an agreement between two or more parties to conduct a business for profit. Each partner shares in the revenues or losses to the extent that is stated in the agreement. Partners are taxed on all the earnings of the company in proportion to their share in the company. To that extent, it is similar to the proprietorship.

In a partnership, responsibility for all aspects of the business is borne jointly and severally by the partners regardless of the capital contribution of the individual partners. This means that each partner can be held responsible for all liabilities incurred by the business regardless of each member's investment.

There is a special type of partnership referred to as a "limited partnership" in which there may be one or more general partners and one or more special partners. The title "limited partner" means that the partner cannot act on behalf of the company or be held responsible for the liabilities incurred by the company beyond the extent of the investment. Limited partnerships are very specialized and not used very often in small businesses. Their main purpose, because of tax advantages, is to finance real estate syndications.

Registration of a limited partnership is required. A certificate of partnership must be filed with the appropriate provincial government department (the same office that handles registration of companies) and a notice published in the *Canada Gazette*, the official publication of the provincial government.

Legally, there is no difference between a proprietorship and a partnership except that in a partnership you have other people with whom to share the liability.

Both these forms of doing business share the common problem of "unlimited" liability. This simply means that if the business fails, your creditors and other claimants can seize your personal assets if the assets of the business are not enough to cover their claims (and they usually aren't).

In a partnership, the creditor can claim against one or all of the partners. (In other words, all partners are jointly and severally liable.) However, if one partner ends up paying more than the others, he or she has a right to claim compensation from the others, provided the partners are equal. However, this is not too effective if all your partners are broke.

A common way of protecting yourself against this kind of risk is to purchase insurance or to transfer all personal assets to someone else, such as your spouse, although this also carries with it some risks because if the marriage breaks up, you cannot claim these assets back.

Another serious disadvantage of the ordinary partnership is that the actions of one partner in

the course of business binds all the others, no matter what the consequences of those actions are. As you can see, partnerships require the ultimate in faith and confidence.

1.2a Saying goodbye to your business partner (exit clause)

If you have or are considering acquiring a business partner, you already know the advantages. Not only do you infuse your business with new cash, new skills, and new business contacts, but you have someone to share in the decision making and brainstorming.

Despite these advantages, business partnerships have a higher failure rate than any other business structure. Some partnerships are designed to last for a set time. Others appear to have been mistakes from the very beginning. When the time comes to say goodbye, many such partnerships end with an animosity matching that found in the most acrimonious of divorces.

The best time to plan for a partnership breakup is in the beginning of your arrangement — before tensions have started to build. By including an exit clause in your partnership contract, you will ensure that the transition will be smoother if and when the time comes. More importantly, partners will be more flexible defining processes at a time when the discussion is theoretical than later on when both are striving to optimize their own ends.

With an exit clause, you will have a clearly defined procedure for winding down your partnership activities. Since a good exit clause will clearly define the rights and responsibilities of each partner at the time of breakup, the path has been smoothed. Moreover, everyone involved understands the consequence of ending the partnership arrangement. There should be no unpleasant surprises.

Naturally, you will want to consult with legal counsel before drawing up an exit clause or any other legally binding agreement. The tips that follow are to be viewed as general guidelines only.

A good exit clause should address a number of issues. First on the list is the matter of business assets and how those assets will be distributed at the dissolution of the partnership. Specify what will be done regarding capital assets, equipment, real estate, client lists, and investments. Don't forget to include goodwill. Although goodwill is an intangible asset and sometimes difficult to measure, it is worth a great deal and should be addressed.

Another issue: Does your business have employees? What arrangement will you make for these people at the end of the partnership?

Is there a restriction on the departing partner hiring personnel from the partnership?

Consider also how warranties, guarantees, and product liabilities will be handled after the partnership is dissolved.

If applicable, include statements around non-disclosure of trade secrets, non-competition, copyrights and patents, and division of future profits.

Many exit clauses include rights of first refusal and shotgun clauses. With these clauses in place, a departing partner can invite the other partner(s) to either buy his/her share of the business or to sell their shares to the dissatisfied partner. Shotgun clauses are usually used as a last resort when relationships have deteriorated seriously.

One last thought: Does your partnership agreement include a conflict resolution clause?

It's not part of the exit clause, but rather a format for resolving conflict throughout the life of the partnership. Who knows? If an ounce of prevention is worth a pound of cure, perhaps good conflict resolution procedures will pave the way for improved relationships and minimize the tensions that often lead to a partnership breakup.

1.3 A corporation

A third vehicle to consider as a way of doing business is the limited company or corporation. There are several advantages and a few disadvantages to incorporating.

1.3a Limited liability

The limited company constitutes a legal entity and is distinct and separate from its shareholders, officers, and directors. This means that no member of a company is personally liable for the debts, obligations, or acts of the company over and above the amount paid or owed for the purchase of shares.

EXAMPLE 1:

John Slip and Jack Shod carry on business as a partnership known as Slipshod Industries.

Slipshod Industries incurs debts of $25,000, while the assets of Slipshod Industries are only $10,000.

If a creditor successfully petitions Slipshod Industries into bankruptcy or simply obtains a judgment against Slipshod Industries, all the assets of John Slip and Jack Shod (as individuals), including their homes and cars, may be executed against to repay the $15,000 debt incurred by the partnership over and above its assets.

EXAMPLE 2:

John Slip and Jean Shod carry on business as a corporation known as Slipshod Industries Limited, with John Slip and Jean Shod being the only shareholders, each having purchased one share at $1 (although any number of shares can be purchased).

Slipshod Industries Limited incurs debts of $25,000, while the assets of Slipshod Industries Limited have a market value of $10,000.

If a creditor successfully petitions Slipshod Industries Limited into bankruptcy, he or she can realize $10,000 on the assets of the company, but has no rights against John and Jean as individuals, regardless of the amount of assets that John and Jean may own outside the company. The creditor is a creditor of the company, not of John and Jean.

In most cases, a bank requires the major shareholder to personally guarantee, sign, and co-sign loans, but trade creditors are not usually so particular.

1.3b The potential of a greater available source of capital

In the case of corporations, it is possible for people to invest money without having to accept any responsibility for the actual running of the company.

Therefore, it is easier to find people to invest in companies than in other forms of enterprises. In fact, legal history tells us that this was the reason these fictitious, legal "persons" were created in the first place. Apparently, British merchants in the 1800s developed the concept of the corporation in their quest for ways of raising capital.

A corporation, as opposed to a partnership or proprietorship, can issue a "floating" charge or debenture, that allows the bank to take security on inventory, work in progress, and raw material, which constantly changes.

1.3c Ease of transferability of ownership

Shares may be transferred without disturbing the management of the business.

1.3d Perpetual existence

Because the company is a separate entity, it does not cease to exist with the death of a shareholder.

1.3e Tax benefits

There is greater flexibility and benefits concerning taxation, particularly when a Canadian-controlled, active small business is concerned. These advantages are discussed in detail in Chapter 14.

1.3f Incorporation procedures

As a business person starting out with your own company, you may or may not wish to incorporate. That is up to you. However, at least you now have some basic knowledge to help you make the right decisions.

If you decide to incorporate your company you have two alternatives. If your business activity will be confined to one province, then you need to incorporate only as a provincial company. Should your business plans include expansion of your company markets to other provinces, you may be required to register in each additional province as an extra-provincial company or you may opt for registration as a federally incorporated company.

Note: The way in which businesses are incorporated in Canada has changed dramatically in recent years. The process has been simplified and now involves filling in forms online, instead of filing lots of paper. When you consider a lawyer's fee for incorporating (which can easily exceed $1,000) is not even tax deductible (making the actual cost much higher), it pays to reduce your expenses in this area to the bare minimum. A less expensive option is to employ a service company to do the online filing for you, but this will still cost you hundreds of dollars in non-deductible expenses. The least costly option is to do it yourself and save a considerable amount of money. The *Resources* section of the CD enclosed with this kit provides a link to free information on the Self-Counsel Press website to help you incorporate your company yourself.

A company may be organized either as a "private" or a "public" company. A public company is generally one that has any of its securities listed for trading on any stock exchange. The requirements for operating a public company are much more stringent than those for a private one. Almost everyone reading this book would be interested in the private corporation, which is designed to suit the needs of the small business person.

To incorporate your business as a federal company, you must comply with the *Canada Corporations Act*, the statute applying to companies incorporated under federal law. The administering body is the Federal Incorporations Branch of Industry Canada in Ottawa, but its regional offices can accept applications and assist with name searches.

Most people want to incorporate federally because they think it will protect their trade name. For example, suppose you have a hot new franchise idea for the fast food industry and you want to protect the name "Duffy's Donuts." You might then go to your lawyer and ask to be incorporated federally. However, this does not protect your name. The only name protection a company registration gives you (federally or provincially) is that it prevents someone else from incorporating under that name.

Legal protection in the marketplace is only possible if you are the first person doing business under "Duffy's Donuts" or if you register your name and trademark under the *Trademarks Act* in Ottawa.

In the first situation, your only recourse is to sue the offender under what is called a "passing off" action. To be successful, you have to show an actual loss of trade or damages. This can be complicated, expensive, and impossible to prove if you are not actually doing business in a particular area.

Therefore, incorporating a federal company under "Duffy's Donuts" will not prevent someone else from doing business under that name unless you can show you actually started doing business in that area first.

Also, if you opened an outlet in Hamilton, Ontario, that would not be sufficient to stop someone else from opening in Swift Current, Saskatchewan.

If you have a unique name and/or logo, the only way to protect it is to register under the *Trademarks Act*. Registration under this act gives you the right to sue any infringer regardless of whether or not you can show any damages. The

Act also allows for "cease and desist" orders so that you can effectively stop the infringing party from continuing to use the name.

If your company is already incorporated in one province and you wish to do business in another, you must register with the Corporate or Companies office as an extra-provincial company. An extra-provincial company, which would include a company incorporated under the *Canada Corporations Act*, must (with certain exceptions) be registered within 30 days after that business has begun operating in a province. All extra-provincial companies must comply with provincial legislation regarding licences and taxes, so you should contact the Companies office in each province in which you plan to do business.

A "foreign" (i.e., out-of-province) company may locate in any province simply by making application for registration as an extra-provincial company. When you send in the application, you must also file a certified copy of the company's incorporation document and a certificate of status from the jurisdiction in which the company was originally incorporated.

If you are not a Canadian citizen or permanent resident, or if you have a non-Canadian company, you may come under the jurisdiction of the *Investment Canada Act*. (See section 5. for more detailed information.)

You may wish to transfer certain personal assets into your incorporated company in exchange for cash or a promissory note. You may transfer cars, trucks, and other assets to the company's inventory of assets within one month of incorporation without paying provincial sales tax.

However, there is no substantial tax advantage in doing so because, while the company is allowed to deduct depreciation, you are allowed to charge your company a fee for the use of any

vehicle if you retain personal ownership, and this includes the cost of depreciation, so the net result is the same. Also, the transfer of vehicles may trigger provincial taxes.

Again, I must stress that proper professional advice is vital to the proper structuring of your business procedures.

To summarize, there are three main legal forms an organization can take. These forms and their individual characteristics are outlined briefly below for quick reference. Please note that most of the points raised on taxes are explained fully in Chapter 14.

SOLE PROPRIETORSHIPS

Characteristics

- Unincorporated.
- Owned by one person.

Advantages

- You avoid the costs of incorporation, filing of reports, added professional fees, etc., which a corporate entity requires.

- You have a lower rate of taxation than the lowest corporate rate where the income of the entity is very low.

- You can offset business losses against your other income. There are exceptions to this rule. Check with your accountant.

Disadvantages

- You are personally liable for all debts. Creditors have a legal claim against your personal assets.

- You may have higher taxes where the income results in a tax rate higher than the fixed corporate rates.

- You may not be eligible for government loans or guarantee programs, many of which are limited to incorporated companies.

- You may have difficulty should you decide to sell your business. Sole proprietorships are often perceived as short-term rather than long-term business ventures and can lack market credibility.

- You are limited in the forms of employee compensation plans that you can make available, such as deferred profit sharing, group term insurance, and stock option plans.

PARTNERSHIPS
Characteristics

- Unincorporated.

- Owned by two or more people.

- The acts of one partner in the course of the management of business are binding on the other partners.

Advantages

- It may be the only legal form available (e.g., for professionals).

- Income earned by the partnership retains its nature (e.g., interest, rent, dividends) and flows directly to the partners. Each partner declares the income personally.

- You may draw up a partnership to meet the specific needs and wishes of the partners.

- Your spouse, in certain circumstances, can be a bona fide business partner and share in the income or losses of the business.

Disadvantages

- You may have a lack of flexibility in gearing business deductions to suit individual tax planning requirements.

- Unlimited liability for general partners for debts of the partnership.

- Rules to determine the adjusted cost base of a partnership interest are complex.

- Accounting for partnership changes can be cumbersome.

- The partnership dissolves upon the death or withdrawal of any partner or upon the acceptance of a new partner.

CORPORATION
Characteristics

- Incorporated in most provinces by Memorandum of Association or Articles of Incorporation.

- Exists as a separate legal entity.

- Shareholders are liable only to the extent of their investment and the callable shares they hold in the corporation.

- Has perpetual existence.

- Has virtually no limit to the number of shareholders.

Advantages

- The shareholders are not personally liable for the corporation's debts unless they have signed a personal guarantee.

- Often advantageous tax considerations such as availability of small-business tax rates for Canadian-controlled private corporations. The small business deduction has been lowered from over 21 percent to 11 percent (tax year 2008) and applied to a larger amount of net income ($500,000 versus just $200,000 a few years ago).

- The corporate structure provides a better vehicle for retaining profits within the company, since the full tax effect on earnings is not realized until dividends are paid to shareholders.

- There is no disruption to the business upon the withdrawal or death of a shareholder.

- A corporation is more readily financed and can be eligible for government funding and loan programs not available to either proprietorships or partnerships.

- A corporation is more easily saleable.

- A corporation is perceived as having more status and credibility in the marketplace.

Disadvantages

- There are added costs incurred due to the complexity, legal requirements, etc., that arise when a corporate structure is used.

- Operating losses and tax credits must remain within the corporation and cannot be used by individual shareholders against personal tax.

- Allowable capital losses incurred may only be written off against taxable capital gains.

As you can see, there are pros and cons for each of the three business structures. Think carefully about each of them. Discuss the subject with a professional and select the one that is best for you. Remember, it is possible to switch from one business form to another as your business grows and changes.

1.4 What to do if it is a husband/wife business

Many small businesses begin with the husband or wife taking an active part in keeping the books or running the office. Usually (at least in the beginning) little or no salary is paid to either.

So, now you ask: "How can each spouse's interest be properly protected if the business succeeds but the marriage fails?" My answer is that each party's contribution to the business should be recognized and protected from the start.

This is simple to do. In the case of an incorporated business, you can simply divide the shares according to the contribution of each spouse. Actually, this is a bit of a simplification, and you should really consider entering into a buy-sell agreement, which provides that one party can buy out the other according to a predetermined formula. In addition, this is a very effective estate planning tool that can provide ready cash to one partner to buy the shares of the business if the other partner suddenly dies. In many instances, of course, the deceased spouse would leave his or her interest in the business to the other spouse, in which case a funding plan would not be necessary.

Furthermore, this money can come from life insurance by each party insuring the other's life. At any rate, although it sounds complicated, it is something worth considering when starting a small business. (See Chapter 15 for further details.)

Another point to consider is that many provinces have enacted, or are in the process of enacting, changes in family law that provide that each spouse is entitled to one-half of the property — including business interests — if the marriage breaks up. A marriage contract spelling out what each partner is entitled to is the best way to protect a business from unplanned division of this kind.

In the case of a partnership, some sort of agreement must be entered into to reflect the contribution of each party and what is to happen if the partners split up.

According to law, the partnership is automatically dissolved if any one partner retires, dies, or quits. Therefore, it is doubly important for you to have some arrangement for one party to buy out the other.

Who buys out whom and at what price? You might provide for a specific arrangement — such as the husband buying out the wife at a price of one year's gross sales or three years' net profits. There are endless formulas you can use to determine the net worth of the business. My favourite if there are two equal partners and if either one of them could run the business is the Russian roulette formula. This simply provides that if there is a major dispute, one party shall buy out the other. One party makes an offer to sell the business to the other. (Which party makes the offer is decided by flipping a coin.) The offering party must set a price for his or her one-half interest. The other party then has the option of paying that amount to buy out the other person or selling his or her interest for the same price.

The only problem with this formula is that it puts a severe onus on the party making the offer to "price it right" because, if the offer is too low, naturally the other partner will buy. On the other hand, if it is too high, the offering party has to come up with a lot of cash.

Remember that these are only ideas. You must work out your own formula and have it tailor-made to suit your business. You would be well advised to seek some professional advice from a lawyer, business consultant, or insurance expert who specializes in buy-sell agreements.

2. FEDERAL REQUIREMENTS AND REGULATIONS YOU SHOULD KNOW ABOUT

2.1 Goods and services tax (GST)

The Government of Canada levies a sales tax (currently 5 percent) on almost all goods and services. Your business will almost certainly be subject to the provisions of the Goods and Services Tax (GST), which means that you will have to charge the tax on the goods or services you provide, as well as pay it on the purchases you make.

The GST has a great many aspects that will affect your business, too many to cover in detail in this volume. What follows is a brief description of some of the most important elements of the GST that you should consider when formulating your business plans.

Registering for the GST is almost the first thing you should do for your business. Realize that the GST is a consumer tax, which means that once you are registered, every penny of GST that you spend on business purchases is recoverable by you, provided you track it carefully. It also means that the net price you pay as a business for supplies and equipment will be 5 percent less than the price you pay as a consumer for the same items, which is why it is important to register early on.

If you expect your gross revenue to be over $30,000, you are required by law to register for GST purposes and to charge and collect the tax. But if you expect your gross revenue to be under

$30,000, you have the option of registering, and there are both advantages and disadvantages to doing so.

The introduction of the GST has changed business and consumer buying habits across the country. In very general terms it has encouraged the purchase of goods and discouraged the purchase of services. You should consider whether this factor will have any effect on the way you plan your business in the near future.

2.2 Federal excise tax

An excise tax is a tax levied on specific classes of goods whether manufactured or produced in Canada or imported into Canada. The list includes things such as tobacco and alcoholic beverages. Complete details can be found in the *Excise Tax Act*, a copy of which may be obtained from the government's authorized bookstore agents.

Canada Revenue Agency (CRA), Excise Branch, requires that all people or firms manufacturing or producing goods subject to an excise tax operate under a manufacturer's registration. You can obtain this registration from the regional or district Excise Branch of the CRA in the area in which you choose to operate.

The procedure for filing returns and paying excise tax is similar to that for the GST. If you are in any doubt concerning your status under the *Excise Tax Act*, write to the regional director of the CRA Excise Branch nearest you.

2.3 Customs duties

Any business that imports products from abroad must be aware of customs duties that are levied against goods upon entry into Canada. There are regulations concerning invoicing, classifying goods, rates of duty, and reductions and exemptions for special classes of articles. You should obtain a ruling on the classification, rate of duty, and valuation before starting to make shipments.

If you are a foreign exporter or a Canadian importer, you will require complete information covering the rules for exporting out of or importing into Canada. Approach the Regional Collector of Customs, CRA, who has jurisdiction over the Canadian port of entry for the majority of your goods. You can also talk to a customs broker. If you intend to ship either into or out of the country, you will need one.

Since 1989, the implementation of the Goods and Services Tax (GST), the Free Trade Agreement (FTA), and the North American Free Trade Agreement (NAFTA) has affected the rules related to customs duties and their procedures.

The FTA and NAFTA are agreements between Canada and the United States, and between Canada, the United States, and Mexico, respectively, which are meant to create trade between the countries that is essentially free of customs duties. Existing tariffs will be eliminated over a period of several years. Further free trade agreements with countries of Central and South America are possible.

The goods and services tax has changed the procedures that you follow related to customs duties. Where before you might have been able to import certain items on an exempt basis and so pay no duties, that option has almost entirely disappeared. Similarly, the complicated procedure for recovering duties and excise included in the costs of goods for export has also been simplified. Ongoing changes to these regulations are another reason to use the services of a good customs broker.

2.4 Federal income tax

The federal government levies both personal and corporate income tax on money earned in Canada. Income taxes are applied on income received or receivable during the taxation year from all sources inside and outside Canada, less certain deductions.

Individuals and branches of foreign companies carrying on business in Canada are also liable for income taxes on profits derived from these business operations. Small businesses qualify for special tax rates (see Chapter 14 for further information).

If you are an employer, you are required to deduct personal income tax from the paycheques of all employees on a regular basis. Remit these funds monthly through any branch of a chartered bank or to your local tax centre. You must start to deduct employee benefits when the employees begin to work for you.

The federal income tax regulations outline the rules for allocating income to provinces when individuals earn business income in more than one province.

For specific information about federal income tax, contact the nearest office of the CRA. You can visit its website at www.cra-arc.gc.ca.

2.5 Employment insurance

In Canada, workers who become unemployed may qualify for employment insurance benefits under a federal government program. The program is administered by Human Resources and Social Development Canada.

With few exceptions, all employment in Canada is insurable. Therefore, most employers and employees must make employment insurance premium payments. The employer must collect each employee's premiums according to the current premium scales. All matters relating to deductions, remittances, and rulings for employment insurance premiums are handled by the CRA. The rules are stringent, and there are penalties for those employers who send the payments late or, worse yet, fail to remit at all. Contact your local CRA branch and ask them to send you their *Employers' Guides* — and follow the rules. Alternatively, go to www.cra-arc.gc.ca/tx/bsnss/tpcs/pyrll/menu-eng.html.

Note: If you are a proprietor or a partner, or if you and your spouse own over 40 percent of the shares of a company between you, you are not eligible to collect employment insurance benefits. You can, however, contribute to the Canada Pension Plan (CPP).

2.6 Canada Pension Plan

The Canada Pension Plan is designed to provide a basic retirement pension for working Canadians. Employees between 18 and 70 in most types of employment are covered by the plan and must contribute to it unless they are receiving CPP benefits. There are few other exceptions.

Employers are responsible for making the deductions from all eligible employees and they must match these deductions with similar contributions. The CRA can supply you with an explanatory book and all the information necessary to calculate and properly remit the deductions.

Note: A person who is self-employed is responsible for his or her entire annual contribution to the CPP. If you are incorporated and pay yourself a wage, as far as the CPP is concerned you are not self-employed. You should deduct the normal amount from your wage and the company will also contribute as the employer.

2.7 Privacy Acts

Yes, Acts. The Federal Government has the *Personal Information Protection and Electronic Documents Act* (PIPEDA). Alberta, British Columbia, and Quebec have provincial laws that are substantially similar to the federal law.

In all cases, the law says that an organization may collect, use, or disclose personal information only for a purpose that a reasonable person would consider appropriate in the circumstances. Generally, the provincial rules will apply if your company is doing business in a province that has its own privacy act.

If your business plan includes collecting substantial amounts of information on customers, suppliers, employees, or other businesses, you should take a very careful look at the details of the privacy rules that apply to you.

If your business will only be recording information necessary to transact a sale or purchase, or hire a person, the following rules are what you should be concerned about:

- Organizations are accountable for the protection of personal information under their control.

- The purposes for which the personal information is being collected must be identified during or prior to the collection.

- Personal information may only be collected, used, or disclosed by an organization with the knowledge and consent of the individual, with limited exceptions as specified in the legislation.

- The collection of personal information is limited to what is necessary for the identified purposes, and it must be collected by fair and lawful means.

- Personal information must only be used and disclosed for the purposes for which it was collected, except with consent or as required by law. It can be retained only as long as it is necessary to fulfill those purposes.

- Personal information must be as accurate, complete, and up-to-date as is necessary.

- Personal information must be protected by adequate safeguards.

- Information about an organization's privacy policies and practices must be readily available to individuals upon request.

- An individual has the right of access to personal information about himself or herself and has the right to seek correction. Both these rights are subject to some exceptions as specified in each statute.

- Organizations must provide the means for an individual to challenge an organization's compliance with the above principles.

- If you operate in more than one province, you may have to comply with more than one statute, depending on the jurisdiction.

Note: The information above is a summary of PIPEDA and related legislation. With increasing incidents of data and identity theft, it is certain that both the storage and use of personal information, and who has access to that information, will come under a lot more scrutiny in years to come.

3. PROVINCIAL GOVERNMENT REQUIREMENTS AND REGULATIONS YOU SHOULD KNOW ABOUT

3.1 Licensing

If your business is located in an unorganized territory, you are required to obtain a provincial government trade licence, which is issued by the nearest government agent or the RCMP under the *Trade Licences Act*.

There are certain specific provincial acts containing licensing regulations and requirements that apply to specific businesses. While it is impossible to list all the provincial acts and the businesses to which they apply, here is a list of areas that fall under provincial jurisdiction and about which you should be concerned if you operate a business in these areas:

- Door-to-door sales, pyramid schemes, and franchises

- Firms that loan money or are involved with the consumer finance business in any way

- Manufacturers (especially regarding labour laws and factory standards)

- Anyone who handles or processes food

- Anyone who is in the transport (goods or persons) business

- Anyone who is dealing with natural resources, such as forests, minerals, or water

- Anyone in the fish processing business

- Anyone who is affected by pollution standards

- Anyone who does business on provincially owned land, such as parks and beaches

3.2 Sales tax

Every provincial government, with the exception of the one in Alberta, imposes a sales or social service tax, which the seller collects from the consumer. This is a sales tax that is levied on virtually all tangible personal property that is purchased or imported for consumption or use.

If you are going to be buying merchandise for resale, you need to apply for a provincial tax number. Upon application, a registration certificate assigning a tax number will be issued by the provincial consumer taxation branch. This certificate grants exemption from the payment of the tax on merchandise purchased for resale purposes or merchandise that will become part of tangible personal property intended for resale. Contact your nearest provincial government tax office for further details.

Some provinces are considering extending the scope of their sales taxes to include services, in large part to synchronize with the GST. At the time of writing some provinces had announced plans for such standardization, and it is likely that eventually other provinces will follow.

4. MUNICIPAL GOVERNMENT REQUIREMENTS AND REGULATIONS YOU SHOULD KNOW ABOUT

4.1 Licensing

The *Municipal Act* authorizes municipalities to license all businesses within its boundaries, and incorporated centres issue licences and permits based on local bylaws. Communities can control aspects of zoning, land use, construction, and renovation for all types of business activities, including the licensing of commercial vehicles.

Contact the local city hall or municipal office for information in these areas. If you are setting up a business in any unincorporated area, even in your home, contact the nearest government agent or RCMP detachment.

When checking out business licence fees, be sure to ask if the fee includes all charges for the year. Some municipalities charge a small-business licence fee and then add on a substantial fee or occupancy charge based on the annual rent or, if you own the building, fair market rental value. This has hurt many people as this extra charge can range up to 10 percent of the annual rent.

4.2 Municipal taxes

Municipal governments levy direct taxes on real estate, water consumption, and business premises.

Property taxes are based on the assessed real value of the land and improvements as determined by provincial assessment authorities. Annual notices of assessments are sent out with provision for appeal.

Local business taxes are applied directly against the tenant or the business operator. The business tax is generally based on a percentage of the annual rental value, the property assessment, the size of the premises, or the number of employees.

4.3 Building requirements

All three levels of government have some responsibility for regulating commercial buildings. Any construction that is proposed must satisfy all the requirements of the three governments.

The city hall or municipal office brings together all the various building codes and inspections, making it possible for the approval of any planned construction to be obtained at the local level.

The municipality controls the type of building you may construct. Municipal building and zoning regulations control the physical structure and the final use of your building. The municipality also has the power to enforce building regulations.

Before starting the construction or renovation of a structure, you must obtain a building permit from the municipality. To apply, you must submit preliminary sketches for approval and, when the sketches have received approval, submit complete construction drawings, which will be examined to ensure that they meet the federal, provincial, and municipal building standards. If approval is given, then you will be issued a building permit. Once construction has begun, various stages of the construction must be inspected before the project can continue.

Because each municipality controls certain aspects of construction, the requirements vary from one area to another, so you should contact the building department of the municipal government office for specific requirements.

4.4 Hospitalization

Some provinces require that regular amounts be paid into a province-wide hospital plan. These payments may be made by the employees directly or as a payroll deduction by the employees and employer together in some shared fashion, or by the employer on behalf of his or her employees.

Check with your local provincial government office for the regulations that apply to your business.

5. MISCELLANEOUS INFORMATION YOU SHOULD BE AWARE OF

5.1 Weights and measures

Industry Canada is responsible for the approval and initial inspection of all weighing and measuring devices, such as scales and fuel dispensers that are used in trade.

Measurement Canada must inspect all new trade devices prior to first use. If you acquire used weighing equipment for commercial use you should notify Measurement Canada.

Those devices requiring installation before being inspected (e.g., vehicle scales) must be inspected on-site when operational. Movable devices may be factory inspected prior to shipping, and the department must be notified when this equipment is in place. Any relocation of the equipment must be reported to the department to ensure that regular inspections can continue to take place.

The period between inspections varies but is usually every two years. You should note that you are responsible for the cost of the initial inspection.

For further information or to arrange for an inspection, contact the nearest Measurement Canada office of the federal department of Industry Canada.

5.2 Packaging and labelling

Any prepackaged consumer product, including food and inedible items, is subject to the packaging regulations of Industry Canada.

Prepackaged products require a label stating the product's net quantity. The information must be declared in metric units and must appear in French and English. The identity of the product must also be given in both French and English.

The identity and principal place of business of the manufacturer or the person for whom the product was manufactured must appear on the package in either French or English.

In some instances other information may be required. For example, hazardous or dangerous products must be properly marked according to the *Hazardous Products Act*.

Textiles must be labelled to show the fibre content according to the *Textile Labelling Act*. This act provides for the mandatory labelling of such textile articles as wearing apparel, fabrics sold by the piece, and household textiles. It also regulates the advertising, sale, and importation of all consumer-textile fabric products.

Articles such as jewellery, silverware, optical products, watches, pens, and pencils, made wholly or partly of precious metals, are regulated by the *Precious Metals Marking Act*.

There are restrictions on the permissible size of the packages and for certain products only specific sizes are allowed.

For more detailed information regarding packaging, you should contact your nearest Industry Canada office.

5.3 Patents, copyright, trademarks, and industrial designs

The laws concerning patents, copyright, trademarks, and industrial designs are very complicated and you may find professional help useful. Registered patent and trademark lawyers specialize in these fields and consultation with them will ensure you get maximum protection and benefits.

5.3a Patents

A patent is a contract between the federal government and an inventor. In exchange for full disclosure of the invention, the government grants the inventor the exclusive right to make, use, or sell the invention in Canada for 20 years.

Patents are granted for inventions that are defined as some technological development or improvement that has not previously been considered. If you have not yet completed your invention and are concerned that others might patent it, you may file a description of the invention as far as it has been developed with the patent office. The document filed is known as a caveat. You, the "caveator," will be informed if anyone else files an application to patent the same invention in the year immediately following the filing of the caveat.

The caveat may also have some value in proving when your invention was made. It does not give you any right to exclude others from using the invention, and it is not until you have filed an application and been granted a patent that you are entitled to any exclusive rights. Because a caveat is not an application for patent, its value is somewhat limited.

Because of the complexities involved in filing for a patent, hiring a patent agent is strongly recommended. The cost can be steep — be prepared to spend thousands.

If you wish to apply for a patent you must make an application to the Commissioner of Patents in Ottawa, Canada. The application must meet all the requirements of the *Patent Act* and the Patent Rules.

5.3b Copyright

The *Canadian Copyright Act* recognizes the exclusive right of an author to reproduce every original literary, musical, dramatic, and artistic work he or she creates, provided the author is a Canadian national, a British subject, or a citizen of a country that adheres to the Universal Copyright Convention when he or she produces the work.

The author's rights are recognized as existing once he or she has produced the work. This exclusive right lasts for the life of the author and 50 years after the author's death. In the case of records, discs, and photographs, the term of protection is 50 years, irrespective of the life span of the author.

To register a copyright, you must send your application to the Registrar of Copyright in Ottawa on the form prescribed in the Copyright Rules.

5.3c Trademarks

A trademark lasts for 15 years and is renewable. The *Trademarks Act* outlines the types of symbols that can or cannot be used.

When sending an application for registration of a trademark, you must include the filing fee and, after the application has been examined, a further fee for the registration of the mark is necessary. The application may be submitted by you, the owner of the trademark, or your authorized agent.

There are no forms for a trademark application, but the information must be supplied as required by the government. If you use a lawyer or registered agent (see "patent agent" in the Yellow Pages), it will cost anywhere from a few hundred dollars to $2,000 or more to register a trade name and trademark.

5.3d Industrial designs

An industrial design is any original shape, pattern, or ornamentation applied to an article of manufacture. The article must be made by an industrial process. An industrial design may be registered in Canada if the design is not identical or similar to others registered.

Registration provides you with exclusive right to the design for a period of five years and it may be extended for one additional five-year period. To register a design, you must file a drawing and description with the Registrar of Industrial Design in Ottawa. A search will be made of earlier designs to determine if the design is novel.

Note: Inquiries about copyright, patents, trademarks, and industrial designs should be directed to —

Industry Canada
Canadian Intellectual Property Office
Place du Portage I
50 Victoria St., Room C-114
Gatineau, QC K1A 0C9
By courier: J8X 3X1
Toll free: 1-866-997-1936

5.4 Product standards

Any product you make for sale in Canada must meet certain standards to ensure that it is safe and to protect the consumer against faulty construction and misleading sales practices.

Your product will probably have to be inspected by one of the following:

- The Canadian General Standards Board sets standards for many products ranging from hair dryers to mobile homes. Most electrical goods must conform to its standards. Apply to the CSA (Canadian Standards Organization) Testing Laboratories nearest you — you will find the office listed in the white pages of the telephone book.

- The Underwriters Laboratories of Canada sets standards for fire protection equipment, building materials, and related products. Apply to —

Underwriters Laboratories of Canada
7 Underwriters Road
Toronto, ON M1R 3B4
Telephone: (416) 757-3611
Toll free: 1-866-937-3852

Industry Canada, Legal Metrology Branch, is responsible for testing and approval of weighing and measuring devices that are used in trade.

Health Canada is responsible for all phases of selling, manufacturing, and importing food, drugs, cosmetics, and medical equipment. Emphasis is placed on the control of plant facilities, ingredients, formulas, and packaging. For further information, contact the health protection branch in Ottawa or the district office nearest you.

If you're not sure where to go, contact —

Standards Council of Canada
270 Albert Street, Suite 200
Ottawa, ON K1P 6N7
Telephone: (613) 238-3222

5.5 Immigration and citizenship

If you are established in business in a foreign country but wish to live and establish a business in Canada, you must contact the Canadian immigration representative in your country.

You have to apply for permanent resident status while you are still outside Canada. If the feasibility of your business proposal satisfies the immigration officer and you meet all other immigration requirements, it is possible that you will receive permanent resident status. Canadian citizenship is usually not needed for employment in Canada except in certain areas of the civil service and some professions.

If you are considering employment that is not just temporary, you must apply for permanent resident status before your arrival in Canada. Full citizenship can be applied for after three years' residence in Canada.

The duty-free entry of effects that are owned by people prior to coming to Canada is provided by Canadian customs regulations. You may not sell or dispose of these goods within 12 months of your entry without paying duty.

If you plan to bring with you tools or machinery necessary for your business or profession, be sure to make arrangements before you have them shipped. Customs duty and sales tax are applicable to equipment, and you should be aware of the requirements.

Further information may be obtained from the nearest Canadian embassy or consulate or by writing to Citizenship and Immigration Canada in Ottawa.

5.6 Foreign investment

The *Investment Canada Act* requires that the government review foreign investment and encourage investment that offers significant benefit to Canada. Under this act, if you are a foreign investor and are considering an acquisition in Canada that is above the minimum size outlined in the act, you must demonstrate that a significant benefit will accrue to Canada.

The *Investment Canada Act* does not apply to all investments, but if you are not a Canadian citizen or permanent resident you must notify Investment Canada of the establishment of any new business:

Director of Investments
Investment Review Division
Industry Canada
C.D. Howe Building
235 Queen Street, Room 301B East Tower
Ottawa, ON K1A 0H5

Investors can contact the nearest Industry Canada office (see the blue pages of your telephone book), as well as Canadian embassies and consulates. Telephone (613) 954-1887 for more information.

5.7 Consumer protection

Business practices are strictly regulated by both the federal and provincial governments, and you should be aware of your rights and obligations under the various laws.

In many provinces, for instance, high-pressure selling may get you into trouble if your customers complain. Contact your nearest

Industry Canada office (see the blue pages of your telephone book) and ask for their literature on the subject.

Contact the departments of your provincial government that deal with business practices and consumer protection to get as much information as possible about the regulations that govern the way you are supposed to do business. It can save you a lot of headaches if you make yourself familiar with the subject.

5
FINANCIAL FORECASTING FOR A NEW BUSINESS

A carefully prepared income and expense forecast is one of the most useful and meaningful tools available to you as a prospective successful business person. It can help you spot opportunities and learn more about your business. It might also point out things about your business of which you were not aware and force you to operate with a game plan.

It may not be accurate, but it can be adjusted from time to time. Merely having a forecast forces you to think. Besides, you need one for the bank. Furthermore, income and expense forecasts reduce the number of surprises you will get and will, therefore, increase your chances of success.

Even after you have considered the whole matter exhaustively, you will likely still find many "iffy" areas remaining in your forecast.

This will be so with many small businesses, especially those that involve new technological developments or new products. Even so, information obtained in preparing a forecast can eliminate some of the areas of uncertainty that can cause a business's quick failure if it is established with a "damn the torpedoes!" approach.

All too frequently the business established with this approach does not fail because of a single catastrophic event, but rather slips away into quicksand after causing "close calls" or equally unceremonious deaths for some of the other businesses that have extended it credit.

1. MAJOR ITEMS TO CONSIDER

The following discussion provides only some of the questions that you should answer before producing your forecasts.

1.1 The market

Who will your customers be? The type of business you are considering will, in part, determine the answer to this question.

If you are thinking of a fishing camp, your market will be the angler. If you want to make widgets, you need to know who uses them. If you are a widget manufacturer, for example, you might ask yourself additional questions, such as the following:

- Is the market for widgets growing, decreasing, or stable?

- If your widget has superior wearing qualities, a further question might be, "Will a longer-wearing widget be attractive to my customers?" You might find that your possible customers are not interested in longer-wearing widgets, which are more expensive than the ones they now use, because the existing type of widget lasts as long as the equipment in which it is used. It might not make sense for prospective customers to purchase a product they do not really need.

- Where are the customers located? This may affect your decisions regarding the location of the business, advertising, and the number of salespeople you will employ.

- How do the customers order? Regularly or irregularly? In a few large orders or several small ones? What is the frequency of rush orders? Answers to these questions will affect your inventory requirements, the scheduling of production, and possibly the number of employees (if any) you will need.

1.2 Prices

What are the prices of competitive products? Do these prices include freight costs? Are discounts given by competitive businesses? What price structure do you need to make reasonable profits?

1.3 Materials

What is the cost of the materials you need? How well established are your suppliers? What is their reputation for quality, service, and delivery?

1.4 Competition

Who are your competitors? Are they large or small companies? How are they likely to respond to your company's entry into the widget-making business?

Are they likely to cut the prices of their own products, improve their service, or develop their own longer-lasting widget in response to your possible threat to their businesses?

How long might it take them to develop such a widget? In other words, how much time do you have to become an established widget supplier? Could you still compete effectively if competitors were to "take a run" at you? Can they afford to do so? How many widgets can you sell and at what price?

1.5 Facilities and equipment

What kind of facilities do you need? What are the costs of facilities and equipment? What are the relative costs of leasing and purchasing facilities and equipment? Is adequate equipment available? When, and under what conditions, can equipment be obtained? What are the reputations of the various manufacturers of the equipment?

1.6 Employees

What skills will your employees need? If you have decided on a location where you would prefer to establish your business, is there an adequate supply of possible employees with the skills you need?

Can these skills be readily taught? Is there a training facility in the area or will you have to do the training yourself? What wage rate and benefits will you have to pay?

What relationships do other businesses in the area have with their employees? Will you pay by the hour or on some other basis, for example, piecework or commission?

Also, you should be aware that, on the average, each employee costs you 25 to 30 percent more than the actual wages paid because of fringe benefits such as holidays, sick time, medical and dental benefits, and employment and pension contributions.

To avoid these problems (and others) with employees, you may consider setting up as many as you can as freelance contractors. By doing this you would pay each "employee" a flat total fee for hours, days, or weeks worked. Your "employees" would then make their own tax, Canada Pension Plan, and other deductions.

Of course, in this situation, you lose some control over your people because legally they are not your employees anymore. Despite this problem, there is no question that more and more employers are choosing to go the "independent contractor" route.

Remember, don't hire help until it is absolutely necessary. For more ideas about employees, see Chapter 17.

1.7 Production costs

How much will the material to make a widget cost? Will there be a difference in the cost of the material if you produce larger (or lesser) quantities of widgets? What will power cost and how much will be needed to operate your equipment and to heat and light your facilities?

How many widgets can an employee produce in a given time? How many widgets do you need each employee to produce to sell the volume expected? What regulatory authorities will you have to deal with? What are the regulations you will have to obey? How much, if anything, will adherence to these regulations cost?

1.8 Financial considerations

What kind of record-keeping system should you have? Will you need a bookkeeper and/or a full-time accountant? If you need to borrow money, can it be obtained and, if so, on what terms? (See Chapter 6.)

1.9 Working capital

What inventory level will you need in raw materials and in the finished product? What is the amount of accounts receivable you can expect to have on your books at any one time? What payment terms would apply?

What are the payment terms of your suppliers? How long would it take for the purchased material to be sold as a finished product? What proportion of your sales would be for cash or immediate payment? Is working capital support available if you need it?

This list of questions you want answered when starting a new business is by no means complete, but it gives you something with which to start.

Plainly, these questions can be answered only with considerable effort. Your accountant and banker, local board of trade, library, various government offices, and, yes, even your competition may be able to help you.

2. BE SURE OF YOUR SOURCES

If you were to hear a statement like "The average annual profit of businesses at Bedrock is $400,000," your first reaction might be "Bedrock, here I come!" Only after further questioning might you find out that this figure includes the large profits of, say, a major mining company and the more modest profits of many other businesses.

The vital point to remember is that averages and other statistical information can sometimes be meaningless. To make such information meaningful, it is important that you know the basis on which the information is meant to be conveyed by the statistics you are using.

Statistics Canada is a good source of statistical information for and about Canadian business. This federal government department publishes a catalogue that lists the more than 900 publications produced by Statistics Canada each year. The catalogue also contains a section of helpful advice on how to use Statistics Canada's services, and how to read and interpret statistical information.

You can browse the catalogue online at www.statcan.gc.ca, or order it from your regional office (find the number listed under Statistics Canada in the blue pages of your telephone directory) or by calling the national toll-free number: 1-800-263-1136.

The website or the voice mail system at your regional office will lead you through a list of services and provides an up-to-date schedule of workshops and seminars. As well, there are Statistics Canada libraries in many major cities in Canada, where you can study the agency's publications without having to purchase them. Staff can help you find and interpret the information you need.

The census reports (called census profiles) are particularly useful. They offer complete demographic studies of any region or city of Canada. They show you the social and economic characteristics of a marketing area — useful information when you are planning advertising or starting a new business. The costs of these studies vary, but all are reasonable and should be looked into.

Small businesses can solve basic problems by taking advantage of Statistics Canada's Advisory Services. For example, one manufacturer seeking to diversify a product line learned how to estimate the market and assess the performance of potential competitors. Another used the statistics on housing starts and completions to decide whether or not to expand. Ask your regional office about Advisory Services, call the toll-free number (1-800-263-1136), or write to:

Statistics Canada
Advisory Services
Arthur Meighan Building
25 St. Clair Avenue East
5th floor
Toronto, ON M4T 1M4

Also, every province compiles useful business statistics. Contact your provincial government department responsible for small business. (See the blue pages of your telephone book.)

If you have obtained accurate information, you will already have the solutions to many of the problems that might otherwise cause the business early difficulties. These problems will arise very quickly if you are simply determined to be very independent and put all your faith in luck or your own capabilities to surmount them.

While the success of Slipshod Industries, whose forecast is shown in Sample 1 (at the end of the chapter), would not be guaranteed, its chances of success would be good because the owner was prepared not only to work hard at the business but, more important, was prepared to think hard about it.

3. WHAT FORECASTS DO YOU NEED AND HOW DO YOU PREPARE THEM?

Because you are a professional, you will need three types of forecasts, and there are good reasons for each of them:

- Income and expense forecast
- Cash flow budget
- Break-even analysis

3.1 Income and expense forecast

An income and expense forecast can be described as the operating statement that you would expect to see for your business at the end of the period for which the forecast is being prepared. Generally, this period would be a year. For a new business, the forecast would show what revenues and expenses you expect the business to have in its first year of operation.

It can be very useful, of course, to prepare a forecast for a period longer than one year, but it is not strictly necessary.

Preparing an income and expense forecast for a new business is more of a problem than preparing one for an existing business simply because in a new business there is no historical record to go by. For this reason, the preparation of this forecast for a new business is an even more essential, interesting, and rewarding experience than doing it for an existing business, even though time and effort will be required.

The question of whether you are going to make money at your enterprise is answered by this analysis. It need not be lengthy; it need not be difficult. Obviously, the more detailed the better, but because of the necessary allowance for error, don't go overboard.

As you can see from Sample 1, the first figure to estimate is income (sales). In many respects it should be the last because at this stage it is the most uncertain of all. However, because you need this figure in order to calculate "cost of material," you have to plug in something. Be conservative — better to underestimate than go hog-wild.

You can sometimes obtain guidelines on revenues and costs for a particular type of business by looking through magazines and periodicals or asking firms engaged in the type of business you are considering. By reading a lot and talking to many people you could develop a forecast of income and expenses that might seem to be entirely reasonable.

However, as is pointed out in most articles on the subject, a financial forecast for a new business cannot be divorced from the location of the business, the type of product it sells, the market the business serves, the physical facilities, and the actual capabilities of the owners and employees. Guidelines are just that and individual circumstances will determine their relevance.

Your main concern is to nail the expenses down as accurately and in as much detail as possible. This, then, gives you a target or break-even figure toward which to work.

Fill in whatever amounts you would expect to see opposite each item for a year's operation. It may be, of course, that some of these headings are not suitable for your kind of business, or that others should be added, but the example illustrates how you should proceed in setting up an income and expense forecast.

3.2 Cash flow budget

A cash flow budget measures the flow of money into and out of the business. It is important to you and your banker.

Most businesses I know of operate seasonally. In other words, there are slow months and busy months. Therefore, there are occasions when you are cash poor and others when you are cash rich. (This is the theory at any rate.)

A cash budget gives you the numbers you and your banker need to know to help you properly finance your operation. It tells you in advance if you have enough cash to get by. This is very important.

A cash flow budget need not be fancy. It should be prepared a year in advance and contain monthly breakdowns. Sample 2 (at the end of the chapter) shows an example of a format to use.

3.3 Break-even analysis

A break-even analysis is a critical calculation for every small business. Rather than calculating how much your firm would make if it obtained an estimated sales volume, a more meaningful analysis determines at which sales volume your firm will break even.

The other statistic is really pie-in-the-sky because the estimated sales volume is very questionable. Don't assume a sales volume and determine your so-called profits; do it in reverse: determine the sales volume necessary for your firm to break even.

Above the break-even point, your firm makes money; below it, it loses money. A break-even point, then, is a level of sales volume over some period of time (e.g., "My firm broke even on $10,000 a week in sales").

The calculation of a break-even point for every small business is one of the crucial financial pieces of information. Above the break-even sales volume it is only a matter of how much money your business can generate; below the break-even level of sales it's only a matter of how many days the business can operate before bankruptcy.

Knowing your break-even point gives you a very real and meaningful figure to work toward. A break-even analysis might be required every few months to reflect your business growth.

Note: In a small business, there is no such item as a truly fixed cost. No costs are fixed forever. Insurance can be cancelled, executives fired, rent renegotiated, or the business moved. So a fixed cost should be thought of as a fixed cost only over a period of time or over a finite range of production.

Here is an example of a break-even analysis for Slipshod Industries Ltd., which produces only one product: widgets.

Assume the following:

- The fixed costs are $20,000 per year, including lights, power, telephones (utilities), rent, insurance, and administrative salaries. These costs are fixed for over

10,000 units to 15,000 units manufactured annually.

- The variable costs over the 10,000 to 15,000 unit range are —

  $1.50   material
  .25   labour
  .75   overhead (50% of material)
  $2.50   per unit

- Sales price per unit is $4.00 per unit

  Total costs (TC)=
  variable costs (VC) +
  fixed costs (FC)
  TC = VC + FC

Total costs are all costs of operating the business over a specified time period.

Variable costs are those costs that vary directly with the number of products manufactured. Sometimes called "direct costs," these typically include material and labour costs plus a percentage of the overhead costs.

Fixed costs are costs that do not vary with the number of products produced. Also known as "indirect costs," these costs typically include executive salaries, rent, and insurance, and are considered fixed over a relevant range of production.

The break-even point is where total costs are equal to total revenues.

The break-even chart (also known in more optimistic circles as a profit graph) translates the three facts you know into linear terms: the fixed cost of $20,000, the variable cost of $2.50 per unit, and the sales price of $4.00 per unit (see Sample 3).

The fixed costs line is horizontal because the fixed costs are $20,000, regardless of production volumes. To determine the revenue line, calculate that at 10,000 units the revenue is $40,000 ($10,000 x 4), and that at 20,000 units it will be $80,000; and draw a line through those two points.

From the revenue line, you can determine the revenue if you know the number of units, or you can determine the number of units if you know the revenue.

The total costs line is determined by calculating what the variable costs would be at any two volumes, adding the $20,000 in fixed costs to each of these numbers, and drawing a line through the two points.

The total costs at 10,000 units are:

(10,000 x $2.50 = $25,000)
$25,000 + $20,000 = $45,000 and at
20,000 units the total costs are $70,000.

The total costs line through these two points shows the total costs at different volumes.

When you have drawn the fixed costs, revenue, and total costs lines you can see that the break-even point is around 13,000, which is the intersection of the revenue and total costs lines. At volumes greater than 13,000, there will be a profit because revenues will be greater than total costs.

Your goal, then, is to sell 13,000 units. If you exceed this figure: PROFIT. If not: time for a hard look at the operation.

INCOME AND EXPENSE FORECAST

SLIPSHOD INDUSTRIES LTD.
Year Ending December 31, 20—

INCOME

20,000 widgets at $4.00 each	$80,000

EXPENSES

Materials at $1.50 per widget	30,000
Wages and benefits:	
Two employees (including owner at $15,000 per year)	30,000
Depreciation (on equipment costing $5,000)	1,000
Overhead (power, heat, light, and water)	2,000
Equipment repairs	500
Delivery and freight	1,000
Advertising	500
Insurance	300
Rent	2,400
Interest	200
Telephone	800
Taxes	900
Accounting and legal	500
Travel and entertainment	2,000
Miscellaneous	1,200
Total expenses	$73,300
Net profit	$6,700

SAMPLE 2
CASH FLOW BUDGET WORKSHEET

	Month												Total
	1	2	3	4	5	6	7	8	9	10	11	12	

Cash at beginning of month
In bank and on hand
In investment

TOTAL CASH
Plus income during months
Cash sales (include credit cards)
Credit sales payments
Investment income
Loans
Other cash income
Total income

TOTAL CASH AND INCOME
Expenses during the month
Inventory or new material
Wages and benefits
  (including owner's)
Rent
Licence and permits
Business taxes
Telephone
Equipment, repairs, and rentals
Accounting and legal
Utilities
Advertising
Sales commissions
Delivery and freight
  (including postage)
Vehicle expenses
Travel and entertainment
Insurance
Loan repayment
Other cash expenses

TOTAL EXPENSES
Cash flow excess (or deficit)
  at the end of month
Cash flow cumulative (monthly)

SAMPLE 3
BREAK-EVEN CHART

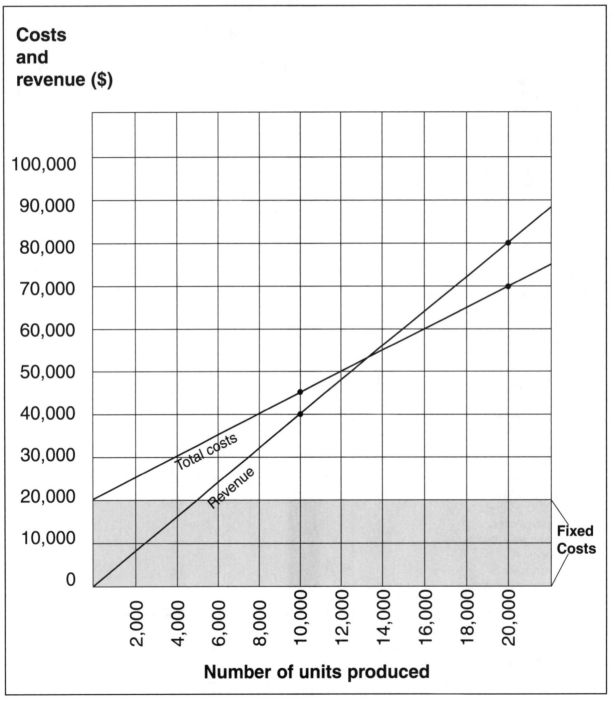

6
HOW TO GET MONEY

You have decided to take the plunge and start your own business. However, you need money and you don't have any.

Naturally, as with most people, you ask yourself, "How much money do I have to invest?" That is the wrong approach. What you should be asking is, "Where can I rent money, at reasonable rates of interest, that will allow me to expand, pay back the loan, and still make a profit?"

Now, the first thing to get clear in your mind is that you should never think in terms of "borrowing" money, because the very word "borrowing" is bad for morale. It could create a feeling of inferiority.

For too many people, the word "borrowing" leaves a bad taste in the mouth. Why should you, a self-made business person, harbour a sense of failure, just because you know it is necessary to use somebody else's money rather than your own?

For example, if you are taking a holiday, and you and your family rent a boat for a day or a week, does that feel like borrowing? Of course not! In reality you are doing the marina a favour. It earns its living by "renting" boats and motors.

If you rent an apartment suite in a fancy new high-rise building, do you feel "cheap" because you are renting? Hardly. You know full well that the people who built the apartment complex in the first place made the investment so that they could rent luxury suites at a good profit.

So, why feel "bad" about renting money, especially when you rent only from people who need your business?

Firms such as banks, credit unions, finance companies, and other "money rental" operators need your business in order to exist.

"Renting" money is a sound and recognized way to do business. Therefore, starting now, get used to the idea, and rent money the same way you would rent a car, boat, or summer cottage. Money is just another commodity, so use the money rental system to become financially independent.

One word of warning: never rent money just for the sake of having a few bucks in your jeans. You should rent money only when you have a definite and sound money-making plan where you can use some other person's cash to build up your business.

Let's get started in the game of renting money to make money for yourself.

1. WHAT FINANCING ALTERNATIVES DO YOU HAVE?

Before looking at where you can get financing, you should understand some basic ground rules about how a business (any business) operates.

A business obtains money by the owners investing their savings (this is called equity financing) or by borrowing. In order to borrow money, you post security by pledging certain defined, fixed assets (land or equipment), or you use a "working capital" loan or a "line of credit" under a floating charge.

This means that the inventory and receivables of a business are pledged as assets. As you can readily understand, it would be impossible to nail down security on inventory and receivables that are constantly being turned over or processed. Hence the term "floating."

So, the banks have devised a method to allow businesses to raise money by pledging these assets. Because the levels of inventory and receivables fluctuate, the amount of the loan fluctuates also. You will often hear that banks will lend up to 75 percent on "good" receivables and up to 50 percent on inventory. These are only rules of thumb, however, and fluctuate considerably, depending on the situation.

Note: Your business must be incorporated to be eligible for this type of loan.

1.1 Equity

The money you personally put into a company or business is called equity. This includes all money coming from your own resources, including savings and personal loans from financial institutions, friends, relatives, or business associates. As time progresses, earnings are retained in the business to increase equity.

If you have formed a limited company, you can buy one or more shares and lend the money to the company; this is called a shareholder's loan.

In a new business there is usually little, if any, equity value, but you may interest someone in buying a share in the potential equity of your business, which amounts to speculation in its simplest form.

1.1a The advantages of using equity capital

If you use equity capital, you will then be able to —

- expand the borrowing power of the company (a larger equity base permits this),
- improve the company's credit rating with its suppliers,

- spread the ownership of the company (and, consequently, the risk) to include more shareholders who may be more venturesome than only a few owners, and

- gain the experience and counsel of new shareholders.

1.1b The disadvantages of using equity capital

Using equity capital, however, can also mean —

- a possible lessening of flexibility and increase in interference because of shared ownership,

- the dilution of ownership interest of the original owners, and

- possible increased expenses such as costs incurred in issuing the stock, dividend payments, and accounting.

Remember, if you are the sole owner of a business, you enjoy complete flexibility in operating and complete power in making decisions. You do not need to consult anyone; you can take risks that a financial partner may not wish to share. In short, you are your own boss.

By selling stock to new investors, you are really admitting new partners to the business so that you have to share control with others. In effect, you probably become an employee of the company's owners, of whom you are one.

In addition, selling partial ownership in a business by introducing new investors reduces your share in the company's profits.

The premature sale of stock in a growth company could subsequently make the original owner reluctant to further reduce his or her

ownership interest, even though the new funding is vitally needed.

The sale of a portion of the equity usually involves additional expenses. Legal fees may be involved. The business's accounting system will probably have to be expanded for the protection and information of the new investor co-owners. A more disciplined standard of conduct may be forced on you when you reduce your share of the ownership by selling part of it to others.

On the other hand, refusing to sell additional shares could impair the growth of the business or allow competitors to overtake it.

1.2 Borrowed money

Remember that there are two types of loans you can go after: term loans (fixed asset financing) and demand loans or line of credit (working capital financing).

1.2a Fixed asset financing

If your business owns or is going to buy something that will last a long time, such as cars, buildings, land, machinery, equipment, or shelving (fixed assets), then you could use these assets as collateral for a term loan.

These are the typical characteristics of a term loan:

(a) It is repaid over a period of time that is generally related to the "useful life" of the asset. (Thus, if you used a car as collateral, you might be given 3 to 5 years; if you used land and buildings, you might be given up to 30 years.)

(b) The lender will only give you a percentage of the value of the asset. (So, for a car you might be given 80 percent, while for property you might be given up to 90 percent.) The other 10 to 20 percent of the cost of the asset generally must come from the equity you have in the company or from the new funds of shareholders.

You will see after reading the following section on "Where do I go to rent money?" that there are many, many sources for this type of loan. However, there are some things to be aware of here:

(a) All lenders will want your personal guarantee on the loan. Instead of meekly agreeing to this, try to negotiate a limited guarantee, such as the amount of the loan plus three months' interest. Also, once you have repaid the loan in full, be sure you go back to the lender and obtain a release of the guarantee.

(b) If there are any loans from shareholders to the company, a "postponement of claim" may be requested. This is simply an agreement by the company that it will not repay the shareholders until the lender has been repaid in full, and it is quite common.

(c) An "assignment of life insurance" on yourself or any other key management person may be requested. This is called "key-person insurance." If it is a condition of a loan, the policy may be taken out by the company and the premiums will likely be tax deductible. (Consult your accountant.)

One term you are likely to run into when applying for this type of loan is the "leverage" or

"debt-to-equity ratio." This is the ratio of the money you owe to the money you put into the business.

For example, assume that your debt picture looked like this:

Owing to suppliers	$2,000
Bank loan	$4,000
Total debt	$6,000

And your investment in the company was $3,000, then your debt-to-equity ratio would be $6,000 divided by $3,000, or 2:1.

Generally, the lender's assessment of this ratio is discretionary, but if you are starting a new business or just building a reputation, it is unlikely that a lender will want to go beyond a 2:1 or even a 1:1 ratio.

1.2b Working capital financing

If you deal in inventory and receivables you will probably encounter the situation in which you are requested to pay for this inventory and other current bills before you receive money from the sale of your goods. This cash lag can be financed by a demand loan, generally called a bank line of credit.

The main characteristics of this type of loan are as follows:

(a) The loan goes up and down according to your needs and the level of your assets and inventory.

(b) It is generally available from banks.

(c) The lender uses accounts receivable (the money owed to you by customers) and inventory as security. As a rule of thumb you can get 50 to 75 percent of the value of your accounts receivable, not including any amount unpaid for longer than 90 days (this is called the "advance value" and is up to 50 percent on inventory). It is also possible that a higher advance value may be given on accounts receivable if inventory is pledged at "no advance" value.

2. PLAN YOUR FINANCIAL REQUIREMENTS

Many borrowers come away from the bank or lending institution frustrated because they can't get an answer or they have been turned down. In many cases, this happens because they have not answered the banker's crucial questions:

- How much money do you need?

- What are you going to do with it?

- How will you repay it?

- Do you have enough security for the amount of loan you want?

- If you do not have enough security, what can you do about it?

Be prepared to answer these questions in specific terms. It's best to have a written proposal that you can leave with the lender. While it does not have to be elaborate, a proper presentation goes a long way toward showing the lender that you have given the matter a good deal of thought. A substantial factor in the decision is the lender's assessment of you as a manager and planner.

To make your presentation, you will need the following:

- A ONE-page summary answering the questions above.

- A cash flow budget for the term of the loan (i.e., for a line of credit, your budget would be on a monthly basis for one year; for a five-year term loan, you would show the annual cash flow for five years). It is an added advantage to make up a projected income and expense statement. (See Chapter 5 for detailed instructions on how to prepare a financial forecast.)

- Financial statements (if applicable). If the business has been in operation for a number of years, statements for at least two years should be submitted. If it's a brand new business, a properly prepared forecast is even more important.

- A history of the company and your experience. Prepare a written summary, no longer than two pages, in which you do the following:

(a) Briefly describe the type of business you are in.

(b) Indicate whether the business is a sole proprietorship, partnership, or a limited company, and state the date of incorporation, who the owners are, and what percentage of the business they own. If it is a limited company, give the authorized and issued shares and show who owns them.

(c) List all the directors and the key management people, giving age, background, and number of years with your business.

(d) List the principal products or services provided, with a description of their strengths and weaknesses.

(e) List your major customers.

(f) Show what your potential market is, who the competition are (give specific names), what your present share of the market is, and what your selling items are.

(g) List your major suppliers and their terms.

(h) Give references, including the name and branch of any banks or financial institutions with which you have dealt, details of present lines of credit or loans, and the names of your accountant and lawyer.

If all this seems to be a waste of time — it isn't. You will be surprised by the insights you gain by having to do some hard thinking about your business.

A properly prepared cash flow budget, for example, will serve as an invaluable guide during the crucial formative years. It will help to pinpoint the problem areas immediately.

Even the exercise of placing a brief description of your business on paper is useful. It forces you to justify your plan to hard-headed but objective advisors.

It may cause you to do some rethinking or even to revise or change your plans. Good — that's what it's supposed to do. And even if your presentation passes with flying colors, you will be glad that someone else believes you have a fighting chance — especially when that someone controls the money tap.

In my experience, most business people make the mistake of asking for too little rather than too much. Business people are notorious for overestimating revenues and underestimating costs — and underestimating the length of time needed to reach the break-even point.

I discuss preparing a business plan in more detail in the Appendix, and there are some useful worksheets you can install from the CD included with the book.

3. WHERE DO YOU GO TO RENT MONEY?

An important consideration for every business person looking for money is not only, "How do I approach someone for money?" but "Who do I approach?"

Canada's "money stores" vary greatly, depending on what they will lend money for, how much they will lend, what terms they will offer, what security they want, and what they want in your presentation.

In recent years, many foreign banks have opened their doors in Canada resulting in increased competition for your business. I've noticed that our local financial "stores" have become much more receptive to the small-business person in the past few years. This means you can shop around and negotiate terms in your favour.

Remember that you are not dealing with one-product vending machines that all look alike — faceless and mysterious — but rather with a supermarket of financial services, all offering different products. It is up to you to match the needs of your business with the lending institution best equipped to meet those needs. The institution offering the lowest interest rate may not be the best for you and your business.

How should you make the choice? To begin with, investigate the person you will be dealing with. An aggressive bank manager might be more willing to take a chance on an up-and-coming firm than a more cautious person might be.

As well, investigate lending limits. Very often loan requests are turned down simply because a manager's lending authority is limited. Small suburban bank branches, for instance, may not be authorized to lend more than $50,000 without approval from upstairs. A loan officer at a large downtown branch, on the other hand, might be working with a lending limit of $500,000 or more.

It's also important to find a lender who is familiar with your special requirements and peculiar problems — particularly if you operate in a specialized industry. Shared knowledge and understanding are important in your lending relationships.

Ask your lawyer, accountant, or business acquaintances about the strengths and weaknesses of various lenders. These people should be able to provide you with enough leads to help you find a lender who is right for your needs.

It's useful to understand how lending decisions are made. Usually, a lender will base decisions on a risk assessment — an analysis of the borrower that determines the likelihood of the loan being repaid. Risk assessments are based on a number of factors, including the following:

- Length of time in business

- Management expertise displayed by the borrower

- Security and guarantees offered

- Trends within your company's industry and in the overall business climate

- Special factors peculiar to your type of business

Most lenders are not dogmatic about risk assessments, however. Even though other factors are not positive, risk can be moderated if a firm shows promise. An exciting, unique product line, a number of long-term contracts, and a history of successful business ventures can all tilt the risk assessment in your favour.

3.1 Personal sources

While potentially the most attractive because of the low or even non-existent interest and flexible pay-back schedule, personal friends and rich uncles or aunts should be avoided if possible.

My experience is that the reason your rich aunt will cough up is that she likes you personally. However, you are running a business, and money lent on any other basis should not have been lent in the first place.

Also, if you have such a sound, profitable idea, why won't the bank or the credit union lend you what you want? At least that's what I would ask if my son-in-law came to me. And, it's not being cheap; I would be doing him a favour. You wouldn't want to have your personal relationship ruined because of a few dollars, would you?

If, by chance, you have someone who is dying to put some money into your little enterprise, or you simply cannot turn down the chance for cheap, easy money, make sure it is all done on a proper, businesslike basis with the proper security, interest payments, etc. If you cannot avoid the personal involvement, at least you can cut down the risk of personal problems.

Besides family and friends, you may also consider employees, suppliers, and customers. (After all, who knows your business better than a major supplier, customer, or your employee?)

If you are fresh out of personal sources, try talking to people who have contacts with money, such as accountants, lawyers, and insurance salespeople.

Other factors to consider when weighing the pros and cons of this source are the following:

(a) The source usually has limited funds, and if you contemplate needing further financing down the road — forget it.

(b) You usually have to give up some equity.

(c) There is no such thing as a "silent" investor of this nature, so you're better off with someone knowledgeable about the business. (In case you ever get into trouble, there's nothing worse than Aunt Minnie or Uncle Bob looking over your shoulder into the affairs of your business!)

(d) If considering employees as a source, one of your main objectives will be to lock in the incentive to see that the business does well. Therefore, your employees must be prepared to pay for the equity they are getting (even if at a discount) because simply giving stock to them will not accomplish this. Furthermore, you'll have the employees running the show (not a bad idea sometimes) with no stake in the outcome. Remember, you can always arrange to buy back the shares if the employee leaves.

3.2 Banks

The first thing you should know is that it is far more important to know your banker than your bank. All the television ads in the world mean nothing — it all hinges on the outlook of the manager you are dealing with. So, when you find a good one, keep to him or her for as long as possible.

Second, because there are so many banks, you can use the leverage of competition — with a certain amount of discretion. In other words, you can shop around but not indiscriminately.

Suppose you have located — or already know — a manager whom you think will be receptive to your proposal. You have prepared a sound cash flow budget and proposal for funds (see Chapter 5). Don't approach your manager and say, "Harry, I've made my pitch to three other banks as well as to yours, so I trust you will act accordingly." Unless bank competition in your area is very fierce and yours is a very attractive account indeed, this approach will likely backfire. Generally, bankers don't like to be pressured in this manner and are more likely to turn down your proposal outright.

It is better to approach one banker at a time, allowing him or her a certain amount of time to approve your proposal, hinting that you need the money by such and such a date and that you need time to approach other sources if you get turned down.

Third, if you are turned down by your banker, never go on to the regional branch without his or her knowledge, because the managers there will always back up the branch manager.

Fourth, invite your banker to see your operation. It is surprising how many bankers never get out of their offices to see who and what they are financing. It's a free public relations gesture that may make all the difference to your banker's outlook.

Fifth, banks normally deal only on a short-term, demand basis, with changing interest rates. So, if you anticipate that you will need to return to the well several times, and if your receivables and inventory fluctuate wildly, banks may not be your best source of rented money.

Of course, if you are going to be a frequent, regular borrower of small amounts, then you will appreciate the convenience of establishing a line of credit with your bank. This is the maximum amount of credit a bank will allow you at any one time, and provided you do not exceed that amount, it is always available without requiring a separate application.

Banks also grant revolving credit, a system similar to the consumer revolving credit accounts offered by large department stores. This allows you to borrow the maximum, reduce it by payments, and borrow up to the maximum again. This can be useful as an intermediate- or long-term credit system.

Sixth, banks like security and will take all they can get. *Don't give away more than you have to.* If you cannot give the bank security for a loan, and if you do not own real estate or equipment of substantial value, the bank will loan on receivables and finished inventory.

A common misconception is that banks will only loan up to 50 percent of the receivables. This is not true, as I have seen 75 percent credit lines loaned frequently.

The common question is "How good are the receivables?" Generally, banks do not like accounts receivable older than 120 days. For new businesses, banks naturally like to see that the owner (you) has some equity in the business. Even if it is not much equity, it shows a commitment on your part.

If you do not have any of your own money invested, be ready to answer this question before approaching your banker: "Why should we lend you business capital when you don't believe in it enough to put your own money in?"

Finally, if you live in a province that has provincially sponsored banks (i.e., Alberta) it would be wise to approach them first because they have the lowest rates available. Their loan decisions, however, are sometimes dictated by local economic considerations.

3.2a What you need to know about what can serve as security for loans

Every small-business person should know about the flexibility banks have to finance manufacturers, wholesalers, and retailers. They have the power to take security on assets that historically could not be identified or pledged as credit. In other words, banks can take security or legal control on a "floating charge" basis. (This is a claim on all assets going in or out of the business.)

The security held by the bank under a floating charge loan is tantamount to ownership. The bank acquires the same rights to any crops, fish catches, implements, goods used in manufacturing, or lumber that it would have under a bill of lading or warehouse receipt describing the goods that secure the debt upon default.

Farmers also may obtain loans for the purchase of agricultural implements or the installation of an electrical system by using the implements or electrical system as security.

Building improvements may be financed in a similar way. (Note that any improvement that becomes affixed to real property, such as fencing or drainage systems, must be registered in the Land Registry in order to retain the bank's priority.)

Fishermen may obtain loans on the security of ships, fishing equipment, supplies, or their catches in order to finance something like a new fishing vessel or repairs.

Wholesale purchasers, shippers, or dealers may use the products that they customarily purchase, ship, or deal in and any materials used in packing these products, as security for loans.

Because the banks want as much security as they can get, in nearly all cases where it is possible to do so, a bank will take security of assets with a floating charge. (In Canada, this type of security is third in popularity behind promissory notes and mortgages.)

Here are some more examples that will give you some idea of the variety of things that will serve as security for a loan:

(a) Manufacturers may use the goods that they produce (including goods produced at the time of the loan, and those that will come into existence later) or the goods they obtain for use in the process of manufacturing.

(b) An owner of a timber licence (a logger) may use, for example, the pulpwood that will be produced as a result of the work.

(c) Farmers may use their crops or livestock to obtain seed grain, fertilizer, or binder twine. (The security may be the livestock, or it may be the crop that is grown from the seed and fertilizer and harvested using the binder twine.)

3.2b What you should know about the Small Business Loans Act

The *Small Business Loans Act* was passed in 1960 to help owners of small-business enterprises obtain term credit for a wide range of business improvement purposes.

A business is eligible if its estimated annual gross revenue does not exceed $5 million. Groups not eligible include farms, businesses renting real estate or purchasing real estate for resale, and charitable or religious enterprises.

Loans under the *Small Business Loans Act* are made at 1.25 percent above the prime rate, plus an additional charge.

You should also know that a lender may, at its discretion, charge an additional 1 percent of the business improvement loan as a one-time, front-end fee. The lender then pays that fee to the federal government.

i. Where can loans be obtained?

All chartered banks and Alberta Treasury Branches are authorized to make business improvement loans under provisions of the *Small Business Loans Act*. In addition, loans may be made by credit unions, caisses populaires, or co-operative credit societies, trust companies, loan companies, and insurance companies that have applied and have been designated as lenders under the act by the Minister of Finance.

Banks and other lenders can advise applicants if they qualify for loans under this legislation and how their particular credit needs can be arranged.

ii. Loan purposes

Business improvement loans can be used to finance the following:

• The purchase, construction, renovation, improvement, or modernization of premises

- The purchase of land necessary for the operation of a business enterprise

- The purchase, installation, renovation, improvement, and/or modernization of new or used equipment

- Debt incurred to acquire fixed assets purchased during a period not exceeding 180 days prior to applying for the loan

iii. Terms and conditions of loan

The detailed terms and conditions of a business improvement loan are worked out between you and the bank. In establishing the loan terms, the bank will take into account the type of business, the purpose for which the loan is to be made, and your ability to repay. In all cases, however, the following conditions must be met:

- The loan must be repaid within ten years.

- Subject to the $250,000 loan maximum, loans can be used to finance up to 90 percent of the asset acquisition costs.

- Banks are required to take collateral security in accordance with their usual commercial practice. The one exception is that personal guarantees may not exceed 25 percent of the original amount of the loan and may not be secured by personal assets.

iv. Security for loan

It would be a classic understatement to say that banks are "security" conscious. This is by far the most important factor in a banker's mind when he or she is assessing your proposal. Needless to say then, all business loans must be secured. For equipment loans the bank will take a "chattel mortgage," and for premises loans the bank will take a mortgage on the premises.

In the case of a land loan, a first mortgage on the land purchased is mandatory. In some cases additional security may be required. You are also required to personally sign a promissory note.

In general, banks are expected to make loans with the same care that is required of a bank in the conduct of its ordinary business and to use normal banking practices in drawing up agreements and servicing the loans.

v. Interest rate

The interest rate charged on a floating basis cannot exceed 1.75 percent over the prime lending rate. In addition, the interest rate may be fixed at a rate not exceeding 1.75 percent above the bank's base residential mortgage rate for the applicable term.

vi. Government fee

There will be a one-time front-end fee of 2 percent of the loan which the bank must collect and pay to the federal government. The fee may be charged to the borrower and may be added to the amount of the loan.

vii. Application for a loan

If you are interested in a business improvement loan, you may simply discuss your financial requirements with the manager of the lending agency of your choice. You may obtain duplicate copies of the Small Business Loan Application form (form B-1) from your lending agency and, when they are properly completed, return them for processing (which normally takes less than a week).

Shop around for your business improvement loan as you would for any other. But if the loan is not granted, you should insist on a letter listing the reasons for rejection. If the reasons don't make good business sense, or if the manager is unwilling to process the application form, you should write or telephone your Member of Parliament and give him or her the full details of the problem encountered applying for a loan under this federally sponsored program, preferably with photocopies of the correspondence.

Remember, if you feel you are eligible there is no reason why you shouldn't get this cheap money, although there is some discretion open for the banker to determine your eligibility.

3.3 Institutional term lenders

Institutional term lenders engage in the financing of fixed assets such as property and equipment, including mobile units (e.g., trucks and boats). They are also involved in related fields, such as leasing, which is really another form of financing. Term lending is available from various sources including the Business Development Bank of Canada (BDC), most chartered banks, and many credit unions.

Typically, institutional lenders like to see long-term loans (of a minimum of three years) with an interest rate ranging from reasonable to high, depending on the security. Their rates would be comparable to the Business Development Bank of Canada rate.

One thing to be careful of is the floating interest rate that is hinged to the bank's prime rate. Most business people like to know what their interest costs are, and a floating rate leaves this question unanswered. Avoid it, if possible.

3.4 Credit unions

There has been a tremendous expansion of credit union activity over the last two decades. While most of this activity is because the number of consumer loans has increased, there is no reason why a small business cannot borrow from a credit union, as long as the company is prepared to join the credit union as a member.

Typically credit unions are a bit more flexible than banks and will deal in both term and working capital loans. Their rates are normally a shade higher than banks. However, their flexibility and relative informality may be worth the price.

4. USING YOUR HOME TO RAISE MONEY

If you own your own home, you may be in luck, even if you are making mortgage payments. As you are aware, mortgage interest payments on private residences are not tax deductible in Canada as they are in the United States. So, in addition to the fact that we end up paying for our home about three times over during the life of the mortgage, to be really accurate we should add on another 30 percent to 50 percent because we make these payments with after-tax money.

In simpler terms, in order to make a $1.00 payment on your mortgage (95 percent of which is interest), you have to earn between $1.30 and $1.50 depending on your tax rate. Sounds unfair? It is, but there is a way around it.

If you own your home free and clear, simply arrange to have it put up as security against the loan for your business. The interest then becomes tax deductible. Even if there is a mortgage already registered against your house, you may use the remaining equity as "collateral" security, which means that the value of the house less the value of the mortgages registered against it would act as a "backup" or "extra" level of security for the lender. Offering collateral security often makes the difference in a loan deal.

5. OTHER SOURCES OF MONEY

As I mentioned at the start of this chapter, there are many, many sources of capital in Canada. Below I briefly outline some other sources to give you an idea of the scope available and to widen your horizons accordingly.

5.1 Leasing

The idea behind leasing is to concentrate on how much money you make on your assets — not on the fact that you own them. Leasing provides more flexibility than purchasing, and all costs are normally tax deductible. The price you pay is a relatively high interest rate.

5.2 Accounts receivable (factoring)

Under the accounts receivable method, receivables are sold at a discount to a factoring firm. It's relatively expensive and not usually a viable alternative for a young firm just starting out.

5.3 Venture capital

There are numerous investment companies in Canada that specialize in venture capital financing. Many specialize in certain fields of investment, such as technology companies or transportation businesses, so you should research which venture capitalists might be interested in your kind of business before you approach them.

For more information you can contact —

> Canadian Venture Capital Association
> MaRS Centre
> Heritage Building
> 101 College Street, Suite 120 J
> Toronto, ON M5G 1L7
> Telephone: (416) 487-0519

There's no sense in approaching a venture capitalist to borrow $10,000 to open a corner doughnut shop. Don't even bother asking for $50,000. The smallest amount that most of them will lend in practice (ignore what the brochures say) is $100,000, and they feel right at home in the $250,000 and up range.

The word "venture" also tends to conjure up ideas of "new" and innovative. Paradoxically, however, most venture capitalists avoid bankrolling start-ups. They are more comfortable financing the rapid expansion of a young business.

If you're still interested, be prepared for a gruelling analysis. Typically, venture capitalists purchase a minority equity position with possible conversion to debt or majority interest if things go badly. In some cases, they may set a target of having your company list its shares on a stock market after a specific revenue goal has been reached and they will see that Initial Public Offering (IPO) as their time to cash out and take their profits.

They also demand a say in the running of your business, which may be a major stumbling block. The plus side of that coin is, they often have access to specialist managers and can help you obtain the services of those people on a consulting or more permanent basis.

The venture capitalist's general approach to life is that their security is in the management and its performance, which is their only downside protection (many venture capital investments are in private companies and there is no market for their shares, although the IPO scenario mentioned above is fairly common for fast-growth businesses in "hot" business sectors).

They look for growth in excess of 20 percent per year compounded and they are more interested in capital gains than in earnings on debt, despite the fact that many venture capital deals involve a mixture of debt and equity or convertible debt.

5.4 Angel Investors

When funding is difficult to arrange through a bank or venture capital firm, many owners of small firms look for an "angel."

Angel investors are people who invest money in dynamic, young businesses. Usually successful business people themselves, they are capable of making good business decisions and of recognizing when a venture has good potential. Some angels invest because they enjoy the excitement and challenge of being involved with the launch of a new business venture. Others are clever and cautious investors whose main motivation is to receive a good return on their investment. Angel financing is sometimes known as *informal venture capital.*

Should you look for an angel if you want to raise capital? Consider the following:

(a) Venture capitalists turn down the majority of applications that they receive. Since there are many more angels than there are venture capitalists, your chances of getting the financing may be better with an angel.

(b) Most people who arrange angel funding find angels who are operating businesses locally. Geographic proximity makes the deal more appealing to many angels, who may prefer to invest in their own community, or who may simply feel more secure knowing that you are located nearby. Look for angel investors in your social or professional network or by placing an ad in your local newspaper.

(c) The angel will have a rate of return and a security level in mind. These rates may vary wildly, but you will have to convince your would-be angel that investing in your business will be more rewarding than if he or she used the money for other purposes. In other words, you will have to convince them that putting money in *your* business idea will be better for them in some way than if they put that money in the stock market or saved it for their retirement.

Some angels may be looking for psychological rewards as well. They may be motivated by the idea that they can invest in an exciting new concept; they may be interested in being the wise mentor; they may enjoy the feeling of power that their investment will give them — and so on.

Your job is to identify that motivation and address it.

(d) Since most angels are successful business people, they are able to offer guidance and coaching in your business operations. The degree of involvement will vary, but given that you are using their money, expect to find that your angel doesn't just take a back seat. Some people find that their angel wants more involvement and a stronger voice in the decision making than they prefer. Others complain that their angel is a demanding taskmaster who more closely resembles a devil.

(e) If your business is not doing well, the angel is likely to step in and take over. He or she has an interest in protecting the investment and probably will not hesitate to act if he or she thinks it is needed.

Since the angel market is unregulated, both you and the angel will want to exercise caution. If you choose to go this route, with all of its pros and cons, the important thing is to try to understand in advance the role that your angel will want to play, and decide if this role is within your comfort level. If not, you will have to make a hard decision as to whether this is the right relationship for you.

5.5 Private placement (minimum $500,000)

The expression "private placement" is used to describe financing where stock is placed with a handful of institutions. Although it can be done directly, frequently an intermediary such as an underwriter or broker is involved. The amount involved is rarely less than $500,000 and is usually greater.

Frequently a deal too large for a single venture capital company will end up becoming a private placement in which one or more venture capital companies may participate, alongside typical purchasers such as pension funds, banks, life insurance companies, trust companies, etc.

Private placements go in and out of vogue, depending on the condition of the stock market. They are generally in vogue at times when the stock market is slow and new stock launches (IPOs or Initial Public Offerings) are difficult. Under these circumstances, it is cheaper and less complicated to place the stock with informed purchasers who understand the vagaries of the market and are prepared to take their chances in return for a reasonable discount.

There is less work because there is frequently no need for a prospectus; a lower fee, which is usually on a commission or agency basis; and less stringent requirements with exchange commissions.

Again, it can be seen that primarily because of the need for size, this particular type of financing is rarely available to the small business — and certainly highly unlikely if your financial needs are under $500,000. A typical range for private placements is in the range of $500,000 to $3 million.

5.6 Franchising

Yes, franchising can be described as an alternative way of financing a business. For the small-business person, however, franchising also represents the golden key to independence and riches. For this reason I have devoted an entire chapter to franchising (see Chapter 7).

5.7 Going public (minimum $1 million)

Many people who start small businesses dream of "going public" with their business. The pot at the end of the rainbow is the reason — and this certainly was true in the heady stock market days of the late 1990s when new technology and Internet issues were selling for huge multiples of their often meager and sometimes non-existent earnings. (The owner retains a good chunk of the stock and then sells to the public at inflated prices.)

A rule with new issues, if there are any rules, is to go public early and try to sell your concept to the public when it is just developing and still a pure concept. In a bull market, if you miss the concept stage you will have to wait until maturity when substantial earnings make investment in your company an attractive proposition. The harsh reality of a young company with few sales and a handful of profits — or losses — only confuses investors. The phenomenon is demonstrated in the mines and oil markets where a hole in the ground often attracts more interest than a company solidly in the development stage of its growth. At any rate, today it is necessary to be reasonably large and have a fair record of earnings to justify using the public as a source of capital.

An exception to the above rule has been technology companies. Many new technology stocks have been launched successfully despite the companies having few sales and little or no profits. It remains to be seen whether this trend continues, but if your business will be in the high technology sector or the biotechnology sector and you are planning on seeking venture capital investors, you might find you are involved in discussing an IPO while the business is still at the concept stage.

Among the costs of a market for your shares is full disclosure and a somewhat unpredictable reaction to your company's performance. A further cost, if venture capital is involved, is that the venture capitalists may want quite a large portion of the company's shares in return for their investment because they will view the public offering as their payoff. The benefits are liquidity, access to specialized management skills if venture capital is involved and, from time to time, a higher value on your stock than if it were closely held and not readily marketable.

6. MORE TIPS ON APPROACHING YOUR LENDER

You should plan your requirements well ahead of time. A lender does not want to be approached at the last minute because you have a payroll to meet.

Remember also that the lender needs time to assess your proposal. It is entirely possible that the person you deal with can't approve the loan on his or her own.

Furthermore, it is a good idea to approach more than one lender — but don't go overboard.

What are your needs? You should know what they are in advance, and the only way I know to properly forecast needs is to have a monthly cash flow budget for at least 12 months. Without one, you really cannot deal effectively with your own bank, let alone a possible outside investor.

While it will not be possible to identify all your needs in order of priority right at the beginning, it should be possible, by a gradual process of exposure and feedback, to steadily identify them. For example, if engineering and design is likely to be a continuing problem, possibly it would make more sense to see a supplier or an individual with that type of background than your banker. If planning and money management are weak, then the BDC, with their consulting services, may be a good source.

Do not substitute fanciness for thoroughness. A well drawn-up, pencilled presentation that has been photocopied, is written clearly, and is legible is better than a glossy presentation with no hard facts and a lot of verbal garbage.

Research your sources. While reading articles will give you a general feel for the field, some hard work in terms of sifting through brochures and talking to your accountant, lawyer, or bank manager may be advisable.

You need a short list of those who should be interested in your proposition before you go knocking on doors. Use the advisors you already have. Most businesses have a banker, an accountant, an insurance agent, and a lawyer. It's in their interest to see your business succeed, so don't be afraid to approach them.

If you are turned down or sense that the interview is going badly, do not be miffed. Rather, play helpless, get them to say why and how they look at you and your deal, and get some guidance as to how to make it better and who else to see — then be prepared to rethink your situation before you go to the next source.

For example, suppose you have approached your bank for a $2,000 loan. You feel that a loan will be cheaper than the interest being charged by your supplier. Your presentation includes the following information:

BALANCE SHEET
MY COMPANY

Accounts receivable	$1,000
Stock	3,500
	$4,500
Owing to suppliers	$4,000
Equity	500
	$4,500

Loan requested: $2,000

Purpose: to pay suppliers

Repayment: from Christmas sales (cash flow, showing that sufficient funds would be available, was provided to the lender)

Security: accounts receivable and inventory totalling $4,500

Your banker will likely decline this proposal. You do not understand, as the money will be there to repay the loan and there is sufficient security. You ask why. Your banker replies that the business is undercapitalized. Now you have two choices. You can walk out the door wondering what on earth he or she really means by undercapitalization, or you can *ask* what he or she means. (This seems obvious, but many people are reluctant to do so.)

Your banker will explain that your investment in the company is too small. Your debt-to-equity ratio is 8:1 (you owe your suppliers $4,000 and your equity is just $500). However willing to be a partner in your business, the banker likes to see you take a reasonable share of the risk.

In this case, if the business is not successful, the bank will lose $8 for every $1 that you lose. To the banker, this risk will be unacceptable.

Consequently, he or she suggests that if you invest another $1,500 in the business, the bank will be "prepared to look at your proposal again."

This is the point at which you must re-examine the entire proposal. Some of the questions you can ask yourself:

- Do I have the $1,500?

- Can I take in a partner or borrow the money from friends?

- Can I wait and pay the suppliers after my Christmas sales are in?

- Can I approach another lender?

In this situation you should likely continue to use your supplier's credit until after the Christmas sale period. If this period has been successful, new earnings will have been generated by the business to increase the equity and at the same time cash will have come in to pay the suppliers.

The cost to you is some overdue interest charges. (This is a good time to implement "the cheque is in the mail" strategy.) You can then approach the bank before the next buying season. Plan your requirements for the next year.

7. GOVERNMENT HELP

There are government programs, both federal and provincial, that are designed to help business. It's worth some of your time to seek them out. While budget constraints have eliminated many of them, there is still some valuable assistance available.

If you have never applied for a government grant before, or you are simply uninformed about the programs available, you may assume that you are ineligible. However, unless the program you are investigating is entirely foreign to your situation, it may well pay you to apply.

You can start by writing to the appropriate government department and asking them to send you any information they have on assistance programs for small businesses. They will be happy to send you their literature.

One more piece of advice — if you are seeking government assistance, don't make any commitments elsewhere concerning your project; that includes signing leases, ordering materials, and contracting builders. If you do, the government will realize you have already decided to go ahead with your idea whether or not you get government assistance.

The government is a source of last resort and is there to make your dream possible only if you have exhausted all other sources for funds and would give up your idea if not for its help.

Because of the multitude of government programs, I have outlined below the benefits of the two major federal agencies involved in helping businesses:

- Business Development Bank of Canada

- Industry Canada

I have also outlined the other federal programs in alphabetical order by subject and provide a suggestion about provincial agencies that offer help.

7.1 Business Development Bank of Canada

The Business Development Bank of Canada (BDC) is a federal Crown corporation set up to help create and develop Canadian small- and medium-sized businesses. BDC offers a variety of specialized financing and consulting programs and support to fit each stage of a business's growth.

BDC's financial services include everything from micro-business and flexible term loans to working capital loans and venture capital. This wide range enables the bank to provide the right kind of financing, at the right time, to support the long-term growth of Canadian businesses in all sectors of the economy, including knowledge- and export-based industries.

In order to design a loan agreement that will best help a business succeed, BDC does everything possible to structure repayments according to a client's ability to pay. The bank offers a variety of flexible terms and conditions, such as stepped principal payments, seasonal payments, and, in some cases, deferred principal repayment.

For further information, call 1-877-BDC-BANX, contact your local BDC branch (listed in the white pages of your telephone book), or visit the website at www.bdc.ca.

7.2 Industry Canada

Industry Canada is the arm of the federal government devoted to the care and nurturing of Canadian business. It is concerned with trade issues, technology, productivity, and business development. It also works in conjunction with your provincial government via provincial Canada Business Service Centres. You can call these centres, or your provincial small business bureau, for up-to-date information on government services and programs.

Another route to information is Service Canada at 1-800-662-6232 (1-800 O CANADA). Service Canada can give you addresses and telephone numbers for information on all federal government programs and services.

7.3 Specialized federal programs to help you

7.3a Agriculture and Agri-Food Canada

The *Prairie Grain Advance Payments Act* makes interest-free cash advances available to producers, as does the *Advance Payments for Crops Act*. Agriculture and Agri-Food Canada also sponsors programs for the distribution, storage, processing, and marketing of agricultural goods.

Of interest to the small-business person establishing a farm is the *Farm Credit Canada Act*, which allows for farm loans for qualifying applicants. The loan can be to buy land, make improvements, buy breeding stock and equipment, or to consolidate debt: it is amortized over a period of up to 30 years.

Finally, the *Farm Improvement Loans Act* makes it easier to get term loans to buy equipment or to carry out a wide range of farm improvement projects. Under this Act, the federal government guarantees lenders against losses incurred in loans made in accordance with the act.

Only a farmer may borrow, but it is not necessary in all cases to be the owner of a farm to be eligible. A farmer who is a tenant may apply. The borrower must be in possession of a farm and the operation of that farm must be the borrower's principal occupation.

All chartered banks and the Alberta Treasury Branches are authorized to make loans under this Act. Loans may also be obtained from credit unions, caisses populaires, or other co-operative societies, trust companies, loan companies, and insurance companies that have been designated as lenders under the act.

The detailed terms and conditions of the loan are arranged between you and the lender. The lender will take into account the type of farming carried on, the purpose, the life of the asset being financed, your income, and your ability to repay.

The loan must be secured. Security is usually a first charge on the item purchased or a mortgage on the farm property. You must also sign a written promise to repay the loan.

You should plan your proposed investment carefully and consider its implications on the overall productivity of your farming enterprise. Where appropriate, discussions with your local agricultural extension agent or farm management specialist would be beneficial.

Refinancing of existing debts, purchase of marketing quotas, or working capital requirements are not eligible.

Further information on farm improvement loans is available from your local bank.

7.3b Canada Mortgage and Housing Corporation

Loans for new house construction and to investors in rental housing development are insured up to 90 percent under the *National Housing Act* through the Canada Mortgage and Housing Corporation (CMHC). These loans are negotiated through your chartered bank and other financial institutions and mortgage companies; therefore, you must meet the requirements of the lending institution and convince them of the viability of your income property plan.

CMHC also does extensive research in home technology covering design, innovation, and environmental issues. This research is available from each regional office. Call the office nearest you or check out their website at www.cmhc-schl.gc.ca.

7.3c Export Development Canada

Export Development Canada (EDC) is a Crown corporation that provides a wide range of insurance and bank guarantee services to Canadian exporters and arranges credit for foreign buyers to facilitate and develop export trade. EDC also provides guarantees to banks that finance exports through buyer or supplier credits.

The most widely used insurance service is export credits insurance, which protects the exporter against nonpayment by the foreign buyer. The most widely used export credits insurance service is Global Comprehensive, which covers both political and commercial risks and can be used for worldwide exporting.

EDC's financing services support the sale of capital goods and services — those financed on credit terms of one year or more. EDC will lend up to 85 percent of the contract price to support the sale.

For information on EDC services, contact the regional office that serves your province or territory; there are 13 offices throughout Canada. Or contact —

Corporate Communications Department
Export Development Canada
151 O'Connor Street
Ottawa, ON K1A 1K3
Toll free: 1-866-283-2957

7.3d Fisheries Improvement Loans Act

This *Fisheries Improvement Loans Act* program makes it easier to get term loans for a variety of fisheries improvement projects. The act authorizes the Minister of Finance to guarantee term loans granted to commercial fishing concerns.

Only if you fish commercially may you borrow under this program. A loan may be made for buying, building, or repairing a boat; for new fishing equipment; or for new shore installations.

Security and a promissory note are required. For more information contact your local bank.

7.3e Indian and Northern Affairs Canada

Indian and Northern Affairs Canada (INAC) operates programs that support economic development in First Nation and Inuit communities, and encourage aboriginal people's participation in the economy through business development. Programs such as Aboriginal Business Canada provide funding and assistance for aboriginal entrepreneurs, for both new and existing businesses.

INAC also provides resources to those businesses (both Indian and non-Indian) that are a viable source of employment for Indian people. Contact your local Canada Business Centre (see the next section) for more information.

7.4 Provincial programs

Most provincial governments sponsor seminars and workshops for the small-business person, and I have always found these worthwhile. For details just keep your eye on your local paper or contact the agency involved.

Because there are so many programs offered and because they change all the time, the most practical thing for you to do is to contact the agency that would be the most help to you and ask for details about the current programs offered.

7.5 Confused? Call your local Canada Business Service Centre

Helpful as these and the many other kinds of programs are, trying to sort out who to contact about what kind of assistance can be the biggest headache.

One of the most useful things the government has done is set up Canada Business Service Centres in each province to provide easy access to the federal, provincial, and even some private programs that affect business. In most provinces the Business Service Centre is a joint effort of the provincial and the federal governments, and in some cases, collaborates with not-for-profit organizations.

Province-wide toll-free numbers put you in touch with an extensive information bank and staff experts who will find the information you want. Your local Canada Business Service Centre is listed under Government of Canada in the blue pages of your telephone directory or visit their website at www.canadabusiness.ca.

8. EMPLOYMENT INCENTIVES

Governments are always interested in increasing the quantity of people employed in the workforce, as well as developing their quality. Both the federal and provincial governments have programs to accomplish these goals, and municipalities may sometimes introduce incentives on a local basis as well.

The purpose of these programs may be to create new jobs, to encourage skills training, or to encourage the hiring of various hard-to-employ individuals.

8.1 New jobs

In some areas of the country, usually those with high unemployment rates, there will be grants available to help businesses get started. The funds that come from these sources can often be applied to the purchase of equipment, renovation of facilities, and occasionally even working capital rather than directly on wages, but the granting agencies will only make such money available if you are creating new employment as part of the process.

Some provinces also have programs to encourage job sharing. Job sharing is where two employees might share one full-time job for a total of 40 hours a week. Such programs are usually designed to prevent layoffs from larger more established companies rather than extending existing part-time employment, but as the rules are often changed, you should not discount this type of program as helping pay for the labour or support you want.

8.2 Skills development

It is to your benefit to maintain the abilities of your employees at the highest possible level, but such training naturally costs money. Fortunately, governments recognize that it is to Canada's benefit to upgrade the knowledge of its workers, and there are ongoing programs to do this.

The incentives may be aimed at encouraging very specialized skills, such as welding, machine-repair or programming, or more everyday abilities such as teaching or upgrading computer skills.

Incentives may vary from the underwriting of course fees and associated costs to the subsidy of wages for time spent on courses on or off the job. They may be spent on existing employees, or to hire new ones, particularly for apprentices who want real work experience.

Incidentally, in order to give students similar "real world" experience, many colleges and universities have co-operative programs to place their students or graduates in jobs. Such programs may vary from "practicums" where the individual will work for you free of charge for 40 to 60 hours, usually on a specific project, to assistance in interviewing and selecting qualified candidates in marketing, sales, and design.

8.3 Hard-to-employ persons

Individuals who have physical disadvantages, such as blindness or lack of a limb, often have difficulty finding a job due to the prejudices of employers, as well as the problems they face of transportation or needing special work facilities.

Others who have difficulty are those with no appropriate training in basic skills, as well as those who find themselves in a vicious circle of welfare, availability for employment, and finding the necessary qualifications and experience to get hired.

In both cases, governments will pay to encourage you to hire people with these disadvantages. In broad terms, such payments may be up to 100 percent of their salaries, and may last as long as a full year, or may pay for the cost of special equipment, but you should contact the appropriate agency for the complete details. You usually must provide a comprehensive training plan that demonstrates that the person you hire will benefit from the job experience.

These types of programs offer a tremendous opportunity to give you an employee paid for in part or in full by the government. But it also imposes a large responsibility on you to select the potential person very carefully, as well as to thoroughly train him or her.

7
WHAT ABOUT FRANCHISING?

If you are starting a small retail or service business of your own or even if you just want to expand your present business, you may consider franchising.

The concept of franchising is sound. It offers the novice entrepreneur a chance to own his or her own business and helps to minimize the chances of failure. Failure rates in franchising are estimated to be 80 percent lower than independent small business. But the main reason to consider buying a franchise is that it allows you to take advantage of the franchisor's business experience and to capitalize on proven business systems.

The purchase of a franchise, like all business, does entail risk, so do some research before you put your hard-earned money on the line. Not all franchise operations are good ones so check them out carefully. The purpose of this chapter is to help you do just that.

The cost of a franchise varies and can run from a few thousand dollars to close to a million. But a small investment can make you the boss of a franchised crafts store, campground, candy store, cleaning establishment, coin-operated service, counselling firm, employment agency, fast food outlet, hearing aid distributorship, motel, printing service, roadside stand, or tool rental agency. And that's only a partial list.

The initial cost of a franchise normally includes the franchise fee and the cost to set up the operation. Ongoing costs include royalties and advertising.

A good rule of thumb to follow if you are considering the purchase of a franchise is to ask yourself, "Is the money that I am required to invest equally offset by the training, advertising, and general initial costs incurred by the franchisor?" If the answer is yes, you can assume that the franchisor is genuinely interested in the success of the business and you.

If not, you can assume the franchisor makes a profit from selling franchises and not from the product or service — so beware!

By the way, if your plan is to buy an existing franchise, one already in operation, be sure to contact the franchisor. Don't just assume you can take over under an existing contract. In most instances, a contract will be null and void without the franchisor's approval.

1. WHAT IS FRANCHISING?

Franchising is essentially a system of distribution under which an individually owned business is operated as though it were part of a large chain, complete with trademarks, uniform symbols, design, equipment, and standardized services or products. Franchising can be used for almost any type of business.

As a marketing technique, franchising is uniquely North American. It began before the turn of the century, when automobile manufacturers and petroleum refiners licensed new car dealers and gasoline service stations to retail their products in assigned areas. These retailers were supported with nationwide advertising and publicity.

From these beginnings, the idea was picked up for fast food service places, car rental businesses, drug stores, and auto parts stores. Such services as dance studios and janitorial services were soon added.

Franchising began to flourish after World War II because opportunities were offered to small investors to operate franchised roadside businesses (primarily drive-in food and ice cream stands). When such drive-ins began to spread all over the landscape, franchising became a magic word.

Today, hundreds of companies market many products and services through franchised outlets. Moreover, some of the best known and oldest names in industry are using franchised stores to expand into new markets with new or established products and services.

If you are a small investor, franchising can minimize your risk of failure by allowing you to start a business under the image of a corporate name and trademark and by offering you training and management assistance from experienced personnel.

Sometimes you may also be offered financial assistance so that you can start a business of your own with less than the usual amount of cash. In addition, franchising makes it possible for you to be associated with a regional, national, and sometimes international organization. From the standpoint of the companies offering franchises (the franchisors) this type of business operation makes their rapid expansion possible.

Whether or not you are ready for franchising depends on several things, including your present situation. Are you thinking of closing out your present business and opening a franchise business or do you intend to start a franchise operation from scratch? Maybe you are considering the possibility of adding a franchised line, or lines, to an existing business. But before you decide, think carefully of how much of your independence you would have to give up.

As with any other type of business undertaking, your returns in franchising are related directly to the amount of time and money you invest. Contrary to what some people may think, franchising is not a get-rich-quick deal, nor is it an easy road to expansion for the franchisor. There are dangers in franchising for both franchisor and franchisee.

2. ADVANTAGES AND DISADVANTAGES

Generally, the principal advantage of franchising is that it enables you, as an investor, to capitalize on experience that you might otherwise have to obtain the hard way — through trial and error.

The parent company uses its experience in business locations, management, advertising, publicity, product research, and development to enable its franchisees to start and operate its outlets with optimum efficiency, maximum profitability, and minimum friction. When the company's products are proven and well-known products, your business has an instant pulling power. On your own, it would probably take years of promotion and considerable investment to build such an identity and goodwill.

Yet by franchising, you will lose your personal identity to that of the parent company, which has tremendous sums of money invested in building and maintaining its identity for your use. So, if you enjoy having your business known by your name, a franchise business may not be for you. On the other hand, consider the increased sales and profits you might make with a franchise arrangement.

Remember, though, that in a franchise operation you cannot make all the rules. Contrary to the many "be your own boss" lures in franchise advertisements, you may not truly be your own boss. The extent to which you are the captain of your own ship depends on the franchise contract. You may have no effective voice in deciding your own future or the products you want to sell. Even your hours and days of business may be specified in the contract. You have to live by the rules of your franchise contract; so, be sure that they are acceptable to you before you sign it.

Perhaps a brief look at the parent company's side will be helpful in understanding some of the rules that are in the contract.

Manufacturers or distributors start franchising operations to trade proven experience and known product acceptance for your money and time. Thus their sales can be increased at lower cost than if their companies, alone, had to put up all the money.

A big problem for the franchisor is that of picking the right kind of people to run the franchised outlets. The parent company has the disadvantage of having to deal with individuals who, when they become successful, may forget about the parent company's "helping hand" that boosted them to prosperity. "They've got nothing to offer me," is the way some of these business people feel at this stage, thinking that they could have been successful without the parent company.

Even when the right kind of people are chosen, the franchisor has serious problems in administration and control. After all, the franchisees are individual small-business people — not company-employed managers. Therefore, a reputable parent company tries to use a contract containing rules with which both the company and the outlet operator can live in a team framework, if not in a team spirit.

3. BEWARE THE HARD SELL

Just as in any other business, some franchise operators can be highly unethical. Beware of anyone with flashy advertisements that promise you huge profits with little commitment. If anyone tries to rush you into signing a contract without fully explaining the proposal to you, back off until you have the chance to check things out.

Also, be careful of newspaper or magazine ads offering to sell a business at a loss. Of course, with the number of bankruptcies today, many of these ads are legitimate. But some are written by unscrupulous business people who will try to lure you into buying without reading the fine print of the contract.

For tips on how to screen opportunities, see the next chapter.

4. WHERE DO YOU START?

A good place to begin looking for franchise opportunities is the business section of your local newspaper. There you will find several franchises offered on a daily basis. Also, franchisors frequently run ads regarding opportunities available in trade magazines and the national press.

Because, typically, most franchising operations begin in the United States, you may want to have a look at Thursday's Wall Street Journal, which has several franchise-opportunity ads. For a wider survey of US franchises, write to —

International Franchise Association
1501 K Street, N.W., Suite 350
Washington, DC 20005
Telephone: (202) 628-8000
Website: www.franchise.org

There is also a Canadian association. Write to —

Canadian Franchise Association
5399 Eglinton Avenue West, Suite 116
Toronto, ON M9C 5K6
Telephone: (416) 695-2896
Toll Free: 1-800-665-4232
Website: www.cfa.ca

Also, your Chamber of Commerce will be able to tell you if any business shows are going to be held in your area in the next few months. Sometimes franchisors attend these shows to try to attract new franchisees. There, you can find out what is expected of you as a potential franchisee, and you can compare various franchise companies to see which would be best for you.

If you are interested in a very popular franchise, for example, a well-known fast food chain, all you need to do is go to a local outlet and ask for the address of the national headquarters. Then you can write for further information on that particular franchise.

Remember that it does take some time to start into a franchise. Once you have received the preliminary information from your choice of franchisors, you must apply for business and go through a thorough investigation to satisfy the franchisor. If you are accepted, you may have to go through a period of training before you are let out on your own. Any franchise that offers you a business overnight is one to check out carefully.

5. CHECK OUT THE FRANCHISOR

After you've made some preliminary enquiries and tentatively expressed interest in one or more companies, the next step is to check out the franchisor's reputation. Remember, the franchisor is proposing marriage, and the honeymoon soon ends after you sign the contract. You don't need the headaches and expense of a messy divorce a few months down the road.

A reputable company's most valuable asset is just that — its reputation. So, regardless of who is right or wrong in a particular situation, or even what the contract says, you stand a lot better chance of getting a fair shake from an established franchisor. Check with your Better Business Bureau, Chamber of Commerce, and bank. (A telephone call will probably produce more information than a formal letter.)

Also try to obtain a full credit report on the company offering the franchise and on its principals. Contact your bank for references here.

One of the best techniques for checking is to ask the company to provide you with a list of its existing franchisees in the area you are considering. From this list, you should select several names and visit their offices during business hours.

By spending at least a few hours at each location, you can get an idea of what's going on. How many customers come in? What do they buy? What amount? And so on. You should also take time to ask the franchisees about the business. Most good parent companies encourage their franchisees to answer all questions of prospective investors.

Before committing yourself to a franchise business, be sure you have all the facts. Remember that information is your greatest tool when selecting the franchise that would be best for you.

From the franchisor's point of view, the final selection of franchisees depends on many things. Some parent companies, for instance, will not select any franchisee who does not agree to accept a minimum period of training. Others require psychological or aptitude tests. Still others rely entirely on comprehensive questionnaires and personal interviews. Sometimes, the process begins with a parent company representative interviewing the prospective franchisee in his or her home. This interview is followed by a final interview at the parent company's headquarters.

If you refuse to travel to headquarters for this interview, many franchisors will disqualify you immediately. They feel that such a refusal indicates a lack of real interest in the opportunity they offer.

6. THE FRANCHISE CONTRACT

The licence, or franchise contract, is your key to franchising success. But it can also contain the seeds for disappointment and discontent, which can cause failure for both you and the parent company.

In effect, a franchise contract is an investment agreement between the franchisor — sometimes known as the parent company — and the franchisee — the investor.

Contracts may range from a simple one-page memorandum of agreement to highly complex documents in which every conceivable detail of business operation is spelled out. You should bear in mind that there is no standard franchise agreement any more than there is a uniform code of business practice.

Furthermore, there is no special significance in a simple contract as compared with a complex one. A great deal depends on the type of business being franchised and the method the parent company uses for selecting franchisees. In all cases, however, you should never sign a franchise contract without legal counsel. Today, the most reputable franchising companies insist that prospective investors do not sign until they have consulted their lawyer or at least close family advisors, or their accountants or bankers.

For a more detailed evaluation of the pros and cons of buying a franchise, see *Buying a Franchise in Canada*, another title in the Self-Counsel Business Series.

8
WHAT ABOUT BUYING A BUSINESS?

One shortcut to success is to buy a business. By buying instead of starting a business, you avoid many of the initial problems and you already have a proven market and profit picture. However, there always seems to be a price to pay, and in this case there are really two prices. One is money, and the second is time and effort.

If you buy a prosperous business, the money you lay out for goodwill is paying for these advantages. This may be money well spent. On the other hand, it may be entirely wasted if the business is really a failing one or has unforeseen problems. The lesson here is, again, before you invest — investigate.

Buying a business is like buying a house. You should look at many, many prospects before making an offer. By doing this, your perception of what you really are looking for is increased immeasurably.

Each day hundreds of small Canadian businesses change hands. For buyers and sellers alike, such changes of ownership are major events. The process is complex. A clear understanding of it, and careful planning of each step are needed for a logical, unemotional, and good decision. The transaction can then be closed in proper legal form, safe and fair for both parties.

This chapter outlines some of the key considerations involved in both buying and selling a business. For simple illustration, the case of a proprietorship is used, although similar considerations will apply to partnerships and to companies. In any case, it is essential that both the buyer and the seller invest enough effort in preliminary work in order to avoid a waste of everyone's time and money.

1. ADVANTAGES OF BUYING

If you have enough capital to buy a business that you want, you should probably go ahead and make the move. Here is why:

(a) You don't have to worry about all the problems of starting up a new business. All the supplies are there, and customers don't have to be introduced to the business.

(b) The previous owner will be able to give you valuable advice on business trends, failures, and successes. He or she will let you know how the location of the business affects sales, advertising, and prices.

(c) You will inherit suppliers, service people, and employees who all know the business.

2. LOCATING AND PURCHASING A BUSINESS

There are a number of things to bear in mind when locating and purchasing a business.

2.1 Select carefully

Select the size and type of business best suited to your interests, character, available capital, and prior experience. The selection of the type of business is a personal one, and the important considerations to keep in mind were discussed in Chapter 3.

2.2 Seek opportunities

Seek out opportunities that meet your requirements. This may be done in several ways.

2.2a Word-of-mouth contact

Word-of-mouth contact is the best way to begin. Many people never actively advertise that their business is for sale. Instead, they just quietly pass the word in the business community that they are looking for interested buyers. If you let people know that you are in the market, you may be able to get in on one of these deals.

You can also directly approach a business that you might want to buy. There's nothing wrong with entering, for example, a ladies' boutique and asking the owner if he or she has ever considered selling. The owner may say no, but he or she may also know of another boutique that is looking for a buyer.

2.2b Real estate brokers

If used properly, real estate brokers can provide valuable information about possible sellers and sources of financing. It is important to remember, however, that a broker is an agent of the seller, and, therefore, will be highly optimistic about the profits you can make by buying a particular business.

If you want to use a broker, look in the Yellow Pages under real estate agencies. Some do business brokerage on the side. Some will specialize in a particular type of business and others will handle almost any type of business. It is usually a good idea to call first and ask what type of businesses they handle.

2.2c Trade publications

Many trade publications advertise businesses specializing in the particular trade they cover. (If you are looking for a particular kind of business, this method eliminates a lot of time.)

2.3 Properly evaluate each opportunity

Sometimes people grab the first opportunity that comes along, rather than cautiously measuring their own capabilities and suitability for that particular business. These are the same people that are the first to lose money in their business and go bankrupt.

The evaluation of each opportunity on a comparative basis is the most crucial stage. Make sure you have satisfactory answers on all the following:

- The reason the business is up for sale

- Its assets and liabilities

- Its history, location, and potential

- Its profit record, operating ratios, and projections

Normally, small businesses do not sell overnight, so do not rush investigations; taking the time to get the necessary information will pay off when deciding whether to purchase and what price to settle for. Many successful business owners report that they considered alternatives for a year or more before deciding to go ahead.

An adverse trend that is apparent from the financial statements may reveal the true reason for selling; and you should establish the reasons for such a trend and determine whether it is reversible or whether, for example, changes in the character of the neighbourhood are responsible.

One of the principal assets often involved in a change of ownership is the inventory. A physical count, preferably by an independent appraiser, should be taken to establish a fair price for it, taking into account its salability, its condition and style, and making due allowance for any items that would have to be cleared out at a loss.

Similarly, accounts receivable should be analyzed for quality and aging. This simple analysis is an indication of the seller's credit and collection policies and of the level of operating capital required to support day-to-day operations.

If real estate is involved, a professional appraisal of its value might be money well spent, since its condition and versatility should be reflected in the price offered. What alterations are needed and at what cost? Similarly, the furniture, fixtures, and equipment should be assessed.

Gather all the competitive information you can. If, for example, you are considering a retail business, you will want to know if a Real Canadian Superstore or a Wal-Mart is moving into your market area.

Also, be sure to determine that there are no hidden liabilities such as unregistered liens against equipment, back taxes, or pending lawsuits. (A lawyer's help at this stage would be wise.)

The agreement of purchase and sale should spell out that all claims not shown on the balance sheet used as the basis of sale are the responsibility of the seller.

2.4 Establish a fair price

Establishing a fair price is the biggest problem. The seller understandably tries to put a price on the effort and money invested in the business. However, you are mainly interested in the ability of the business to yield a good return on your investment after allowing for a reasonable salary. In other words, you want to do more than just buy a job.

Therefore, the future potential is of primary interest when determining whether the business will yield a return on investment at least equal to, if not better than, alternative sources. If such is not the case, you shouldn't offer more than the value of the tangible assets. As the term suggests, these are assets that can be touched, weighed, or measured, and have real value.

You would not ascribe any value to "goodwill." Goodwill can be best described as that amount in excess of what the business is worth.

Convince the seller to forget about his or her prior investment and base the price realistically on present and future factors. The following steps might be useful in determining a price formula:

(a) Establish the tangible net worth of the business (i.e., assets less liabilities, ignoring any intangible assets such as goodwill).

(b) Estimate what dollar return (perhaps 20 percent) an outside investor would get on this amount if it were invested elsewhere with approximately the same degree of risk. This is called "earning power."

(c) Add a reasonable salary for yourself.

(d) Establish from the operating statements the average annual net earnings before taxes (net profit before deducting owner's drawings) for the past few years. This gives a means of comparing the historical earnings with those you could get from alternative sources open

to you. The trend of historical earnings is the key factor.

(e) Deduct the earning power (b) plus reasonable salary (c) from the average net earnings (d) to determine the business's "extra earning power."

(f) To value the intangibles, multiply (e) by the number of years of profitable operation. A well-established and successful business would justify using a factor of five or more; a less well-based enterprise might be fairly priced at a factor of one to three.

(g) Final asking price equals tangible net worth (a) plus value of intangibles (f).

Example:

Apply the price formula described above to evaluate two businesses up for sale.

	Business A	Business B
(a) Tangible net worth	$140,000	$140,000
(b) Earning power — 20% of (a)	28,000	28,000
(c) Reasonable salary for owner	20,000	20,000
(d) Average net earnings	58,000	32,000
(e) Extra earning power: (d) minus (b) and (c)	10,000	16,000
(f) Value of intangibles — (e) times no. of years	30,000	Nil
Final asking price (a) plus (f)	$170,000	$140,000

In the case of business A, the seller should get a substantial price of $30,000 for the intangibles (mainly "goodwill") because the business is well established and is probably earning more than you would likely get elsewhere with comparable effort and risk.

You would, in this example, recover the cost of goodwill (f) in three years. The reasoning is that if the business continues to average $58,000 net earnings per year, you will realize your 20 percent return on net worth, a salary of $20,000, plus $10,000 extra earnings each year. This last amount would equal, in three years, the $30,000 you paid initially for the goodwill.

For business B, there is no goodwill value because there is no extra earning power (e), and you might even conclude that the business is not worth its tangible net worth (a) because of the poor return on an investment of that size. Intangible assets often include patents, franchises, organization expenses, trademarks, and goodwill.

2.5 Location is important

The location of the business is very important. Consider the following factors.

2.5a First, check the lease

It is not uncommon for a lease to contain a clause that prevents a business person from selling the business. Read the fine print carefully! Also, you will want to clarify other terms of the lease. What kind of lease is it? Are rental payments fair in comparison to businesses nearby? If you have the wrong rental terms for you, you might see a quick end to your business.

2.5b Second, evaluate the location

Location can make or break your business. Try to evaluate the area by the traffic flow. What are the peak hours? Do people walk by or drive by? How well are the surrounding businesses doing?

The general rule is that the best area for a new business is a prosperous and growing one. However, sometimes a location off the beaten track can do just as well. For example, a waterfront business may be far away from the busy downtown, but if your city attracts a lot of tourists who like beaches, fishing, and water sports, it may be a lucrative location.

2.6 Ensure that the transaction is handled properly

Making sure the transaction is handled properly is very important. But, provided you have followed the preceding steps, you should not be far off the track.

You should keep two other points in mind, however. First, when negotiations look as though they're getting serious, contact a lawyer and an accountant. Make sure both have experience in this area — because many do not.

You need a lawyer to make sure that you are getting what you are paying for, and you need an accountant to arrange everything to your advantage in paying taxes (see 2.7 below). Again, if you don't know a good lawyer or accountant, ask your friends who are in business. They will be in the best position to know, and are almost always willing to help.

Caution: In case the business you intend to buy involves the sale of liquor in any way, make sure that you do not close any sale until you have received a liquor licence in your name. Liquor licences are not automatically transferable. Factors completely beyond your control may dictate denial of a licence to a new owner.

2.7 Tax considerations in buying a business or franchise

It is a sad fact today that tax considerations have become of prime importance when considering any business acquisition. This is especially true for you, the prospective purchaser. Properly structuring a deal tax-wise can literally save you 50 percent of the acquisition price — so it is imperative that you enlist the help of experts.

The point of this section is not to go into great detail on what you should and shouldn't be doing but to give you some basic guidelines about what you should be thinking about.

First, if you are buying a franchise, have the deal structured so that the franchise fee can be written off over a period of years. To do this, the franchise agreement must be related to a certain number of years and not be left open-ended. In other words, if you pay $20,000 for a franchise, the term of the agreement should be as short as possible. This way you can write off your investment over the period. But, you may not want to lose your franchise after a short time. You can protect yourself by including in the contract the automatic right to renew for further periods.

Second, if you are making a fire sale purchase, you should try to preserve these losses wherever possible by maintaining the legal structure. This can be done if the selling business was incorporated by purchasing the shares rather than the assets.

Third, if you are dealing with a proprietorship or partnership where goodwill is involved, try to have the assets valued higher (except land, which is not depreciable anyway) and the goodwill lower. This is because you can depreciate all the assets, while goodwill is only half depreciable — and at a lower rate than most assets. Offsetting this is the fact that if you live in a province that has sales tax (everywhere but Alberta) you will have to pay sales tax in the transfer. Sales tax can be substantial in some cases and may be an important consideration. There is a way of avoiding this tax through the use of a limited company which the seller uses to purchase the assets (this transaction is tax free) immediately before the sale and then the purchaser buys the shares of the company interest of the assets (also tax free).

Fourth, if you are purchasing shares, you should be incorporating a second company (holding company) to purchase the operating company. (I'm not deliberately trying to complicate your life.) This works as follows.

If you are borrowing the purchase price, say from a bank, you will be expecting the business to pay the interest and eventually the principal out of its savings. If you borrow the money personally to purchase the shares of an operating company, the only way to repay the principal part of the loan is to draw out salary or dividends — both of which are taxable in your hands. So you end up paying back the purchase price in after-tax money and, depending on your tax bracket, this could be up to 50 percent more.

However, if you form a separate holding company and have that company borrow the money to purchase the shares in the operating company, dividends can flow tax free to your holding company, which can then pay back the bank.

Even if you put up the purchase price personally, you are better off to lend the money to a holding company owned by you or your family and then you can have the loan repaid to you tax free. (Actually, since presumably you've already paid tax on the money you have, you are not really avoiding tax — just avoiding paying twice.)

Finally, keep in mind that what's good for you tax-wise will likely be bad for the seller — so in many cases it comes down to good old head-to-head negotiations.

3. FINANCING THE TRANSACTION

The financing of the transaction must now be considered, assuming that you and the seller have reached an agreement on the price. Remember not to put all your funds into the purchase price! You will need enough left over for operating capital and personal expenses until the business can begin paying you a salary.

The best way to pay for a business is to have the previous owner finance it. The reasons for this are the following:

(a) It locks the previous owner into ensuring the new owner succeeds. (After all, most owners after selling don't want to see it go bankrupt and end up owning it again.)

(b) You avoid having to justify prices to outside lenders because the owner has already done his or her best to convince you of the worth of the business and its assets, so he or she can't very well dispute the valuation.

(c) You avoid outside audit checks, loan applications, etc. This is really an extension of the second point, but don't underestimate it. The time and costs of securing outside financing can be significant.

(d) You can often negotiate better terms from the seller than from an outside source. In cases when the seller is anxious, it is relatively easy to negotiate advantageous financing terms, such as lower interest rates and extended terms.

(e) In case the seller misrepresents anything, you have an automatic right of setoff without having to initiate legal action. In this situation you can simply deduct your damages from the monthly cheque you send to the seller. **Note:** Make sure your financing agreement allows for this right of setoff.

The main thing to remember when buying a business is to insist on full disclosure of all facets of the business you are interested in purchasing. Do not be stampeded into making a snap decision. Insist on adequate time to do the necessary research.

9
LOCATION — HOME OR OFFICE?

Some of you may not have much choice when deciding where to set up shop. For example, if you want to get into the auto-wrecking business, there are very definite zoning restrictions on where you can operate. The same is true for any heavy industry or business that involves a physical plant of any size or that may cause a nuisance in a residential neighbourhood.

On the other hand, your location needs may be dictated by access to other facilities such as railway lines, an airport, or highways. In the retail goods or service business, pedestrian or vehicle traffic patterns may be your prime concern.

Needless to say, for some people it is one of the most important decisions. For others, it is not, and those people should consider locating in their home if lease, tenancy, and neighbourhood

regulations allow it. More and more people are finding it practical, convenient, and less costly to work at home. Furthermore, the advantages of today's technology make it not only easier, but often more efficient to work at home.

You must have a firm business address, a place where you can receive mail and customers, and somewhere to stock supplies. You must have a telephone. Why not operate at home, at least until your business grows to the point where you need more space? If you are willing to take a fast survey you'll be amazed at how many people are getting rich operating home-based businesses.

Operating a business from your home is not very different from operating a business from an office, warehouse, or shop anywhere else. But the advantages to be gained from doing business at home are almost too numerous to mention. The main advantages are these:

- You do away with traffic problems.

- You save money because you travel less.

- You don't have to dress up every morning.

- You can claim a portion of your home expenses as a tax deduction. (See section 3. of this chapter for further details.)

- You save time.

You can operate almost any kind of business from home. The majority of home-based businesses, however, fall under one of the following headings:

- Services (professional or specialized labour)

- Mail order

- Light manufacturing, distributing, or wholesale

Hence, one of the first and most vital decisions you have to make is whether to operate out of your home or whether to rent outside space. Again, sometimes you will have no choice if, for example, you are starting a retail business or manufacturing concern, which simply cannot fit into the basement.

Perhaps you live in a small, one-bedroom apartment and it is simply impossible to expropriate space for your business.

If you employ outside help, it will be more difficult to operate out of the house unless, of course, you employ only salespeople who are on the road all the time.

Consider also that you will need a business licence, and each city has regulations regarding the type of business you may operate out of the home. These regulations are not normally enforced too strenuously unless you become a nuisance to a neighbour, in which case the city has to act. So be careful not to be a nuisance.

Besides these considerations, the choice should be based on your personal needs and requirements. You may feel that you need office space for reasons of prestige, or you may feel that you simply do not have the self-discipline to avoid the many distractions that exist at home.

However, one of the main reasons for even starting your own business is to cut expenses, avoid heavy traffic, and make more money. Moreover, the time you spend driving from home to office or factory is wasted time.

For argument's sake, let's break down the factors involved in this decision. (The same method can be used even if comparing two rented premises.)

1. RENTED PREMISES

You have to pay rent, spend money on reasonable office furnishings, travel to and from your place of business, and pay hydro and telephone bills.

Let's break this down even further. Time is money. The time you spend travelling to and from your rented office is lost time. Also, travelling expenses will eat into your profits.

What if your new business doesn't pan out as expected? The money you laid out for rent, telephone, heat and light, office furniture, and travelling is lost money. But, if your business grows and makes money, you still have those fixed expenses. They cannot decrease.

Most likely, your expenses will increase, eating even deeper into your profits. You will have to earn more money in order to meet these fixed expenses. Any money that you pay out for the fixed expenses described above is money lost — money that you earned but cannot use.

2. OPERATING AT HOME

Here's some proof to show you that you save money and make more money working your business in your home. Let's list the monthly expenses involved in operating from a rented office downtown.

Office rent	$750
Telephone	150
Hydro	150
Travelling	200
Lunches	250

You could possibly save $1,500 per month by operating at home — maybe more if you evaluate your time lost in travelling.

So, if your aim is to make $1,000 per week running your own business, then isn't it more profitable to operate at home? Haven't you already made $1,500 a month because you saved these expenses?

The fact that you operate from your home can add two hours per day to your working time. Suppose you work for someone else from nine to five. That's eight hours. Add travelling time and expenses, and you will see what I mean.

You use up at least ten hours of every day with two hours unpaid time wasted! If you waste two hours each day travelling to and from your place of business, this adds up to many hours down the drain in one year! Just by working at home you can add those wasted hours to

your business or use those hours in leisure time with your family.

Here is something startling. Very few home businesses fail. Why is this? By operating at home you cut expenses and you do everything yourself. You know and control every phase of your business and you waste very little money on employees who are interested only in their own welfare!

All right, you've decided to operate from home, at least until growth and profits demand larger premises. Pick a room in your home, maybe in the basement, attic, or even your bedroom, and set up an office. You'll need a desk, a computer, letterhead, envelopes, business cards, pens, pencils, and a planned method of operation.

Finally, don't forget to get a business licence from your local city or municipal hall. After all, you are now operating a legitimate, profit-making business.

3. TAXES AND YOUR HOME

The general principle here is simple. If you are operating your business from your residence (either rented or owned), you are entitled to deduct a reasonable portion of the house expenses from your business income. To deduct such expenses, your home office must be your principal place of business. Recent amendments to the *Income Tax Act* will deny deductions unless it is the only office from which the business operates.

The expenses that relate specifically to the business part of the house may be claimed in full. Those that relate to the building as a whole (e.g., taxes and insurance) may be claimed only as a proportion of the business part to the whole building.

The amount of these expenses that apply to the business part must be reasonable. You can figure it out by dividing the square feet or number of rooms of the business part by the total square feet or number of rooms of the building. You may take whichever calculation is more beneficial to you. For example, if you have a seven-room house and use one room for an office, the business part is one-seventh of the total. But if the size of that room is 300 square feet (a basement office for example) in a house of 1,800 square feet, then the business part is one-sixth of the house.

If you own your own residence, you are also entitled to claim as an expense your mortgage interest and depreciation (or capital cost allowance) of the building. For capital cost allowance (depreciation) purposes, the price of one building and improvements should be figured out. You are entitled to a 10 percent yearly depreciation cost on the portion used for business.

Warning: If you claim capital cost allowance on the business part of the building, you will lose your principal residence status on that part and have to pay capital gains tax when you sell your house. Therefore, a better way to handle this is to ignore the capital cost allowance and simply have your business pay you a reasonable rent based on factors other than depreciation. This rent is tax-free to you because of the offsetting expenses and you retain your principal residence status on the whole building. (See Chapter 14 for additional information.)

If you use your personal telephone for business purposes, you cannot deduct the monthly cost. You can, however, deduct all long distance calls made for business purposes as well as the cost of any addition to your home telephone (i.e., extension lines for an extra telephone or for your computer modem).

4. YOUR PERSONAL LIFE VERSUS YOUR BUSINESS LIFE

If you operate your business in your home, you will be faced with the problem of how to govern your social and business obligations to maintain a sensible level of control over both. The only way you can control this problem is by allocating certain periods of times for business activity and other times for social engagements. Naturally, your business must come first because if your business fails, you won't have any money for social affairs.

If you work at home you must not allow yourself to be distracted by household chores or by your family. You must not let others use you to run errands or drive them to the dentist during allocated business hours. This is where you must be able to refuse people firmly. Have a set schedule for doing business and adhere to it.

Explain to your family that even though you are working at home you are not available every ten minutes for chats about household problems. Leave all home chores until after you've accomplished your work.

Make it clear at the start that when you go into your "office," you are not to be disturbed. You must have more self-discipline when you are your own boss than when you work for someone else.

10
SALES AND MARKETING

Marketing should be the number one priority of your business. You should be asking yourself, "What does the market want to buy?" instead of thinking only about what you want to sell. In other words, to be most successful, you must consider your business from the customer's point of view.

Ask these key questions:

- What are you selling?

- Who are your customers?

- Where are they?

- How do they buy?

As your business grows, the answers to these questions will help you determine the best way to maintain and increase your market. Should you sell outside the country? Should you sell directly or through retail stores? Should you expand your line of products?

If you always keep your market in mind, and you have the right products and provide the right service, you will attract an increased clientele.

1. PRODUCT OR SERVICE — WHICH DO YOU SELL?

Everything you sell is either a product or a service. You should understand which is which. Both a product and a service have an assigned value, but a product is something tangible whereas a service is time provided to someone in exchange for something else. For example, if you own a pizza restaurant, your pizzas would be your product, but your home delivery would be the service you sell.

Whether you are selling goods or services, you must keep your customers in mind and give them what they want. And even if you sell products, remember to be service-minded. You might want to refer to other titles published by Self-Counsel Press for more information, such as *Marketing Your Product*.

2. MARKETING TECHNIQUES

To keep your business operating successfully, you must make a profit and satisfy the needs and wants of your customers. You must consider your product, the price, the place, and the right promotional mix for your product. Consideration of these marketing principles, the four "Ps," will help you make your business successful.

2.1 What is the right product?

Simply remember that the right product is what the customer wants to buy and not what you want to sell. The right product will be sure to attract good sales.

2.2 What is the right price?

Again, you must think about your customer. What price is he or she willing to pay? If your prices are too high you will lose customers to the competition.

2.3 What is the right place?

The right place is the one that is the most convenient for the customer. You may have a great product, but if you are located in an undesirable area where there is no parking and little other business to attract attention, you will have trouble marketing your product.

You must also find the right place for your stock. For example, if you own a bookstore, you will want to keep the current bestsellers near the front to attract attention and where they are most convenient for the customers.

2.4 What is the right promotion?

Developing the right promotional mix of selling (direct or indirect), publicity, advertising, and public relations, is crucial to your success. If your customer does not know about your product or service or know how and where it can be bought, you will not sell it.

3. SATISFYING YOUR CUSTOMERS THROUGH SERVICES

Your business depends on attracting and maintaining repeat customers. No matter how good your product is, you won't do well unless you treat your customers well. You and your employees must always keep service-mindedness as your top priority. Your ability to serve your customers well may mean the difference between success and failure.

Service-mindedness means different things to different businesses. The needs of your market and business will change from time to time according to what you sell, where you are located, what the market is like, and the season. For instance, if suddenly there is an unexpected demand for an item at Christmas, you should increase your stock in that particular line and perhaps keep your business open longer hours — all part of service-mindedness.

Service-mindedness is important. Below are two examples:

Example 1:

Two stores — two attitudes

Flora Fisher always shopped at Number One General Store in town for groceries. When Flora sprained her wrist she asked the manager if someone could deliver her groceries. She lived only a little way from the store, so the manager asked a clerk to carry the groceries home for her. Ms. Fisher liked shopping at this store because the people were so helpful. She told all her friends about her pleasant experience and many of them started to do their own shopping there.

When Flora went to Number Two General Store to buy something on sale, she was treated completely differently. Although the store was clean and well-lighted, the clerks were not very helpful and the sale item was difficult to find.

Ms. Fisher doesn't shop at Number Two any more and she won't recommend it to her friends.

Example 2:

Few products or many products

Betty's boutique sells a selection of women's clothes and accessories. She also carries a large line of nurses' uniforms, shoes, and other hospital and clinic apparel. There is a large hospital and medical clinic within a few miles of Betty's store and she has a steady sale of all her goods.

In another town, Bertha's boutique sells a wider variety of clothes for women and younger boys and girls. There are more families than single women in Bertha's town so the children's clothes sell well.

Betty's store was more specialized, and Bertha's more diversified. Both served a need and found success.

The "willingness to serve" is the reason for success of these two stores. Both owners kept a careful check of what sold well in their area and stocked their merchandise accordingly.

Don't try to please everyone all of the time. That is not service-mindedness. It is impossible to carry every kind of product that customers will want. You must make a decision on a few products that will serve the market and market them well.

4. HOW TO ATTRACT CUSTOMERS

The key to attracting new customers is showmanship and dramatization. All types of selling use this technique to market goods. This doesn't mean that you should sacrifice quality goods for gimmicks. All it means is that you should try to find a good sales pitch.

Maybe your product has a feature that no one has thought of using before. Variety stores sold thousands of clothes pins by telling clerks to let customers know that "they won't roll." (This was at the time that the first square clothes pins were introduced.)

Perhaps you can think of a catchy slogan for your product that will attract customers. Or maybe if you changed the name of your business you would do better. This section will give you a selection of such ideas. Adapt them to your business or use them as a starting point from your own ideas.

4.1 Are you reaching the customers?

A small company cannot afford the selling costs of reaching consumers on a nationwide basis. It must sell on a limited, local basis or use an independent middle organization like a broker, a distributor, or a manufacturers' representative (sales agent).

If you are thinking of introducing a new product, make certain that there are selling agencies who will accept your product and sell it on your behalf. Trade journals will tell you who these groups are. Talk to them. Solicit their advice. See whether they are enthusiastic.

You will find that people in independent sales organizations are co-operative and helpful. They know the customers, so listen to what they have to say.

Warning: Sales agents have rules about the things they sell. A single product is rarely enough, unless it is a big ticket item. Agents typically carry many lines by a number of manufacturers. Make sure that your product is compatible with the agent's line of products and that it is not in direct competition with others they may handle.

Many representatives will not handle items with low sales prices, particularly if they are types of articles that are sold in small quantities. It is a matter of arithmetic.

A sales call for industrial products costs anywhere from $50 to $200. The salesperson must earn that much or more in commission for every call. He or she cannot, for example, afford to sell a $200 item on a call that takes three hours to demonstrate the device, unless multiple orders are possible.

4.2 Do-it-yourself advertising

Not very many people starting out in business know enough about advertising to do a good job on their own. There are many sources you can approach for effective and free advertising.

Don't be afraid to ask for free assistance from anyone soliciting your advertising. Often advertising salespeople in the media can provide layouts and designs for no charge.

Also, if you sell the products of a number of manufacturers, remember to exploit their expertise. For example, if one of the items you sell in your general store is toothpaste, you may want to use a special display case or advertising layouts offered by the manufacturer of one of the toothpaste brands. Any display like this will be professionally done and will help draw customers to that product.

Don't forget about the effectiveness of flyers or direct mail campaigns. You can get advice on promotions, as well as large mailing lists from any direct mail agency.

Warning: The Internet mail equivalent of a direct mail campaign — known as spamming — is widely disliked and can easily have a negative result. The same applies to sending unsolicited facsimile messages (which are illegal in some jurisdictions). Both are unpopular because the recipient, not the sender, bears most of the costs.

4.3 Get free advertising or publicity through news releases

Almost any product, service, or professional skill can be pre-sold through using news releases that you write yourself and get printed free in trade papers or newspapers across the country. Also, the new product sections of trade papers and magazines can be a gold mine of free advertising for you.

Again, you write and mail news releases using, where advisable, photographs illustrating your product or service. Suitable news releases may be printed in publications for free — and are a most valuable aid to pre-selling what you have to offer. So, promote your product or service, at low or no cost through the medium of the news release, and the new product pages of suitable publications.

Don't let writing the news release frighten you. You don't have to be a professional writer, a copy writer, or even a journalist to churn out a suitable news release. It is very simple. You use a standard sheet of white bond paper, and you print or type your release, double-spaced. It is important that you include in your news release only the facts about the product or service you are trying to sell.

Usually, the editorial staff of the paper your release goes to will rewrite it to fit it in with their format anyway.

The facts that should appear in any news release are the following:

- Name, address, and telephone number of your firm

- Main selling features of your product or service

- What the product will do for the buyer

- Price of product or service

- How it can be purchased

That's all. Nothing else. If you want to go into a big selling spiel, then you will have to pay for advertising space. The same holds true when you are trying to get free advertising in the new product columns of trade papers. Just be accurate, clear, and short.

If you do include a photograph with your news release, black-and-white is almost always better than colour — it is cheaper and easier for most publications to use. Make sure the photograph is crisply in focus and shows your product on an unobstructed, contrasting background. If you are unsure how to achieve this, spend a little and get a professional to take the photograph.

4.4 Add something — and multiply sales

A sales strategy known as the tie-in, or premium offer, can sell your product by offering something extra to go along with it. One of the best examples of this is McDonald's. Is there ever a time when McDonald's isn't handing out something with their hamburgers? If it's not a game or a toy, it's cutouts or spaceships or balloons. The list goes on and on. The point is that the customers are always taking something home with them. That something will remind them of a good time and act as a memory jogger to come back.

The secret of tie-in success is to link products that complement each other. A manufacturer of travel bags makes a deal with a car rental company to give away a free bag every time a customer rents a car for three or more days. The car rental company benefits because people are attracted by the special offer. The manufacturer of the travel bag benefits because the name and product are put in front of the public and a large quantity of bags are sold to the rental company at a reasonable price.

If your product is good, and the company you tie in with is well received by its own customers, both products will be enhanced. No matter what your business is you should be able to find some way to use the tie-in scheme. If you are in entertaining, give away a free prize to the first 500 tickets sold to an event. If you sell an industrial product, have a free gift incentive plan for your salespeople. Any new idea will help keep your product's name in front of the consumer.

4.5 What's in a name? Plenty!

You may think that your business doesn't have enough "personality" to help promote your product. For example, if you run a hardware store you may wonder what you can do to make it sound flashy. Try using a distinctive color or logo on every item that passes through your store. Use the same logo in all your advertising, on your sales slips, and in all your exterior and interior decorating. People will soon come to associate your logo with quality products.

This system has been proven over and over again. Women buy 20 times more hosiery of a shade "Desert Sand" than one called plain "beige." Just find a phrase, name, or symbol that is different and pleasing to the public.

4.6 Dramatize differences

If you can dramatize the difference between your product and your competitor's, you're on the way to better sales. If there is no significant difference, then dramatize one particular feature of your product that your competitor has neglected to advertise.

This sales technique has been used successfully time and time again. A well-known example

of this is the various torture tests that the Samsonite Luggage Company put its bags through on national advertising. Samsonite took advantage of the fact that no other luggage company had emphasized the durability of its product in an extensive advertising campaign.

What are your product's marketable differences? Find out and use them.

5. THE IMPORTANCE OF YOUR SALES STAFF

Remember to keep your salespeople informed. They can't effectively sell your product if they aren't kept up to date on new business ventures or possibilities of changes in products. Let them know about any of the following:

- Any large order or unexpected high earning

- Any major financial problems of the company, product problems, or recalls (if they know what caused the problem, they can explain it to clients without losing sales)

- Plans for future changes

- New publicity campaigns, ads, or news releases

Your salespeople are hired to tackle new prospects. Often, part of their job is selling to people who don't even want to talk to them. Good salespeople have a number of ways they use to try to break the ice. Some use gimmicks just to get in the door and then explain the quality of their product. Whatever method they use, your salespeople are vital to your business.

After your salespeople have made the initial contact with prospective buyers, you should try to help them out. Have someone in your office send or telephone a thank-you to the customers for their time. Make sure that the customers know that the sale and business are important to you and that you are grateful for their patronage.

Marketing research has proven that customers are generally satisfied with a purchase when they first receive it. But shortly afterward it is not uncommon for them to question their choice. This is the time to call your customers again and remind them about the unique features your product has that makes it the best.

Your salespeople will be well received the next time they call if you can help out this way.

6. USING PERSUASIVE PRICING

The same marketing skills you use should be applied to your pricing policies. You probably think that you should price your products simply according to profit margins, competition, and what your customers can or will pay. However, small variations on how you present your price can make a big difference in your sales.

One owner of a menswear shop always concentrated his advertisements on his inexpensive clothing. However, he never mentioned that he carried the same quality line of men's suits as his higher-priced competitor down the street. When he began to emphasize this fact, he drew some customers away from the other store.

In this case, business was more successful when actual price was tied in with quality. On the other hand, if you sell a standard well-known item that is available in many stores, emphasis on raw price should be given a priority.

A large department store used another technique for selling a new refrigerator. The store ran newspaper ads offering a refrigerator to the person submitting the highest sealed bid. The store felt they couldn't lose because market research has shown that bids usually approximate the wholesale cost of the item. Also, this attracted a number of new prospects into the store who could be sold other items.

6.1 Help a customer unload

Some industrial salespeople get new customers by buying their competitor's unsold merchandise that is filling warehouse space that their own product could occupy. Then they credit the purchase against a minimum order from the customer. This can be quite profitable if you are sure that follow-up sales will justify the concession.

After this step, the dead merchandise can be sold at a close out price or written off as a sales promotion. Remember to tell your salespeople that the expense will be absorbed from their commissions.

6.2 When you cut the price, say why

Walking down the street you may see the following signs on retail businesses: "Overstocked — must clear," "Closing out sale." Because you are given the reason for the reduced prices, you are less likely to suspect a "catch" or lower quality goods.

If you have suspiciously low prices, you have to try extra hard to convince customers that your product isn't junk. It is human nature to distrust unexplained generosity. Either show the customer why you are forced to make the sale, or explain how you will profit in the long run.

7. THE BIG ONE-TIME ORDER — DO YOU TAKE IT?

Whether to take a big one-time order is always a difficult decision to make. Suppose you are doing fairly well in business but you haven't yet seen as large a profit as you would like. You aren't discouraged, because you have a steady flow of regular customers. However, from time to time you wonder if you will ever reach your financial goal.

You are suddenly confronted with the possibility of filling a huge order that will bring in bigger profits than you have ever seen. However, it would require devoting your entire operation to the one order. In the short term, you could make a great profit, but you risk losing your regular customers. In the long run it could mean financial hardship.

In this situation, unless you can make an absolute killing on the order, and unless you are guaranteed further orders by the same client, I would give the offer up.

8. THE GIANT CUSTOMER

Suppose you are faced with the same situation as above, but the client is prepared to guarantee large orders for years to come. What should your decision be now?

Because your entire operation will be devoted to the one client, the nature of your operation will change. No longer will you be serving a wide variety of customers.

The main advantage of agreeing to this proposition is the assurance of yearly sales. This guarantee can allow you to lower your selling and servicing cost.

However, there are some disadvantages to being dependent on one client. The client may take advantage of your dependency and may press less favourable terms on you over the years. You may begin to feel more like an employee of the client, rather than an independent business person.

In other words, you are the one who is in the most vulnerable position. The client is far more important to the success of your business than you are to the client's. Your profits may be better protected by a number of smaller regular clients.

9. YOU NEEDN'T BE BEST

Sometimes simplicity and generic quality can help you sell your product too. For example, suppose you manufacture a component part for word processors. It isn't designed for all word processors, only those that need the few functions that your component offers.

By advertising the lower price, simplicity, and quality of your product, you may attract a number of customers who don't want, or need, the bigger name brands.

10. HOW TO SELECT NEW PRODUCTS

Although product success cannot be assured, the odds against failure can be improved. This means giving up the long shot, the hula hoop, and the pet rock. It means sticking with concepts that have been proven and adding that little extra.

Television producers do this all the time by copying successful formulas. It may detract from the artistic quality of the programming, but it keeps a network from bombing out on a grand scale. On the whole, viewers do not watch drastically different shows. The television producer puts survival ahead of innovation. So should you.

10.1 The "ideal" product for a small business

Here are the characteristics of the product most likely to survive:

- It is similar to other products that people buy in large quantities. (It is easily recognizable and the market is relatively large.)

- It has all the features of competitive products and performs as well or better in all respects. (It is not necessary to explain away any deficiencies.)

- It has at least one significant advantage over its competition, such as a better appearance, more functions, superior performance, or a lower price. (In other words, there is a strong selling point.)

- There is no dominant supplier in the marketplace. (It is not necessary to overcome customer prejudices.)

10.2 Product life

No product lasts forever. It is replaced by better ideas growing out of new technologies or is abandoned as needs change. Be prepared to upgrade your product to keep it competitive and to drop it when it is no longer capable of carrying its load.

Do not keep products to satisfy personal ego. If you make a mistake, admit it and try again. Do not allow your employees to make product life a personal issue. No one likes to see a brainchild die, but there is a time when this must happen.

10.3 Make product appraisal a continual practice

Never take your product for granted. Know it. Look at it frequently. Try it out if you can. Get all the opinions possible — from your friends, customers, salespeople, and end-users. Forget praise. Listen to criticisms, hedged answers, and unspoken words. Find out whether they are valid. Recognize your weaknesses before your competitors can.

Study your competitors. Keep track of their ideas. Try to divine where they are heading.

11. WRONG LOCATION? CAPITALIZE ON IT

If you have been unfortunate and landed yourself an undesirable location for your business, don't give up. Promote!

Try to think of a catchy name for your business, or some feature that will draw customers in, despite the poor location.

Extra-high quality will attract customers in spite of a poor location. However, this happens very slowly if you don't advertise.

If you are in a brand new business in a bad location, you'll need plenty of innovative ideas to attract first-time customers. Or, you can do what is suggested in the next section.

12. MOVE YOUR MERCHANDISE TO WHERE THE CUSTOMERS ARE

A water ski enthusiast opened a skiing accessory shop. He thought he would do well because he was near the beaches, but because there were very few other businesses nearby, he found that customers weren't easily attracted to his store.

To gain popularity, he began going to water ski beaches on the weekends and setting up displays of some of his goods. He handed out flyers with his prices and the store address on it. He soon found that his business improved.

After two years he didn't need to use the display technique — word had been passed that he had a good shop and customers made the effort to travel to the location.

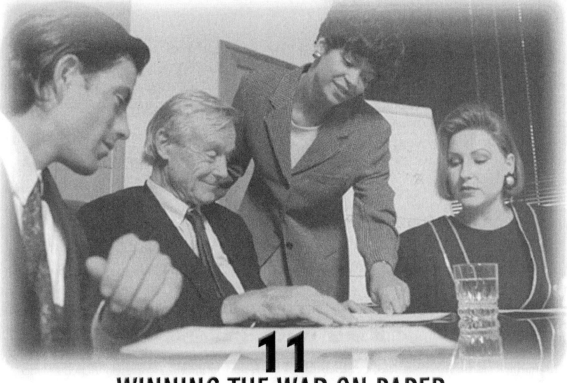

11
WINNING THE WAR ON PAPER

1. DON'T BE A PAPER COLLECTOR

According to *Fortune* magazine "paperwork remains undoubtedly the least efficient operation in ... industry." Don't let yourself become overburdened with costly files that should be thrown away. Too much paper means too little efficiency — which means too few profits.

If you stop to think about it, you will probably realize that you don't ever refer to most of your files. Companies that have drastically cut back on files and paper loads have found no loss or inconvenience to their business.

Admittedly, there is some risk to throwing out files. But the odds are on your side. The increased efficiency that is reflected in rising profits will be far greater than any slight loss by missing a file.

Of course, every business must keep some records because of government requirements or possible lawsuits. (See section 6. of this chapter for details.) However, information that isn't needed shouldn't be kept.

2. KEEP YOUR DESK ORGANIZED

If you don't keep your desk clear of unnecessary papers, you aren't working at maximum efficiency. Here are two simple techniques to help you keep on top of this problem.

The first technique is early screening. Don't let anything get on your desk that doesn't need to be there. Likely, it will just get shuffled under other paper and stay in your way for weeks.

The other technique is simply classifying your papers into priority piles. If you have papers that

95

must be attended to right away, put them on top. Those things that are important but don't need immediate attention should be put underneath. And finally, anything that must be looked at but can wait for a few days should be put at the bottom.

If, after organizing your papers this way, there is anything left over, it should be thrown away or filed.

Don't get lazy when paper is put on your desk. Make yourself look at it right away and make a decision about where it should go. You can save yourself a lot of time and desk space this way.

If you have administrative help, get them to do preliminary screening and sorting of your incoming paper. Then when you receive it you can sort it in your own system. One system you might consider is the following:

(a) Urgent matters for prompt action

(b) Matters that need action soon

(c) Long-term problems that will need careful study

(d) Reading information

Organize your work schedule in a logical sequence that will bring big projects to early completion. Don't waste all your time tidying up small jobs. Often, those small jobs take care of themselves while you work steadily at a big project.

Telephone calls should be handled the same way. Don't return all your calls immediately. Instead, screen them to choose the crucial ones. The others will either call you again or take care of themselves. Again, use your administrative staff to help screen unnecessary calls, or invest in voice mail.

3. Bunch for efficiency

The chores you set out to do at any particular time (e.g., phoning, correspondence, bookkeeping) should be bunched together to save time.

For example, suppose you begin your morning by going through your mail. Some of it requires a reply letter. Some of it will require researching in the files. Other letters ask for payments and will mean looking through the ledgers.

Section this work into categories so that you are doing all your correspondence at once, then your bookkeeping, etc. You will work more quickly and efficiently by concentrating on one thing at a time.

Don't get caught doing too much clerical work. You should be spending your time on things that will help your business grow. An expenditure of enough money to pay for administrative help could be a valuable investment. Let this person work in batches as well. Don't waste his or her time by giving him or her assignments five times a day. Instead, save assignments up for one sitting.

Save up easy yes/no work in one file and work on it at odd moments. Travel time on an airplane is always good for this type of odd job. Similarly, save up problems for a few hours or days. When you bunch them, you'll find that similar problems can be handled with one trip or one telephone call.

4. CUT IT OFF AT THE SOURCE

Remember that cleaning out your files is only one step toward creating a more efficient system. You also have to cut off the problem at the source. Many files don't need to be created in the first place.

5. TAKE SHORTCUTS

With first class postage costs now going out of sight, it makes more and more sense to look at alternate communication methods. Admittedly telephoning costs money. But it often costs more to write and mail a letter, file the copy, and eventually reply. Unless you're sure you need a formal record of what you say, consider telephoning, faxing, or emailing.

And when you receive a letter that needs a written reply, consider writing a brief message in longhand on the face of the original letter, which can then be returned to the sender. If you need a copy simply photocopy the entire letter for your (temporary) files.

It is becoming quite common for businesses to reply to letters by simply writing on the face of the original and returning it by fax. If you want to add a personal touch to this system, you can have letter savers printed up with something like this: "In order to give you the fastest possible response, we have made these marginal notes on your letter. In this case, we think you'll prefer speed to formality."

Email allows still more flexibility and it offers the opportunity for fast response. To save your time, and the time of the person you are emailing, keep your mail simple — resist the temptation to add fancy formatting, "backgrounds," and similar special effects to your email. Email originated as a system using plain text, which did not require any special tools for someone to read it; keep yours that simple and it will be effective.

6. WHAT RECORDS SHOULD YOU KEEP?

In the last decade, governments at all levels have intervened in our private lives and in private businesses on a massive scale. For the small-business person, this has meant a lot of needless headaches. I'm sure each of us has a pet peeve or can relate a particularly gruesome experience with government red tape.

Each of us develops his or her own defence mechanisms to pestering bureaucrats, such as, "It's in the mail" (particularly useful when the post office is on strike), or "I didn't receive it," or "I'm not in charge of that area" (classic reversal of passing-the-buck mumble which government officials use), or "The person in charge of that is away on vacation."

If you don't mind the constant harassment, I suppose this practice can be carried on indefinitely. There is no doubt, however, that the entire exercise becomes counterproductive after a while. My experience is that the best method is to explain to these officials that you are a small-business person starting out and cannot afford the staff or time to comply with their requests.

Occasionally, in these situations, they will offer to send someone over to help you complete the form. This is a great help because then all you have to do is answer questions, which is a lot easier than trying to interpret what they want on a form.

7. USE TECHNOLOGY THAT WILL HELP YOU

Use your computer to its full potential. It can help you take many shortcuts and allow you to exercise greater control over your working life. Ask friends in business what shortcuts they take with their computers — they will often have interesting and useful ideas you can copy.

Also, invest in learning and using a time management system. It will keep you focused on what's important — running a successful business! Hint: Almost everyone I know in business has tried a software-based time management system and almost all of them have gone back to a paper-based system! Why? There was more learning needed to become efficient with the software system and it didn't allow for the quickly scribbled note in the coffee shop or at the bus station.

A few friends have found that a pocket-size PDA like the Palm solves the problem of lugging around a fat time management diary by allowing for scribbled notes. The drawbacks, they say, are the time to learn the input system, remembering to back up their files regularly, and making sure they keep the batteries well charged.

12
KEEPING THE BOOKS

Many inexperienced business people tend to ignore the bookkeeping requirements of their business. "More paperwork," they say and, telling themselves they'll "get to it later," they begin to pile it on an unused portion of their desk. By the time they do get to it the pile can be as high as the CN Tower. Try as you might, you can't ignore the accounting function in your company. For one thing, your friends in Ottawa won't let you. As your business grows so will their demand for proper records.

But, and this is even more important, proper bookkeeping procedures will provide you with an information base on your company. Through time this information will become more and more valuable and will provide the foundation for future sales projections and budgets.

Chances are you are not always going to have time to do your own bookkeeping. After all, you are running a busy, successful business. But do make the effort to understand and implement basic, proper accounting procedures. You won't be sorry.

1. FINDING AN ACCOUNTANT

The books and records of your company will be audited by federal and provincial agencies from time to time. You should have an orderly records and accounts system which will be readily accessible from the beginning. To do this you will need the help of a good accountant.

The best way to find someone is to ask your successful business friends to supply you with names. Then talk to at least three of them before making a choice. When you are choosing the professional services for your business, remember you are trying to establish a long-term relationship. It is important that you are able to communicate easily and effectively. And make sure that the accountant you choose can do the same. If an accountant insists on talking over your head, he or she is not for you. You have a right to understand his or her counsel completely, and it's the accountant's job to ensure that you do.

If you want to learn something about accounting before you talk to an accountant (it always helps to be able to ask intelligent questions), refer to the *Numbers 101* book series from Self-Counsel Press. The first book in the series will teach you the basics of books of accounts; other books in that series extend your knowledge.

You can expect to have your books examined by the following government departments: Workers' Compensation Board; Canada Revenue Agency (CRA) (which will include payroll auditing of employment insurance premiums, Canada Pension Plan contributions, and income tax deductions at source); and CRA, Customs and Excise (for GST). The provincial Department of Finance will audit your books for hospitalization and provincial sales tax (except for lucky Albertans and residents of the territories who have no sales tax).

You must keep your books and records, including supporting documents, such as sales and purchase invoices, contracts, bank statements, and cancelled cheques, in an orderly manner at your place of business or designated records office. Canada Revenue Agency requires that you keep all business records and supporting documents until you request and obtain written permission from the department to dispose of them.

If you wish to destroy company books or records, you may apply in writing to the director of the district taxation office.

Following is a list of what records you should keep and for how long.

(a) Keep permanently:

- Corporate records

- Financial statements

- Journals and ledgers

- Private pension records

- Securities records

- Personal records (e.g., social insurance numbers, job descriptions, Workers' Compensation information)

(b) Keep for fixed periods:

- Records of dissolved corporations — six years after dissolution

- Banking records — six years

- Inventory records — six years

- Personnel records — various periods, depending on class of record

- Canada Pension Plan records — six years

- Cancelled securities — six years

- Sales tax records — various periods, according to jurisdiction

(c) Keep until permission for disposal is granted:

- Federal and provincial income records

2. TIPS ON KEEPING YOUR BOOKS (AND STAYING OUT OF TROUBLE)

First, as I've already mentioned, you will need an accountant and, perhaps, even a bookkeeper, but only when the business is well established. In the meantime, learn to set up the basic records yourself, and that way you will know what's going on, while you will also be cutting costs.

If you need help, use the staff, your spouse, or, as a last resort, part-time help. There are plenty of freelance bookkeepers around who will, for a reasonable fee, come in periodically to review the situation and make sure you're on the right track.

Warning: Do not ask bookkeepers for tax advice. Their expertise is restricted solely to putting business information in the right format for use by you and the government.

Second, never let your bookkeeping chores get so far behind that it looks hopeless. Make a habit of doing your bookkeeping on a regular basis. I suggest that you make a happy habit of bringing your books completely up to date every week. I call it a "happy" habit because you'll be happy if you do so. If you do your books once a week, your record handling will be a relatively minor chore.

There is some good software available to allow a small business to use a computer to maintain its books. If you are interested in this approach, talk to your accountant before you buy such software — your accountant will have a good idea of what you need and which packages best suit the needs of your business.

2.1 Employee pay records

If you end up hiring other people to work with you (including your spouse), you will be required to make certain deductions at the source (from the payroll) and remit them directly to Ottawa or to your local chartered bank.

An employee record book is probably the most important record-keeping item for you to keep accurately and up to date because it's the one thing that can get you in the most trouble with the government. All you need is one complaint from a disgruntled employee to bring investigations from any one of a number of government departments.

So, pick up a payroll book at any stationery store. Make sure it's Canadian, as many of these forms are not and they will mislead you. Also, make sure you use an appropriate payroll book (i.e., one that records the pay periods — weekly, semi-monthly, monthly — that you have decided to use).

The payroll book will list in convenient columns all the deductions you have to make from pay cheques. The major ones are the following:

- Canada Pension Plan (CPP) and, in Quebec, Quebec Pension Plan (QPP)
- Employment insurance (EI)
- Income tax deductions

CPP and EI require contributions from both the employer and employee. Income tax is deducted only from the employee.

To find out how much to take off, you must first open an employer account number with the income tax office. At that time you will be given a book of tables for income tax and another one for Canada pension and employment insurance deductions.

If you employ commissioned salespeople, they are still regarded as employees and you are required to make the appropriate deductions. In this case the deductions will be different for each pay period. In order to reduce bookkeeping, compute the payroll once a month and allow the salespeople a draw at the middle of the month. Don't forget to check with your accountant about GST considerations with commissioned people.

If you are sending employees' deductions for the first time, you should mail a certified cheque or money order for the total amount, payable to the Receiver General for Canada, to your district taxation office. Include your name, the name and address of your business, the amounts you are remitting for income tax, CPP, and EI, and state the pay period this payment covers. The office will send you information and an employer registration form for you to complete and return.

If you are in a proprietorship or partnership and your tax bill for the previous year was more than $1,000, you are required to pay income tax and CPP contributions in quarterly instalments. Instalment payments may be made at your bank or sent to your regional taxation centre. Check the blue pages of your telephone directory for the address of the centre nearest you.

For further information, pick up the booklet *Paying Your Income Tax by Instalments* at your district taxation office.

2.2 Accounts receivable

The next most important things for you to keep straight are your accounts receivable journal and billing system because without them you won't be able to collect any money — unless you operate a cash and credit card business only, in which case you can skip this section.

The type of system you set up will depend largely on how many transactions you handle a month. For example, a plumbing contractor who handles perhaps ten jobs a month can work best with a simple manual system using commercially available preprinted invoice and statement forms. At the end of each year, he or she need merely total up the invoices (less any amounts not collected) and get the "sales" total.

If you have more than, say, 50 active accounts a month, this procedure becomes a little cumbersome, especially when it comes to preparing monthly statements to be sent out. Most businesses in this category use some form of computerized accounts receivable system. There are many to choose from, or you could use one of the commercially available accounting one-write systems.

A one-write system simply refers to an accounting system where all the sales you make are automatically — through carbonized paper — posted to a sales journal and monthly ledger card (for sending out statements) on the receivable side; all the cheques you write are automatically posted to the proper expense journal on the payable side.

You may use either the receivable or payable system, or both. It makes things very simple for you and for your accountant and is particularly useful if you write 50 or more cheques and/or statements each month. The routine handling of invoices is no problem if you have a cash business because you should receive a total sales figure at the end of each day from the cash register.

If you are invoicing, the tax department likes to see all invoices consecutively numbered and they should be filed in numerical order, not alphabetically. This way they are easy to retrieve. There are many types of binding cases available to batch and store old invoices.

If you are printing your own invoices and using two or three copies, there are two options that can make your life easier.

Current software packages for small-business accounting allow you to enter invoice details just once and then the software does the grunt work of posting to the correct records and printing the invoices. Talk to your accountant before you commit to a software system.

If you don't want to use a computer, then check into using carbonized paper. This type of paper can be typed or written on without the necessity for carbon paper. Also, you can then "crash number" the invoices, which simply means that one run through the numbering press using carbonized paper will number all three or four copies of each invoice. The amount you save in printing costs is considerable.

As far as supplying figures to your accountant is concerned, if you operate on a "cash received" basis (in other words, no sale is counted until the payment is received), you can simply supply your accountant or bookkeeper with the bank deposit book at the end of each month (if you are keeping monthly totals).

Be sure to mark clearly in your deposit book any sales that are out of the normal course of business, such as supplier refunds. If you operate on an "accrual" basis (in other words if you include in your sales all accounts receivable less an allowance for bad debts), these figures should be totalled every month.

You would want to know this figure anyway so you are not doing any more work than is necessary. The easiest way is simply to total your monthly statements each month as they are prepared (software will do this automatically).

If using a one-write system, you simply total the columns. This also gives you an "aged" balance (i.e., it shows who owes you how much for 30, 60, 90, or over 90 days).

2.3 Accounts payable

Again, the system you adopt should depend on the number of cheques you are writing each month. For only a few cheques, I suppose a normal cheque book stub is adequate, provided you list the proper description of each cheque on the stub so that your bookkeeper can pick it up.

There is nothing more frustrating to your bookkeeper, or expensive to you, than trying to track down a year later what a $12.46 payment to Joe Blow was for. This is especially so when you write a cheque to yourself for reimbursement of some minor purchase.

As I have mentioned, a one-write system can be very useful if you write more than 50 cheques a month. When you use carbonized cheques, it automatically posts the cheque to a cash disbursement journal and all you need to do is summarize the sheet every 25 cheques. Look into it by contacting the suppliers under "accounting systems" in the Yellow Pages.

Again, a simple computerized system is a real option. The better ones work like a one-write system — you fill in an onscreen image of a cheque and the software does the necessary postings for you, then prints the cheque.

The accounts payable invoices should be filed alphabetically under the supplier's name. You can use a binding case or accordion file. You should keep this file very close to your desk as you will need to review it frequently.

My experience is that you should never delegate the writing of cheques to someone else because only you are in possession of all the information regarding supplier terms, charge backs, etc.

After invoices are paid, throw them in a pile in a convenient spot from which they can be batched and stored periodically. The tax department likes to take a very close look at these invoices so do not destroy them.

2.4 Other requirements

There are endless variations available to make your accounting system as sophisticated as you want. The computer is one of them. Eventually, when your business warrants it, you will want to have one. But when you are just starting out, you only want a system that —

(a) provides the minimum amount of information needed to satisfy government requirements, and

(b) provides you with the operating information you need in the most simplified and direct manner possible.

In the early stages of your business, this is all you need. Any computer professional will tell you that good manual systems are a prerequisite to the successful installation of a computer.

When should you consider a computer? When you have evaluated your business requirements and are satisfied that the benefits of owning a computer outweigh its costs.

It's not as difficult as it sounds, but it is an activity best saved for when you have the time and a solid understanding of your business needs. (See Chapter 13 for more information on computers.)

Always remember that if you don't make money and your business slumps and fails, you won't need books, accountants, or computers. Your big job is to run your business profitably. So, in the early stages, concentrate on making those sales grow and keep a firm grip on expenses.

You will, when your business expands, have to devote more and more time to managing your company's affairs. Then is the time to turn your bookkeeping chores over to a trusted employee or perhaps start window shopping for that computer. Until then run a tight ship and stay in familiar water.

2.5 What you should know about financial statements

A financial statement consists of a balance sheet and a profit and loss (income and expense) statement. These are two very useful tools for managing your business: the balance sheet gives you an overall view of the business as it stands at the time of the statement, while the profit and loss statement shows you how you've done over the past year.

Used correctly, and compared to industrial averages, these statements should tell you what you've done right — and what you've done wrong. When problem areas are pointed out, the solution is sometimes all too obvious.

Also, financial statements are what you show your banker to justify his or her continued support — so make them look as good as possible.

Let me give you an example of a simplified balance sheet (see Sample 4) and a profit and loss statement (see Sample 7) for Slipshod Industries.

The purpose of the examples is to give you some basic information on the structure and use of financial statements.

Sample 4 shows the balance sheet of a sole proprietorship. Each portion of the balance sheet is analyzed.

The net worth section of this balance sheet is then shown for the other two types of business organizations: the partnership (see Sample 5) and the corporation (see Sample 6). This has been done to clearly indicate the different "net worth" sections of each of these organizations.

SAMPLE 4
BALANCE SHEET (Sole Proprietorship)

SLIPSHOD INDUSTRIES LTD.
Balance Sheet
Year Ending December 31, 20—

Assets

Current assets

Cash in bank	$ 2,000		
Accounts receivable	30,000		
Inventory	47,000		
Prepaid rent	1,000		
Total current assets		$ 80,000	

Fixed assets

Trucks	$ 60,000		
Less: Depreciation		30,000	
Book value of truck			30,000
Total assets			$110,000

Liabilities and Net Worth

Current liabilities

Bank note payable	$ 10,000		
Accounts payable	10,000		
Current portion of term debt	5,000		
Accrued wages	5,000		
Total current liabilities		30,000	

Term debt

(Truck purchases)			10,000
Total liabilities			$ 40,000

Net worth

Original amount invested		50,000	
Earnings (or losses) to date		20,000	
Total net worth			70,000
Total net worth and liabilities			$110,000

SAMPLE 5
PARTNER'S EQUITIES
(Part of balance sheet for partners)

SLIPSHOD INDUSTRIES
Statement of Partner's Equities Year Ended

December 31, 20—

	John Slip	Jack Shod	Total investment
Original investment	$30,000	$20,000	$50,000
Additional investment	0	0	0
Profit for year ended Dec. 31, 20—	12,000	8,000	20,000
Total equities	42,000	28,000	70,000
Less: withdrawals	0	0	0
Investment balances as of Dec. 31, 20—	$42,000	$28,000	$70,000

SAMPLE 6
SHAREHOLDER'S EQUITIES
(Part of balance sheet for a corporation)

SHAREHOLDER'S EQUITY

Capital stock — Common retained earnings (from previous years)	$40,000
	10,000
Net earnings before taxes December 31, 20—	20,000
Total net worth	$70,000

SAMPLE 7
PROFIT AND LOSS STATEMENT

Profit and Loss Statement for the
12-Month Period Ending December 31, 20—

Sales	$100,000
Cost of goods sold	60,000
Gross profit margin	$40,000
Less: Administrative and general expenses	20,000
Net profits before taxes	$20,000

ANALYSIS OF THE BALANCE SHEET OF SLIPSHOD INDUSTRIES CURRENT ASSETS

Current assets ($80,000) are any assets that are expected to convert to cash within a year's time.

Cash in bank: $2,000 — cash on deposit in the bank chequing account plus petty cash on hand.

Accounts receivable: $30,000 — sales invoiced and shipped but not yet paid for.

Inventory: $47,000 — merchandise on hand to be sold. (However, in the case of a manufacturing company, it could represent raw materials, work in process, and finished goods. Inventory is usually listed at cost or market value, whichever is lower.)

Prepaid rent: $1,000 — advance lease or rent payments, usually for first and last months.

FIXED ASSETS

Fixed assets ($30,000) — items such as property, equipment, machinery, and leasehold improvements that are permanent in nature and will not be converted into cash in the next fiscal period.

Trucks: $60,000 — the total cost of the trucks when they were purchased new.

Depreciation: $30,000 — the decline in value and useful service of the trucks since they were purchased. (There are several methods of computing depreciation; they can be determined by talking with an accountant.)

Book value of trucks: $30,000 — the value after depreciation is deducted. (This is known as the undepreciated capital cost of the vehicles at the year-end.)

TOTAL ASSETS

Total assets ($110,000) represent the current assets plus the fixed assets of the company.

CURRENT LIABILITIES

Current liabilities ($30,000) are any company debts that must be paid within one year of the statement date.

Bank note payable: $10,000 — money owed to the bank under promissory notes.

Accounts payable: $10,000 — money owed to the company's suppliers. (The company usually has 30, 60, or 90 days to pay these debts and, in some cases, it can receive a discount on the bill if they are paid within ten days.)

Current portion of term debt: $5,000 the amount of debt that must be paid on the trucks within a 12-month period.

Accrued wages: $5,000 — accrued salaries owing to employees, which will not be disbursed until the regular payday.

TERM DEBT

This is any debt due after a year. In this example, $10,000 is the balance owing on the trucks.

NET WORTH (CAPITAL)

This section of the balance sheet shows the equity or ownership ($70,000), which includes the following:

Original amount invested: $50,000 — the amount invested in the company by the owner to start the business.

Earnings to date: $20,000 — the accumulated net profits (before taxes) earned by the company.

In Sample 4, Slipshod Industries is a sole proprietorship. If the company were a partnership, the balance sheet would be the same except for the "Net Worth" section, which would be titled "Partners' Equities."

The only other change necessary would be to change the heading "Liabilities and Net Worth" to "Liabilities and Partners' Equities" on the bottom half of the balance sheet. The partners' equities would be detailed on a separate sheet as in Sample 5 and attached to the financial statements.

The total of the partners' equities is $70,000. Each partner must report his or her own individual tax return and must pay tax on his or her share of the partnership profits, whether or not this amount has actually been distributed.

If the company were a corporation, the net worth (capital) section would be titled "Shareholders' Equity" and would appear in the "Liabilities and Shareholders' Equity" section as in Sample 6.

Corporations are taxed between 18 percent and 23 percent on the first $200,000 of profit per year, and 46 percent on all profits over that amount.

The second statement that makes up a company's financial statement (the first being the balance sheet) is the "Income and Expense" or "Profit and Loss Statement," which is a statement of income and expenses for the current fiscal year. Sample 7 shows a profit and loss statement.

ANALYSIS OF THE PROFIT AND LOSS STATEMENT OF SLIPSHOD INDUSTRIES

Sales: $100,000 — the total dollar amount of orders invoiced for the year.

Cost of goods sold: $60,000 — the cost of raw material purchased, merchandise purchased, and freight costs, as well as direct labour costs.

Gross profit margin: $40,000 — the difference between the sales and the cost of goods sold, which represents the net sales or the markup in the selling price over the cost price.

Administrative and general expense: $20,000 — expenses incurred during the year, such as salaries, travel, office supplies, and insurance costs.

Net profit: $20,000 — the difference between gross profit margin and the administrative and general expenses. The balance left is the net profit, which is carried to the balance sheet as "earnings to date."

If Slipshod Industries is a sole proprietorship, the net profit of $20,000 shown by the business is reported as income on the proprietor's personal tax return.

If Slipshod Industries is a limited company, the $20,000 is taxed at approximately 25 percent. What's left can remain in the business or be paid out to the owners, in which case they pay income tax on the amount received.

It should be noted that categories on the profit and loss statement are usually itemized. For example, the cost of goods sold would be broken down into the various expense items stated above and the amounts for each of these items would be shown. The same applies to administrative and general expenses.

13
WHAT ABOUT COMPUTERS?

I believe that the computer, in principle, is the most remarkable tool invented since the wheel, and the increasing ability of the technology to pack a room-size mainframe's power into a tiny box holds me in awe. But like any tool, it requires skilled use, and that means strategy and training. In the following pages, I try to outline the basic steps involved.

Chances are, the computer you choose will be a personal computer capable of running business applications. The decision will involve purchasing hardware (the physical equipment and components) and software (the programmed instructions that tell the computer what to do). The choices for each seem endless. And while there is a lot of information available to help you make the decision, the amount can seem overwhelming.

Planning can reduce the time and effort you need to reach a decision.

1. PLAN

Despite the publicists' efforts, you may still feel perplexed when you try to decide whether to purchase your first computer. You might well wonder how you will know if you need something if you don't know what it does. The first rule in deciding the appropriate computer configuration for your office is *plan*! Planning will save you time, labour, and money, quite apart from making sure that what you hope to achieve in your office is exactly what is eventually created.

Some of the tasks you may want to computerize, either immediately or in the future, might include the following:

- *Accounting:* Modern accounting software provides general ledger, accounts receivable and payable, invoicing, and more in one package. It will print monthly statements for all your accounts and many programs have job costing and payroll modules. It will also print monthly statements and payroll cheques, although this is not much use to a one or two person operation. Most accounting packages will either include or will work with tax software, and some will work with your bank accounts and credit card accounts — check with your bank to see if they recommend a software package.

- *Word processing:* You can use a computer for letters, typing your invoices (if you don't have an accounting package for this), maintaining a simple mailing list, and any other writing jobs that your business demands. All the leading programs incorporate basic desktop publishing features as well.

- *Spreadsheets:* Spreadsheets are used extensively in forecasting, budgeting, and general business planning. The ability to enter changes and update a cash flow or sales forecast almost effortlessly simplifies what can be a time-consuming task. Spreadsheets can also be used in a small business to track inventory, orders, customers, and sales.

- *Presentation software:* If your business will require you to make frequent sales and marketing presentations, presentation software is designed to make the process fairly simple. It enables you to produce colourful transparencies for overhead projectors, graphics-intense handouts, and simple slide shows.

- *Desktop publishing:* Desktop Publishing (DTP) software enables the user to combine text, drawings, and graphics to produce publishable material. Using DTP, you could, for example, produce a brochure, newsletter, price list, or restaurant menu that will look professionally typeset. Note that most word processing software is capable of performing simple DTP tasks well, and professional DTP software is more powerful (and requires more specialized skill) than what most small businesses need.

- *Database management systems:* This is the one category of software where you are most likely going to need some custom programming work. Examples of database applications include inventory management, telephone directories, client files, mailing lists, and customized order processing. If your business requires that you work consistently with large amounts of information that must be classified, modified, or updated, you may want to consider a database program. 100 addresses is not a large list; 10 times that many is. If your needs are not going to involve processing huge amounts of data, you will find a spreadsheet will work just fine.

You must decide which operation gets moved to computers first, and your plan should help you decide where you will obtain the greatest benefit and what the logical sequence to follow will be.

With input from your staff, prepare a written outline about what you expect to get when you computerize. And while I don't advocate a complete redesign of all your usual procedures, this may also be a good time to see if there are some procedures that could be improved.

Don't try to transfer a bad or inadequate system onto a computer; it will merely be more inadequate, and twice as fast.

When you prepare your outline, answer the following questions:

(a) What operations do you want to computerize?

(b) Why do you want to automate those items?

(c) What is the order of their priority?

(d) What precise benefits do you expect to get?

(e) Who will be involved in the conversion(s)?

(f) Who will be trained to use the programs?

(g) What space and furniture will you need?

(h) How much time will it take to accomplish your plan?

(i) Do you have the budget to accomplish this?

(j) How will you measure your accomplishments?

Take this outline and review it with someone who is knowledgeable about computers and their business applications, someone who will be honest in their assessment of your plan. If you can't find a qualified person to provide this evaluation free of charge, then pay for it. It will be well worth the money spent. If you start with unrealistic expectations, you are bound to be disappointed, and the process of making a comprehensive written plan will lessen the possibility of expecting too much too soon.

Bear in mind, it will take longer than you think to get your office computer systems up and running efficiently, and your staff trained to use them, so allow for this time in your plan.

2. HARDWARE AND SOFTWARE

Computer salespeople probably will not like this, but I firmly believe that your software requirements should drive your hardware decisions. And your software requirements will be driven by the needs of your business and the availability of staff.

Your decisions should happen in this sequence:

(a) Use your plan to identify the tasks you will computerize.

(b) Identify which software applications you will need to complete those tasks.

(c) Identify the operating system these applications run on.

(d) Choose the hardware based on the applications and operating system.

Make your decisions in that order and your choices will become logical and consistent.

2.1 Software applications

Software applications are the tools you and your staff will actually use to produce documents, spreadsheets, web pages, graphics, databases, or any of the other types of data which can be created and manipulated with a computer. Deciding on the applications you will use can make the rest of your computer decisions much easier.

If your business involves producing a lot of graphics, you will need software capable of producing those graphics and you will need staff capable of working with the software. The same applies if your business involves a lot of work with spreadsheets or databases — in either case, you will need specific software to do the job and you will need staff with suitable skills to use the software.

Unless you have a very clear need for it, try to avoid custom-made software. It is expensive to create, more expensive to maintain, and, most important, it will generate ongoing expenses in maintenance and in training staff to use it. When a vendor suggests it will "only" cost a little more to have a software application tailor-made for your business, my advice is to be very afraid.

Whenever possible, be conservative and stay with "mainstream" software applications. Selecting a new, unheard-of word processing package because it is highly recommended by your computer-savvy third cousin may seem like a good idea, but it probably is not. Over a period of a few years, your cost of training staff to use the software will be far greater than the cost of the software itself. Instead, find out which word processor is most popular in your town, or in your industry.

Chances are good, if you choose a popular software package, or a package that is highly compatible with the most popular package, that both existing and potential staff will already know how to use it — choosing a widely used software application can save you a lot of money in reduced training costs.

Be aware that there are two important aspects of software compatibility: file compatibility and user interface compatibility. If package A can read and write files in the format used by package B, then A and B are file compatible. If the menu layout and instructions in package A are highly similar to those of package B, then A and B are quite compatible in terms of user interface. If two packages are 95 percent compatible in this way, then your cost of retraining staff to move them from one to the other will be low.

Software "suites" are packages that offer a word processor, a spreadsheet, and other applications bundled together. They can often be a good choice for an office environment. Software suites sometimes offer a similar way of working with each application in the suite and that may help reduce your ongoing training costs. Suites are also generally a lot cheaper than the sum of their component parts.

Avoid the temptation to select software based on staff preferences. For example: Jane is familiar with word processing software A, which happens to be the one you have elected to buy. A few months later, John joins the staff and urges you to let him use word processing software B, because he is a "power user" of it and would be more productive right away. If you let John use B, you will now have two word processing software packages installed in the office, each potentially generating files that are not totally compatible with the other package. The reality is, the little extra time John will need to come up to speed on package A will be less than the time and cost you might later incur in dealing with not-quite-compatible files.

2.1a Beware of pirated software

You may want to test a program before buying it. Many programs have interactive demonstrations you can download from the Internet or obtain on disks that allow you to get a feel for the program, but unfortunately it is also true that many programs do not have such demonstrations available.

Another option is to try out a copy of the original disk, but please note copying a program without proper authorization or purchase is illegal, and you could be subject to penalties if you are found to be using such copies. I urge you strongly to purchase the copyrighted program from a reputable dealer. You will need the support and access to upgrades that you will get as a registered user, and you will be assured of access to bug fixes and security patches.

Further, you need complete documentation that isn't available from a pirated copy of a disk. And finally, as an independent business person, you should recognize the time and work that has gone into building any product and business and respect the work of software designers by buying their creations through authorized channels.

Note that in buying through a proper outlet, there will still be a wide range in the prices that you can pay, and shopping around for the best software prices can pay off handsomely. Part of the trade-off for a lower price may be the amount of support you receive, but the trade-off is not always in direct proportion to the price reduction.

Also note that you should read the "End User Licence Agreement" (EULA) which comes with your software. Many — but not all — software vendors allow you to install copies of software on more than one computer, usually with the proviso that the two copies may not be in use simulta-

neously. The benefit of this is, if you use a desktop computer in the office and a laptop for travel and home use, you may be able to buy one copy of the software and use it on both computers.

Be aware that the days of receiving a shelf-load of books with your software are gone. Software vendors do have somewhat better online help in their software now, but you may need to set aside a small budget for purchasing key reference books for the software you buy.

2.1b Site licences

Software vendors recognize that while an office may need eight copies of a particular software program, the office often does not need eight copies of every book and document normally supplied with the software.

So software vendors sell "site licences" which supply you with one copy of the software and documentation plus a licence for the number of computers you will use the software on. If you add one or more users later, you simply buy additional licences. These licences usually afford substantial discounts tied to the number of users being licensed. You can take advantage of such licences to reduce your costs of setting up your business.

Another approach gaining a lot of media attention is "Software as a Service" in which you subscribe to use programs such as spreadsheets and word processors over the Internet, and never actually buy and install the software on your computers. It is not clear if this approach will get past the hype stage and become a real alternative. Obvious drawbacks are reliability of Internet service and security of the content being typed into those services. If you are in an area where Internet service is not very reliable, this option is not for you, but if you are in a big city with good Internet access you may save money by going this route.

2.1c Open source software

At the end of the 1990s the term "open source" began to be applied to some software. It means that the source code used to create the software is available for inspection and perhaps modification under relaxed or non-existent licence restrictions. It also means the software is generally free for the individual to use.

Even the media tends to associate open source software with the Linux operating system, which itself is open source. But in fact, a lot of open source software can be used on the Windows operating system and a great deal can be used on the Macintosh.

It is easily possible to acquire and use open source software in place of commonly used commercial software. Some of the options available are mentioned on the CD that accompanies this book.

2.2 Operating systems

The operating system is the software that controls how the computer works. Your application software choices will probably make this decision for you — some software applications are available to run on multiple operating systems, but most are not.

The three most commonly used operating systems are —

- The various Windows systems from Microsoft

- The Macintosh operating system from Apple

- Various versions of the Linux operating system, from a variety of vendors (Linux and Macintosh are closely related)

Microsoft's Windows operating system dominates the office market today while Apple's system has a strong position in graphics oriented businesses such as advertising agencies. Various versions of the Linux operating system are widely used in technology companies, and have begun to achieve credibility in general business use.

Try not to predetermine the operating system you will use. If you do, you will potentially limit your choice of applications software. Instead, once you have selected the software you believe you need, your operating system choice should be obvious.

A word of caution: Using multiple operating systems in the same office will multiply your support and maintenance costs. At least during the start-up phase of your business, using just one operating system is the cost-efficient and sensible choice.

A final and important tip: Computer vendors often "bundle" software with a computer, and can combine the operating system and key applications in a package that affords significant savings over buying the hardware and software separately. If you will be buying one or more computers for your new business, you will definitely save money by buying a hardware and software bundle — just be sure you get the combination you want.

2.3 Hardware

Software and hardware are interrelated. The software programs decide the needed capacity of the equipment, and the operating system decides whether you need computers based on the IBM personal computer (or clones of the PC) or the Apple Macintosh.

If you have made your plan and researched the software and operating system you need, then you will know the kind of computer you need. What you don't yet know are the specifications of the hardware.

2.3a CPU speed

If you have been following personal computer trends at all you are probably aware that processor speeds — the "clock" speed of the central processor, usually expressed as units of gigahertz — increase rapidly and frequently. Yesterday's fast computer is old, and today's faster computer will be replaced by an even faster model in a few months' time.

Is having the latest, fastest machine important? Yes, but only if you will be working with software that can truly take advantage of that speed — if you will be manipulating large audio files or working with photographic quality images, you probably need "hot" hardware and you probably don't need the information in this chapter.

The clients who really drive manufacturers to produce ever-faster computers are game players! For the majority of us, last year's model, or perhaps even the one from two years ago, is more than "good enough" to perform standard office work efficiently. A word processor is not slowed down by a slow computer, it is slowed by the speed of our typing. A really large spreadsheet *might* take an extra second or two to recalculate on an older computer, but so what?

So here's my first rule: don't buy the latest, fastest model computer for standard office work — last year's model will be just as good at the job and it will be a lot cheaper!

2.3b Memory and disk capacity

The next questions are, how much memory should the computer have, and how much hard disk capacity is enough? The "memory" I'm talking about is random access memory (RAM), which is used by application software and the operating system.

Memory is not expensive and more is usually better than less. Modern operating systems and modern software applications like to use lots of memory. I regard two gigabytes of RAM as sufficient for simple work like word processing and four gigabytes is the sweet spot for office suites and most office applications. Windows and other operating systems are moving from memory-limited 32-bit designs to 64-bit designs which can use huge amounts of memory; double each of my numbers above for a 64-bit computer. Image manipulation software is especially demanding of memory and 16 gigabytes is a good buy for a computer using a 64-bit operating system and running image manipulation tools or very large spreadsheets.

Note that for some reason Microsoft tends to under-specify memory and other things needed (such as graphic card capability) for its operating systems. Buying 50 percent more than, or even twice, the amount Microsoft specifies is the safest approach.

Hard disk capacities have been increasing at an amazing pace while prices have plummeted. Do you need the latest, biggest hard drive? No, unless you are doing digital image or digital audio manipulation. So save some money and look for hard drives that are not the latest or biggest on offer. Most hard drives now have so much capacity that it would take literally millions of documents and spreadsheets to fill one.

2.3c Monitors

The monitor is the window to the work you do on a computer. The newest monitors are the so-called flat-panel designs using liquid crystal displays (LCDs). Until recently they came with fancy prices, but that is quickly changing. Standard glass (CRT) tube monitors are big, they chew up desk space, they generate heat, and they consume a lot of electricity.

Monitors range in size from about 15 inches to about 28 inches — the size usually being measured as the diagonal distance between two opposite corners of the screen. Some LCD monitor makers use the horizontal width instead of the diagonal measure, so pay attention when shopping. The actual viewing area or useful dimension of a monitor is always slightly less than the advertised size.

I think the sweet spot in monitors is an LCD with an aspect ratio of 16:9 (looks like a widescreen TV), in the 21 to 22 inch category. These "wide screen" monitors provide lots of space for spreadsheets, word processors, and web browsers to coexist and I believe they improve productivity. I think the 16:9 design has permanently replaced the square screen. I would not buy an LCD smaller than 21 inches. That size lets you view two word processor pages side-by-side in their actual size, or work with large spreadsheets without the need to do a lot or scrolling.

So here is my second rule: Invest in a good-sized, widescreen LCD monitor. Your rewards will include sharply lowered energy consumption, reduced eye strain, and better productivity when working with large documents, spreadsheets, or any other applications which want lots of screen surface area.

2.3d Printers

The most commonly used printers today are laser printers and inkjet printers.

Laser printers use essentially the same technology as the office copier and they produce very high-quality print. They print quickly and they are moderately expensive.

Inkjet printers form images on paper by spraying tiny droplets of ink onto the paper. The result is print quality that is not quite as good as a laser printer. Inkjet printers print quite slowly and their prices are low.

Deciding which type of printer you should buy for your office is not an easy decision. The key to the decision is not the original price of the printer, but the total cost, which is the printer price plus the cost over time of consumables such as laser toner and ink-jet ink. If you expect to be doing a lot of printing, a moderate-price laser printer will save you money because the cost of toner is much less than the cost of ink-jet ink when looked at for the printing of, say, 10,000 or 20,000 sheets.

Two more printing options you should be aware of are colour printers and multifunction printers.

Colour printer technologies include dye sublimation, laser, and inkjet. With the exception of inkjet printers, colour printers tend to be expensive to buy and expensive to operate. My recommendation for a start-up business is, unless you believe you will need a lot of colour printing, avoid buying a colour printer and take your occasional colour work to one of the print service centres that now exist in almost every Canadian city.

Multifunction printers typically combine an inkjet or laser printer with a copier and sometimes also scanning and facsimile functions. While this sounds like a nice way to save some money — the 3- or 4-in-1 product being cheaper than its component parts — the reality is that if one part of the system fails, the whole system fails.

2.3e   Other peripheral devices

The list of devices that can be added into or connected to personal computers is almost endless. I will deal briefly with the most common storage devices for office users.

- *Floppy drives:* The standard is the 3.5-inch, 1.44Mb drive. These are disappearing rapidly from new computers because they have limited storage capacity and the drive costs about the same as a CD-writer. I do not recommend them.

- *Optical drives:* DVDs and CDs can both be used to store and transfer large quantities of information. CDs are being quickly replaced by DVDs in most offices because DVD drives can read and write CDs and the drives are not expensive.

- *High capacity removable media drives:* There are enough options in this category to

make your head spin. If history has anything to tell us, it is that a half or more of this year's crop of these devices will fail to take hold in the market and will be unavailable in two or three years' time. These drives are typically used to transfer large files from one computer to another. If you need to regularly transfer files to someone else's computer (e.g., Postscript files to a typesetter), check what removable media drive they use and buy the same. Some companies also use removable drives to create backup copies of vital data, but in my opinion, using writable DVDs for this purpose is an easier and far less costly approach.

2.3f   Desk or floor?

One of the decisions you will face in buying your office computers is, should you buy a design that has the main box on the desktop or on the floor? While a few computer designs eliminate this decision (everything including the monitor is in one box), most computers separate the monitor from the box that contains the rest of the hardware.

I do not have a cut-and-dried answer for you, but some of the factors you will need to consider are the following:

- Desktop computers reduce free desk space

- Desktop computers make disk drives easier to access

- Floor-standing computers are susceptible to dust, liquid spills, and bumping by cleaning equipment

- Floor-standing computers may not fit under your office desks

3. NETWORKING

If you plan to have more than one computer, you may want to consider networking. Local area networks, or LANS, can offer tremendous abilities to share information, exchange email, and allow flexible use of your programs and such facilities as high-power printers. At the same time, networks are among the most complicated aspects of computer technology, and considerable expertise is needed in configuring and maintaining them.

If your office is new, you should at least arrange to incorporate the *facilities* for a network — channels through which network wiring can be pulled if you do install a network.

Wireless networking is another option for the office. While it has the attraction of not needing wires, a wireless network has the disadvantage of being potentially less secure than a wired network.

Networking computers can range from hooking two computers together with a telephone line and appropriate software, to modular units that can add extra nodes as required, to large configurations using large central servers. Prices range from less than $100 to connect two computers, to more than $10,000 for a network that will support multiple computers and shared peripheral devices. Also, networks are not restricted to any one kind of computer. IBMs and Macintoshes can be connected together, just as microcomputers can talk to minis or mainframes.

First, decide why you want to network your computers. Sharing data is useful, but it may be almost as quick, and a lot cheaper, to do it by exchanging disks if the volume is not large. Sharing printers or tape backup units does not require the building of a LAN. On the other hand, if your business volume is such that you have more than one person working on your computer needs, a LAN may offer you considerable benefits.

You must also consider the security aspects of a network. You do not want everyone to have access to your accounting records, and you will want to protect your database from damage or theft. If your network will also be used for data communication via an Internet connection, you will want to restrict the ability of an outsider to get into your system. And although software can often be shared across a network, you will likely need to buy special network versions of the programs.

In general, the topic of networks is too involved to go into detail here, but again consider it in your calculations, and build it into your plan, if appropriate. You will likely want to pay an expert to install your network, and to ensure it is secure.

4. THE INTERNET

The Internet has become an essential tool for many kinds of business. The popular press has concentrated on the World Wide Web, which is simply a graphical interface to the Internet, but there is a lot more happening on the Internet than just the myriad web pages.

I'll address some of the uses of the Internet first, then discuss the growing range of connection options, and finally make some comments on implementing your connection.

4.1 Business on the Internet

A lot of business is conducted on the Internet. And while some of the high-flying "Internet stock" companies of the 1990s managed to defy gravity, achieving incredible share values even while they were losing amazing amounts of money, the reality of having to make a profit eventually caught up with them.

There are many other companies with much lower public profiles who have found ways to use the Internet to make money and to make their business more efficient. Below are some of the ways these companies do business on the Internet.

4.1a Teleworkers

A growing number of companies are recognizing that they do not need all their workers to assemble in one place to work every day. Some tasks are just as easily done at home, the "teleworker" using email and file transfer tools to send work to and receive work from a remote office.

In the early days of personal computers in the 1980s, teleworkers were a somewhat exotic minority. By the late 1990s this had changed and telework was becoming a fairly mainstream form of employment. I expect this trend will continue. There are clear benefits to the employer:

- Teleworkers do not require office space, saving on rent and all the other direct and indirect costs of office space.

- Teleworkers can be employed on a task-based contract, allowing you to add workers for the time it takes to complete a particular project without adding to your permanent payroll.

The loudest argument I hear against teleworkers is the perceived loss of control. "If Jane doesn't come into the office, how do I manage her?" is a typical manager's response to the idea. The answer, of course, is that it is perfectly possible to manage workers who are not in the office — thousands of companies are doing it

successfully every day, measuring task results, not activity.

4.1b Electronic Data Interchange

Some companies now require their suppliers to have Electronic Data Interchange (EDI) connections which allow buyers to interrogate the suppliers' databases, placing and tracking orders. I know of companies in both the manufacturing and the retail sectors that will not qualify other companies as suppliers unless they have EDI facilities.

Manufacturers, in particular, have found that efficient use of EDI connections together with just-in-time policies have allowed them to sharply reduce their parts inventory costs. Retailers are working toward similar efficiencies, often on a global scale. And suppliers selling via EDI are finding it allows them to better tailor their production to actual demand.

If you are starting a business where such facilities will be required by your clients, you should retain the services of a consultant to help you understand and set up the systems you will need — the topic is well beyond the scope of this book.

4.1c Electronic mail

Electronic mail, or email, is one of the oldest and most widely used applications on the Internet. It allows for almost instant sending and receiving of mail messages across town, across the continent, or around the world.

Used properly, email can be a highly efficient way to maintain contact with remote offices, travelling staff, agents, and suppliers. Used badly, such as mass-mailing unsolicited promotional materials ("spamming" in Internet terminology), email can quickly give your company a bad reputation.

4.1d Research

The Internet, and the pages of the World Wide Web in particular, can be a wonderful research tool. You can use it to find out what your competitors are selling, to find new suppliers, to find new buyers, to track commodity prices, or to check the exchange rate and weather before leaving on a trip.

All you need to do research on the Internet is a good web browser and knowledge of how to search the Web.

4.1e Marketing

The Web was invented as a way to allow academics to share research results and documents. It has quickly evolved into a business marketing tool.

Big companies use websites — a collection of linked web pages at a web address — to promote and sell their products. For example, almost every automobile manufacturer has a website where you can learn about their current model line, check specifications, see what model X looks like in various colours, calculate the price of a car or truck with your favourite options installed, and learn about the latest dealer promotions. You can even place an order at many of these sites.

Small companies can get just as fancy with their websites. In fact, in many ways the web is the great leveller — a small company with a well-designed website can "look and feel" like a much bigger company.

An example: I have an acquaintance who packages and sells gift baskets. When she started the business her clients were local people and tourists, both groups reached through local print advertising. She decided to try selling her gift baskets through a website. Within a year, her business had nearly doubled. She now sells to people all around the world.

Another friend had a similar experience promoting a bed and breakfast on the Internet. The hotel is in a fairly remote area of the east coast. His site promotes both the B&B and the local area, making a virtue of its remoteness and the natural beauty of the area. The result: his occupancy rate has skyrocketed and he now has people visiting from around the world.

A website can be as simple as a page or two promoting your product or service — the digital equivalent of a print brochure — or it can be a full-fledged retail store on the Web, offering visitors the opportunity to place an order, pay by credit card, and receive order confirmation and shipping details by automated, follow-up email.

Setting up a commercial website will cost $4,000 and up for professional design and a few hundred dollars a year for a service provider to host the site. A merchant account (to allow credit card ordering) will add a little more to the cost, but it is very possible to have a retail site up and operating for considerably less than $10,000. Which is not a lot to invest in expanding your business beyond the boundaries of your town or city, if your product or service can be sold to that wider audience.

4.2 Connection options

Through most of the 1990s, the only practical Internet connection for most companies was a POTS (Plain Old Telephone System) modem — most often a 56K modem. Companies with enough money and requirements could spend thousands of dollars a month for a faster connection, which was usually either a 128K ISDN connection, or a "fractional T1 line" — computerese for a shared portion of a medium-speed permanent connection to the Internet.

All this is changing. A variety of vendors have started offering fast, more-or-less permanent Internet connections at quite competitive monthly rates. As a class, these connections are known as broadband — they offer high-capacity connections, versus the low-capacity or "thin pipe" capability of POTS modems. Four types of broadband service are available in urban centres (not all are available everywhere):

- Cable modems
- XDSL modems
- Satellite modems
- Wireless modems

We'll take a brief look at each. Bear in mind, these are new and evolving technologies and it is entirely possible that not all of them will survive to become mature technologies.

4.2a Cable modems

Canadian cable television vendors such as Shaw and Rogers began testing cable modem services in the late 1990s. A modem-like box is installed near your computer and is connected to the cable television network using the same coaxial cable your television uses. The modem is then connected to either a network card in your computer, or to a "hub" — a device that allows the modem to be shared in a LAN.

Cable network connections can be very fast — the cable companies claim "up to 100 times faster" than traditional dial-up modems — but

experience with them suggests the speed can be quite variable, probably because of the architecture of the cable network itself.

Canadian cable modem suppliers were slow to offer commercial connections and concentrated their early marketing efforts on home users. One reason for this was that business users are more likely to demand minimum standards of consistent performance. Business connections are now quite widely available, at a slight premium over what you would pay for home service.

4.2b XDSL modems

Telephone companies such as Bell and Telus began offering broadband services at about the same time the cable companies did. The telephone company system uses a pair of modems, one at your computer and the other in the telephone central office. The two modems are connected using standard copper telephone wire (the same line can be used simultaneously for voice and modem operations). The modem connects to your computer via a network card or a hub on your LAN.

Most Canadian telephone companies seem to be using Asymmetric Digital Subscriber Line (ADSL) technology for their broadband modems, one of the technologies known generically as XDSL.

Telephone broadband connections are offered with various maximum speeds, each at a different monthly price. On paper they do not appear to be as fast as cable modems, but in practice the service speed seems more consistent.

Commercial rental packages are widely available from telephone companies. An important point to note about XDSL service is the maximum speed you will obtain depends on the physical distance between your office and the telephone company's central office (exchange switchgear). If you are too far from the switch, service may not be available at all; if you are near the outer limit of service, your speed may be two-thirds slower than an office that is very close to the switch.

4.2c Satellite modems

Satellite connections to the Internet use a hybrid technology — a small "pizza dish" receiver on the roof or wall of your office receives incoming data while a POTS telephone modem is used to send data. This means that outgoing data is limited to the speed of a conventional, dial-up telephone modem while incoming data is faster, but not as dramatically faster as cable or XDSL — two times faster than dial-up seems typical.

Satellite connections are not yet widely available in Canada. Unless the cable television and telephone companies decide to not offer broadband services in remote areas of the country, I suspect satellite broadband will not be a major player in the future.

4.2d Wireless modems

Wireless broadband modems use a special antenna mounted on the roof or wall of your office to send and receive data. The technology is limited by the need for your antenna to be within a limited radius of the vendor's antenna and your antenna must be in a clear line-of-sight of the vendor's antenna.

Wireless broadband is faster than dial-up, but slower than cable or XDSL. It is not yet widely deployed in Canada.

4.2e Dial-up modems

If your connection requirements are limited to e-mail and occasional web browsing, the most cost-effective option remains the 56K POTS modem and a monthly account with an Internet service provider (ISP). The 56K modem may not be glamorous or very fast, but the technology is well established and both the hardware and the connection are inexpensive.

You will probably want to get a commercial account with an ISP so you can have multiple email accounts for yourself and your staff. If you or your staff will be travelling and will need to access your mail on the road, ask your ISP about "roaming" facilities.

Note: Even if you do not plan to have a company website immediately, you should consider registering a company Internet name and address — typically this will be *companyname.com* or *companyname.ca* — the former indicating a commercial address, the latter a Canadian address. Your ISP will help you with the registration, which is inexpensive. There are two reasons for doing this:

- Your email addresses can use your company name, so they become person@ companyname.com instead of person @ISPname.com.

- You protect your company name from having someone else use it as their Web name.

5. SECURITY

Even if you have just one computer in your new office, you need to be aware of security issues and take the appropriate steps to protect yourself.

5.1 Virus and malware protection

Computer viruses are here to stay. Malware — worms, trojans, key loggers, and root kits — is a fast-growing problem that is overtaking the virus as the biggest danger to computer users. The worst viruses can erase hard disks and destroy valuable data. Malware does not make its presence known so dramatically — it typically hides and works in the background to steal corporate and personal identity information, or uses your computer as a tool to send out spam and malware email. Malware and viruses can get into your computers in a variety of ways, the most common being:

- On a disk someone brings to the office

- As an attachment to an email message

- In a file downloaded from the Internet

The best protection against computer viruses is to install antivirus software and keep it up to date — vendors of this type of software will include tools with the software that allows it to automatically check the vendor's website and download, then install, the latest virus definitions files. I have my antivirus software set to automatically update itself daily — I recommend setting yours to update itself at least once a week.

Antivirus software can be set to automatically scan all files on all hard disks in your computer at regular intervals — I have mine set up to do this daily, too, late at night. If the software finds a problem, it will isolate it and optionally try to repair any infected files, and I get a report telling me what was found and what was done.

Do not rely on your Internet service provider's claim that they have anti-spam and antivirus software on their servers that will protect you from these dangers. Although most service providers do have quite good protection software, it will not protect you from staff bringing an infected disk into the office, or staff opening infected software.

5.1a Email protection

If you will be using email, make sure your antivirus software is set to automatically scan incoming email files.

Most good email software allows you a choice about whether any files attached to the email should be automatically decoded and stored on your disk. My recommendation is to *never* allow automatic decoding of such files. Instead, you (or your staff) should make the decision based on who sent the file and whether it was expected — if you get an email message with an attached file from someone you do not know, the safe action is to simply delete it. If you get an unexpected email message apparently from someone you know, call the person to check what they sent before you open it.

5.1b Software updates

The design of modern software (and operating systems) is complicated, and a single program can often contain millions of lines of code — the computer instructions that make the software work. So it should come as no surprise that most software contains "bugs" — code errors.

Most software bugs are very minor errors the user will never see. But some are flaws that a virus or malware program can exploit to do nasty things.

Software vendors usually release fixes (also called patches) soon after these code errors are found. These are typically available at the vendor's website and may be downloaded at no charge. But sometimes a software vendor may not immediately issue a patch, and then your computers are at risk because virus and malware writers have been adopting a "zero day" approach, trying to produce a virus that exploits the software code problem the same day the problem is found.

Ideally, one person in your office should be made responsible for regularly obtaining software patches and updates and installing them on all users' computers. That same person should also maintain a log of what was obtained and which computers it was installed on, so if he or she leaves, the next person responsible will know what has already been done. Keeping up to date with software patches is becoming an essential part of using computers.

5.2 Backup systems

Backups of your computer data files must be done frequently. Whether you back up the file you are working on every ten minutes or every hour matters little (if you are prepared to do the hour's work over again), but the total data that you record each day should be carefully protected. While antivirus measures will protect your work from malicious software, the only protection you can have against the failure of a computer (or one of its parts, such as a hard disk) is to back up your work — store a copy of it in a different location.

I recommend that you back up every night, or at the very least once a week. If you don't, realize that because the computer has a tremendous speed and memory, it can lose enormous amounts of your information very rapidly. The longer time you leave between backups, the higher the risk that you will lose something crucial. If you need that data to operate, then you could be out of business if it is destroyed.

One other point: if your system does crash and you don't have the expertise to easily restore it, call on an expert. Often the information is there and can be recovered, but only if you have not overwritten it by reloading other data on top of it.

Always keep a major backup of the system off-site, perhaps in a safety deposit box. If your premises are damaged by fire, it will not help you if all five backup copies of your crucial files were stored in the office (though a fireproof safe in the office is a useful place to store daily backups).

I strongly recommend that you use either a tape backup unit or a writable DVD drive for serious backups.

If you have a computer network in your office, be aware there is software available to back up the disks of all computers on the network. This is not very cheap, but what value would you place on, say, losing all the work done in a week by one or more key staff?

If you are unsure what backup strategy to employ, consider retaining the services of an expert consultant to help you design and set up a system — then be sure to follow the system and make sure your staff do, too! Once you have a consultant's recommendation, do not consider only the dollar cost of implementing it. Look long and hard at how much human work will be involved in running the backup system — if the system is labour-intensive, you can expect people to try to avoid the work, and that could be as bad as not having a system at all.

5.3 Powerline conditioning

Modern computers are a lot more rugged than those made in the 1980s, or even those made in the 1990s. They withstand the effects of erratic electrical supply better, and that is good.

Despite these improvements, it is still true that at the heart of every computer are precision components that require a very stable supply of electricity — a sudden surge or drop in the electricity supply can cause unexpected and potentially fatal damage to your data and computers.

If your business will rely on computers, you should seriously consider investing in at least a surge arrestor for each computer — a device that detects a sudden powerline surge and traps it before it reaches the computer. These inexpensive devices (typically less than $50 per computer) are designed to "fail" so that the computer will not fail. The best ones include protection from lightning strikes being transmitted to your computer via a telephone line connected to a modem.

A better, but somewhat more expensive ($200 and up) option is an uninterruptible power supply (UPS) — a box containing a surge arrestor, added circuits to "smooth" the flow of electricity, and a rechargeable battery pack which will provide some minutes of power after a failure of the mains supply, thus allowing the computer to be shut down properly.

The best of these backup power supplies includes software that will automatically close running applications and shut down your computer smoothly in the event of a power failure, even if you are not there. These units also usually come with a warranty that, if your computer is damaged by electrical problems while properly connected, you will be compensated.

How much powerline protection you want to invest in will depend on your budget and how critical the data on your computer will be to your business.

If you are setting up a new office, do try to keep the electric circuit used for your computers separate from other circuits in the office — this isolation should extend all the way back to the main circuit breaker or fuse box.

The reason for such isolation is, other devices in your office that draw large amounts of electricity (refrigerator motors, air conditioners, and power tools, as examples) can affect the entire circuit as they switch on or off — of course, they should not do this, but I have seen it happen often enough to be concerned about it.

5.4 Office security

Two other areas of security you need to be concerned with are theft and malicious damage in the office.

5.4a Computer theft

Computers are *very* popular items for thieves to steal from an office. They are quite portable, high-value, easily resold items that can be quickly stripped to their component parts and made "anonymous" before being sold.

While an overall security plan for your office is essential, it is also a good idea to specifically look at how you can secure the computers in your office. Options include locks and cables (very similar to bicycle locks) that can secure the main box of the computer to the desk or a similarly hard-to-move object.

It is helpful, although not always possible, to place computers in locations in the office where they are not visible from the street — apparently unplanned "smash and grab" thefts of computers from street-front offices seem to have become a feature of our larger cities in recent years.

5.4b The staff threat

It is sad but true that one of the biggest threats to your computers and the data they store are the people who use them. An unhappy departing staff member can wreak havoc very quickly if he or she has unrestricted access to your computers and your data — and it may prove hard to prove who did the damage.

The safe approach is to limit who can access and who can modify the data on your computers. This is especially true for database records. A simple system of user identification and passwords, provided it is properly implemented, can go a long way toward protecting a valuable asset.

If you are unsure about how much security you need, hiring a consultant to do a security audit of your system can be a worthwhile investment.

6. ERGONOMICS AND YOUR ENVIRONMENT

To use your computer system most effectively, you must consider the surroundings in which the computer is placed, as well as the hardware and software.

Computers have changed the way we work in the office, but many offices continue to be designed and furnished as if we still used typewriters and multiple filing cabinets — large desks with "typewriter returns" dominate the space, often with walls lined with filing cabinets.

6.1 Ergonomics are important

Working at a computer is different from working with a typewriter. This may seem like an obvious statement, but I'm continually amazed at how many office designs overlook it, despite the fact that personal computers have been in offices since the early 1980s!

Ergonomics are an important issue — one I suspect will become more important in coming years. Repetitive Strain Injuries (RSI) such as inflammation of wrist joints from poor keyboard positioning and neck injuries stemming from bad monitor positioning will attract increasing attention from insurers, labour groups, and government regulators.

One of the many changes brought about by computers is the amount of time we spend at the keyboard. With typewriters we regularly moved around — to file or mail, to put a new sheet of paper in the rollers, or to perform other, non-typing tasks. The computer has eliminated much of the *need* to move away from the keyboard and I think this is one of the reasons RSI has become an issue. My suggestion is, if you find yourself spending hours at the keyboard, force yourself to take a short break once an hour. Even if you do not have a non-computer task to do, get up anyway, stretch, and exercise your eyes by looking at distant objects — do these things five minutes out of every hour and you will reduce your RSI risk.

6.1a Keyboard and mouse

The keyboard and mouse must sit at the proper height for comfort over an extended period of time. An ordinary desk with a lower side section for a typewriter might provide this, but chances are the keyboard will be too low if placed on the typewriter extension and the monitor will be awkwardly placed on the desktop.

A new computer desk made of veneer and particleboard starts at less than $100 and can be a good alternative to the traditional steel desk.

Check that a keyboard and mouse surface at the right level is available if you look at any of these lower-priced models — ideally, the user should be able to adjust the height of the surface which will hold the keyboard and mouse.

6.1b Monitor

The monitor also must be positioned correctly. It should be able to tilt and swivel in any case, but its initial position should put the top of the screen directly in front of the user at or a little below eye level; if not, the operator may start complaining about an aching neck or back or eyestrain.

When we used typewriters, a desk with good sunlight was attractive; now that we use computers, sunlight can be counterproductive. Lighting for the computer area should be soft and indirect. In situations where you cannot adjust the overhead lighting, use an anti-glare screen for the monitor, and place the monitor so it is minimally affected by other light sources. In offices that receive a lot of sunlight, consider installing dark curtains or blinds which the occupants of the office can easily adjust to minimize glare and reflections on their monitors.

6.1c Chairs

A good-quality chair is very important. We spend as much as six hours a day in our office chairs, but we often choose the least expensive model in the store.

A chair for computer work should be height adjustable, the arms should be short so they do not collide with the keyboard tray or other items when the user turns, and the backrest should provide good lower back support. The "ideal" chair will have adjustable armrests so the user

can rest the upper forearms while typing and the angle of the seat base and backrest should be easily adjusted to suit the task at hand.

6.2 What files?

As someone once said, the paperless office is about as likely as the paperless toilet. But it is also fair to say that computers have both reduced and changed our filing requirements — most offices now rely more on digital databases than on paper files to store records.

In many instances, the paper records that you will need to keep — such as the records your auditors may require — can be stored in a central location and not in each individual workspace. The individual workspace today may only need paper filing for current projects.

The kinds of storage a computer-based workspace does need include spaces for any of the following that you use:

- Backup tapes
- CD/DVD-ROMs
- Paper for printing

6.3 Other considerations

When you are planning the setup for your computer, consider where all the cables will run, especially those to the printer. If the printer is in a different room, or if you are sharing it with other computers, you may be wise to put cables in the ceiling or through the walls rather than across the floor.

If your printer is in the same room you are in, how easy is it to reach? Can you easily replenish or change the paper? Do you have a place to store printer paper near the printer? Do you have at least one replacement ink cartridge (inkjet printer) or toner cartridge (laser printer) stored in the office?

Finally, keep the environment clean. More data has been lost through spilled coffee than electrical storms. Keyboards, monitors, and mice or trackballs should be cleaned at least twice a year by someone using the appropriate cleaning tools. Printers (both laser and inkjet) should also be cleaned once or twice a year — more often if they are heavily used. Office supply stores carry computer-specific cleaners and tools — such as compressed air cans for cleaning keyboards and printers — and staff there can provide useful advice about how to clean.

7. CHOOSING A SUPPLIER

Where should you buy your equipment? There are at least three options: computer consultants, computer stores, and computer manufacturers.

Consultants may sometimes appear to be more expensive, but to stay in business, they must offer you solid knowledge and, unfortunately, you cannot always rely on the knowledge and support offered by many computer stores. Computer manufacturers compete with computer stores by selling via mail order — many have websites where you can order a custom configuration and the computer will be delivered by courier within a day or two.

If you are prepared to take the time and effort to become truly computer literate (and this means primarily a lot of reading and talking to other users), you will find that you will quickly outstrip the meagre knowledge offered by many computer store salespeople.

On the other hand this does take time, and if you can find a good local supplier (and despite

my earlier comments they do exist), they can be a truly useful partner in ensuring that your computer operations live up to your expectations.

How do you discover such a vendor? Here are a list of questions that will help you determine whether they can help with more than connecting the right end of the printer cable to the computer:

(a)   How long have you been in business?

(b)   What are your areas of expertise?

(c)   What warranty do you offer with the purchase of any equipment?

(d)   What does the warranty cover?

(e)   If I don't pay for a maintenance contract and I need service, what will it cost and how long will it take?

(f)   What training do you offer, and can it be custom tailored to my requirements?

(g)   Is training conducted in the store, or can it be provided in my offices if I wish?

(h)   What would you recommend I use for my database requirements and my word processing needs?

The last two questions can be particularly revealing because before you get an answer, you should be subjected to a wide variety of questions about the specifics of the uses you intend, the volume of work, the number of users, etc. If a recommendation is made without an obvious effort to really understand your company and its operations, it means that the salesperson is selling you his or her favourite program (or the one with the largest commission), not choosing the right program to match your needs.

For example, some software programs are far beyond the needs of most small organizations.

This may seem like a minor point until you realize that there is always a trade-off between power and ease of use, and if you buy power you don't need, you will be also be buying a lengthy learning and maintenance curve.

Consider, too, the location of the supplier. If their price is $100 less, but it takes half an hour to reach them, you could spend an hour travelling each time there is a minor problem, and the advantage of price may be outweighed by the time you have to spend in travel.

Finally, of course, *get references* for any supplier you are considering using.

8. TRAINING

Many people assume that once they have obtained the hardware and the software, the battle is almost won. Unfortunately, that is the same as believing that after you have bought the car, driving skills are unnecessary.

Training is the most important part of your computer plan. You should be prepared to spend up to 50 percent (some experts say an additional 100 percent) of your investment in hardware and software on training for you and your staff.

Now, the bad news: After you have trained your star employee to use a computer effectively, he or she is going to be more valuable, and it is possible that your employee will be offered a better-paying job elsewhere. There is really no way of protecting yourself from this aspect of computerization, but it emphasizes why a simple program that a lot of people can use easily may be more beneficial than a highly advanced financial system that no one but your auditor can understand or run.

Having said that, I can now announce the good news: Computers are becoming so wide-spread in commerce that you will have little difficulty finding staff who are familiar with the basics of popular software.

You will have to decide who will be trained on the computer, in what order, on what programs, over what time period, and in what sort of classes (full day, part time, or evening). And realize that no matter how hard you try to arrange matters, training will cause disruptions to your regular workload and schedules.

Don't underestimate the knowledge of your staff. Now that computers are widely used, it is quite possible that someone working for you is an expert — or power user — of the software you use. You may want to encourage this person to help others in the office become more productive with the software.

9. ADMINISTRATION

Setting up a computer system and keeping it going requires a certain number of administrative functions. The most important of these tasks is backup. Others include scheduled cleaning, updating software, and replacing printer inks or toner.

Realize, too, that with the introduction of a computer, job roles and, therefore, job definitions are likely to change. A manager may do more typing, a layout person might get more involved in production, or an administrator may spend more time to properly tackle marketing. Whatever happens, you should plan for such changes even if you can't identify exactly what they will be, and expect a perhaps uncomfortable period of adjustment in the initial few months.

10. RULES

Computers can make a wonderful contribution to productivity. They can also be a wonderful distraction for your staff.

The best thing to do is to set firm rules and stick to them. Make it clear that staff cannot use your computers to —

- browse the Internet that is not for company business reasons

- visit pornographic websites

- download pirated software

- install any software without permission

- send or receive personal email

- send unsolicited commercial email (spam)

- attack or attempt to violate other computers

Draw up a list of computer usage rules and make each staff member read and sign the document. (Kits to create such rules are available commercially on the Internet, including from Self-Counsel Press — see *Small Business Forms*).

If you store customer information on paper or in a database, you should be aware of the Personal Information Protection and Electronic Documents Act (PIPEDA). The best way to learn about it is to visit the Industry Canada website at http://strategis.ic.gc.ca and use the Search tool on the main page to search for the topic "Privacy for Business."

11. CONCLUSION

If joining the computer revolution sounds like a lot of work, you are right — it is. In many cases, it is worth finding an expert to help you through the process. But if you take this route, don't abandon your own involvement. If you don't have a clear understanding about how the whole operation works, it becomes that much harder to evaluate what you have accomplished, and whether that matches your original goals.

What I have discussed here is just a start. The computer revolution has hardly begun, and I believe those who do not become involved will, in many cases, get left behind. If you develop your plan along the lines that are suggested here, you will have made an excellent beginning. Remember, too, to go back to your plan from time to time, modifying it as you and the technology grow.

14
USING TAX LAWS TO YOUR ADVANTAGE

1. INTRODUCTION

Canada's taxation laws and requirements are becoming more and more complex. It is now almost impossible for the small-business person to keep up with the changes. And there are even more on the immediate horizon. Even the experts find the task difficult, and they devote a lot more time to it than you'll have, as you go about the business of making your company grow and prosper. But no matter how difficult (and frustrating) it seems, it is essential that you make yourself aware of the various tax regulations and requirements that relate to your business. You ignore taxation, and its impact on your financial well-being, at your peril.

From the moment you set up in business, you entered into an agreement with the Receiver General for Canada. The government has a stake in your business, and it expects to hear from you on a regular basis. After all, corporate taxes form a major source of its revenue.

And, by the way, the government does not let you off easily if your tax remittances are late or there is any attempt at tax evasion. So don't be dumb — and don't try to be cunning. Get smart. With good tax planning, you *can* legitimately avoid or reduce tax; there's no need for you to pay one cent more in taxes than you have to. That's what being smart is all about.

When it comes to taxation and ways to minimize it, there is no substitute for qualified, professional advice. In this area, your accountant is your best friend. Assuming he or she is good at the job, and most pros are, your accountant can save you tax dollars in the long run. But you can do some research on your own; it will make his or her advice easier to understand and your questions a lot more intelligent. There are numerous sources for tax information. Here are just a few:

(a) *Canada Revenue Agency (CRA):* You might as well start at the top. You'll find the listing in the Government of Canada section of your telephone book. Call or write and ask for the information to be forwarded to you.

(b) *Accounting firms:* Most accounting firms spend thousands of dollars, not to mention labour, on keeping up with the latest in taxation. And most produce booklets and bulletins incorporating the latest changes.

(c) *Public libraries and bookstores:* If you use a library, check the copyright dates of books to be sure the information is current. Outdated information on tax is worse than none at all. Ditto for the bookstores.

Don't let the mountain of information available on this subject scare you; you don't need to be a tax expert to run your business. But you do need to be knowledgeable. If you do your homework and seek out professional advice, you're already one step ahead of most people.

2. INCOME AND TAXES IN CANADA

The Canadian government taxes corporations, individuals, and trusts. But the most common tax targets are corporations and individuals. And that's what this section deals with.

For both corporations and individuals, it is relatively easy to calculate taxes once income is known. In fact, the sections of the *Income Tax Act* that deal with the calculation of taxes are relatively few. On the other hand, those sections that deal with the determination of the income on which those taxes are based take up more than 90 percent of the Act. There is a lot more time spent by taxpayers, their advisors, and the government in determining what income is taxable than there is in calculating the taxes on that income.

In general terms, the government collects taxes on net income, which is the difference between revenue and the cost and expenses incurred to achieve that revenue. Usually, identifying revenue is relatively easy, but calculating and keeping track of deductible expenses can be more difficult. From the CRA's point of view an expense is only deductible when it meets three tests:

- Was the expense laid out to earn income?

- Was the expense reasonable in nature?

- Was the expense capital in nature?

If the taxpayer can answer yes to the first two questions and no to the third one, then the expense is usually an allowable deduction.

So, keep those receipts. Be sure you can back up all your expenses. You can be sure that the tax department will be looking for a paper trail if it does an audit. Keep your records current and complete.

3. MAXIMIZE DEDUCTIBLE EXPENSES

There are many ways to reduce your taxable income, and you are legally entitled to take advantage of every legitimate expense. As a self-employed business person, you are entitled to deduct all expenses incurred for the purpose of earning income.

3.1 Keep every receipt

To deduct all expenses incurred for the purpose of earning income, it is absolutely necessary for you to keep detailed receipts. Every day I meet business people who tell me what a pain in the neck it is to obtain receipts and keep them. Many of them blame the fact that they didn't keep receipts on accountant "friends" of theirs who told them they could claim up to 35 percent to 40 percent of their commission income and they would not be questioned.

They are wrong! The only thing not keeping receipts will guarantee is that when you are audited, your whole claim or a major portion of it will be thrown out the window.

If you are entitled to claim expenses, don't tell me that it is too much trouble to keep receipts. It is not too much trouble. Every time you keep the receipt for $2 you put another tax-free dollar in your pocket.

You *must* keep receipts. These receipts must be itemized and totalled. You must keep all of your receipts and deduct a percentage of the money spent as personal expenses.

There are only two places where you cannot get a receipt for tax purposes: parking meters and pay telephones. In all cases, you should keep a diary of these expenses. They do mount up.

One man guessed that he would spend $50 for these items in a year. He kept a record for the next nine months and in this time he had spent $435, almost as much per month as he had guessed for a year! This meant an extra refund of over $250 tax-free dollars. Remember: that will be every year for many years to come.

Sooner or later you will encounter problems with the tax department if you do not keep receipts — especially if you are running your own business.

Now let's take a brief look at the more important ways of lowering your taxable income.

3.2 Accounting and legal expenses

Accounting, legal, and collection figures are sometimes confusing. People will put down $300 because they did it themselves and, if they hadn't, it would have cost $300 to pay someone else, so they think that they are entitled to the equivalent amount. This really does not make sense. If they could claim the $300, they would just have to add the $300 into their income, making it an exercise in futility.

Legal fees are deductible when incurred to earn or collect income. They are not allowable when of a capital nature. In these cases, they should usually be added to the capital cost of the item to be used as the base for depreciation. Again, please consult competent help.

Note: Legal fees for incorporating are not readily deductible and only one half of their cost ever becomes deductible through the capital cost allowance system.

Collection fees are deductible, but taxpayers tend to try and claim this amount twice in the following manner. (This may be unintentional, but the tax department auditor frowns on it.)

When a business is working on a cash basis, it sometimes ends up with a bad debt that it has to sue for or turn over to a collection agency. When it collects the debt, it reports only the net amount collected and then claims the collection expense as well.

This cannot be done. Report either the net collected amount or report the gross amount as income and claim the collection charges as an expense.

3.3 Advertising and promotion expenses

Advertising and promotion expenses are not as self-explanatory as they may seem. For example, look at the advertising in such well-known publications as *People* or *Money Magazine*.

The *Income Tax Act* says that Canadian businesses cannot write off against Canadian income advertising money paid to foreign publications. Magazines like those above are some of the largest publications in the world and are American owned. Hence, ads in them are not tax deductible, and you can assume that their quoted advertising rates are 30 percent to 100 percent more after taxes than rates for advertising in a similar Canadian publication.

Promotion expenses are another much abused expense area. What is a promotion expense? I have been looking for an exact definition for a long, long time without success and, therefore, can only give you my opinion.

Business promotion can be a very dicey situation. Where does "personal" expense stop and "business" promotion start? If you, as a business person, have a party to which you invite only customers, it would seem clear that you have a business promotion expense. But suppose half the guests are business clients and half old school buddies? Really, it is a matter for your conscience.

If you give a bottle of liquor to a customer or give out wallets or pens with your name on them, these items are deductible if you are a commission salesperson. Again, keep the receipts and every time you give away a bottle, write down the recipient's name on the back of the receipt.

Note: New rules will serve to reduce deductible promotion expenses to 50 percent of the actual costs incurred.

3.4 Business entertaining and meals

In the good old days, a wealthy individual could have a summer cabin, a yacht, club memberships, and other goodies that were all tax deductible for business entertaining. That situation is now very different. Hunting lodges, yachts, and club memberships are specifically forbidden expenses for tax purposes.*

To be deductible now, a yacht or hunting lodge must be owned as a business, not for the personal pleasure or use of the owner. As the average yacht is used about 12 days a year (really!) and a hunting lodge about the same, it is possible for these assets to be converted to business use and rented out, thus making their expenses deductible up to (but not exceeding) the amount of the rental income.

Condominiums at ski resorts, summer cabins, and campers or motor homes also fall into this category.

What does the law say about meals? It is confusing, to say the least. Basically, if you are out of town and buy a meal, it is deductible. If you buy a meal for yourself and a customer, both meals are deductible. But, if you buy a meal for yourself and a customer in town, only the customer's meal is supposed to be deductible. This

---

*Taxwise, you are still better off to have your company pay for your membership to private clubs.

can be very unfair as the tendency of most small-business people of my acquaintance is to buy a hamburger if they are eating alone, and to have an expensive meal at a good restaurant if they are dining with a customer. Therefore, to have to pay tax on half the meal is an undue hardship. It has been my experience that if good records are kept showing the typical meal for yourself, the tax office will allow this as the personal portion of the expensive meal. The CRA considers all meal expenses to be 50 percent deductible.

Again, this points out the need to keep all your receipts so that the personal portion may be deducted. Those taxpayers who keep only the business receipts will find themselves penalized for a personal portion, which is unfair. It is also necessary to keep a note on the back of the receipt showing the who, what, why, and where of the entertainment.

While it is true that the tax office tends to accept claims for "average" meals without receipts, the tax office will not accept a claim for lodgings without a receipt, and the tendency is to not accept much off a claim for meals without receipts.

I advise every person entitled to this claim to keep a reasonably accurate log book with a detailed record of amounts spent for meals. After the initial shock of having to get receipts and learning to write down the amounts, people soon realize how much money they lose by not keeping track.

The usual question at this point is "How much can I legally claim without receipts?" The answer is ... nothing! Without receipts, at the time of an audit, the assessor does not have to allow one red cent for your meal expenses. How

does he or she know that you didn't carry four days' worth of box lunches with you?

As a matter of practice, there seem to be local limits that assessors in different tax offices will allow. For example, one city might allow $10 per day while another district office allows $12 or $15 per day. I think it also has a lot to do with whether or not the assessor had a good breakfast or a fight with his or her spouse that morning. At any rate, there is no set figure you have a right to claim as a business expense. You must keep your receipts and be prepared to produce them at audit time.

I can also assure you that if you keep your receipts you will undoubtedly discover that you are spending more than you thought you were, and your tax refund will be larger. For example, keeping your receipts for just $1 a day more than if you were not would mean a tax refund of about $120 more to the "average" business per year.

3.5 Business tax, fees, and licences

Business tax, fees, and licences are self-explanatory, but here I will give a hint to those contemplating going into business.

Some cities, such as Vancouver, have a very low licence fee. You may have premises renting for $2,000 per month and pay a $10 licence fee and base all budget forecasts on that rate. After a year in business, you receive a nasty surprise when you find there is an additional business tax based on rental value and you suddenly find yourself with an unexpected $2,000 business tax bill. Check municipal rules before you go into business. This has hurt many people.

3.6 Depreciation

Due to normal wear and tear, or obsolescence, the assets of your company are seen to depreciate (i.e., lose value over time). It is standard accounting custom to calculate this loss and write it off against income over a specified period of time.

Surprisingly, many inexperienced business people forget to expense depreciation. Don't be one of them; it can be a very expensive mistake. In most cases, it is a good rule to depreciate an item as quickly as you can. This approach will give you a maximum tax benefit, but like all rules there can be exceptions. Your accountant can advise you.

Your friendly tax department has something to say about depreciation as well. It even has its own name for it: capital cost allowance (CCA). Within the *Canadian Income Tax Act* are specific guidelines covering the allowable depreciation rates by class of asset. The rates range from nothing on things such as land, plants, and animals, to 100 percent for small tools and linen. As you must abide by these rules, you may want to ask the CRA for a copy of the CCA guidelines.

3.7 Car or truck expenses

The main thing to remember about vehicle expenses is that the tax department requires more detailed information than most taxpayers are inclined to give. To claim vehicle expenses, all expenses must be recorded and kept. It is not enough to write down or keep expenses only for the time you were actually working, such as the gas expense when you went to see a supplier in Moose Jaw.

You must keep *all* the year's expenses. In that way, major repairs, tires, insurance, and the capital cost allowance are spread over both personal and business portions. It has been my experience that small-business people penalize themselves when they do not keep proper car records.

"But what happens if I use my car for both business and pleasure?" you ask. According to the *Income Tax Act*, if you use a business vehicle for personal use, you are required to take the personal benefit into your income. Because, in most cases, the personal benefit is hard to measure, a formula is now provided to calculate the benefit.

Before getting into this, however, you should realize that you are considered to have such personal use if you have a vehicle available for such use, regardless of whether you actually use it or not, unless the vehicle is not suitable for personal use (e.g., a delivery truck). Practically, this means that if you take the company car home at night you are caught. The only way to avoid this is to work away from the office and travel straight to the job without calling in at the office.

What is the situation if you have an office in your home? The answer is unclear, but it would be somewhat difficult for the tax department to construct a case that you should be declaring this benefit if you have a personal car as well. If you don't there could be an argument.

The situation is the same if you lease a car — there is a formula provided to calculate the personal benefit. The charge to be included in your income for company-owned cars is 2 percent per month or 24 percent per year, and in the case of a leased car it is two-thirds of the lease cost per month. For example, if you drive a $30,000 company-owned Chevrolet, you must add $7,200 to your income and pay tax on this addition.

On the leased auto the figures are analogous. A car that costs the company $350 a month is a taxable benefit of $2,800 (2/3 x $350 x 12 months).

Currently, the government has provided an alternative for calculating the personal benefit of a company vehicle. The benefit may now be computed at the rate of 50 percent of the standby charge pertaining to that automobile. This means that you can ignore actual operating costs and choose to pay 3 percent per month of the cost of the car multiplied by the number of months the car is available for personal use by the employee.

3.7a To own or lease your vehicle

In effect, the bureaucrats have calculated it so there's no difference in tax between leasing and owning. Whether to lease or own is a question often raised by the small-business person. My experience is that, especially when just starting out, it is important to make your life as simple and uncluttered as possible so that you can concentrate on increasing sales and decreasing expenses.

Leasing today is a complicated business. There are many leasing options to consider, figures to work through, and tax problems to think about. The fine print must be read and contracts must be signed. All this distracts you from your main task at hand.

The second reason for avoiding leases at the beginning is that you are paying more than necessary to "rent" the equipment. After all, the company handling the details and financing has to make a profit too!

And remember to finance the purchase of a major item through your bank rather than through a finance agency appointed by the seller of the item. When the salesperson says, "Don't worry, you can pay over three years by financing through us," begin to worry.

What happens is that the seller gets you to advance a down payment and to sign a conditional sales agreement along with a financing contract. What this means is that some finance company will be collecting 18 percent to 24 percent interest and you do not own the item until the final payment is made. You can find cheaper ways of borrowing money, can't you?

When should you lease? When your personal tax bracket rises to about the 40 percent level, in which case the extra cost of leasing is not important because it is deductible as a business expense, and the benefits of leasing (such as maintenance being included in the cost) can be enjoyed to the full.

Another advantage of leasing (at least where vehicles are concerned) is that no down payment is required. If you are really scrambling for money, this may be important.

Note: Recent rules now limit the capital cost of vehicles for capital cost allowance purposes to $24,000, and the leasing cost cannot exceed $650 per month regardless of the actual amounts.

3.8 Convention expenses and holiday trips

Convention expenses are limited to two conventions per year and, to qualify, the convention must be in the geographic (normal operating) area of the taxpayer.

There may be a point to a geologist travelling from Edmonton to South Africa to learn about diamond mining, but Hammer's Hardware will not get away with a trip to New Orleans.

At one time it was definite that you could not claim your spouse as a "convention" expense. Mind you, it was possible to claim a secretary. It has recently become a policy of many corporations to insist that spouses attend conventions so that they know what is happening with their partners' jobs. In these circumstances, it would seem to be the policy of the tax offices to allow the expenses for both spouses.

One of the few areas left for "creative" write-offs exists in combining business and pleasure trips. For example, if you know you have to travel to Regina on a family matter, try to arrange to do some business there at the same time. This can be done by attending a convention, visiting customers, or contacting a supplier. Even if the tax department disputes the whole amount, you will likely end up with some write-offs.

Likewise, if you are legitimately attending a convention, try to work your personal holiday into the same trip. This will mean big savings to your holiday budget.

3.9 Cost of goods sold

The main thing to remember here is that you will pay tax based on the cost of goods sold and not necessarily on what you spent in the year for inventory. You pay tax on the increased inventory as though it were profits.

Although there are ways you can depreciate inventory, in my opinion it is basically unfair for the government to levy a tax on unrealized gains because it often causes great hardship for small-business people who are struggling to build up their inventory.

Here is the method of showing the cost of goods sold:

Opening inventory	$ 3,500
Purchases	22,500
Total available to sell	26,000
Ending inventory	6,000
Total actually sold	$20,000

The cost of goods sold is $20,000 and this is the figure claimed, even though $22,500 was actually spent during the fiscal year for the purchase of goods to sell.

3.10 Delivery, express, and freight

Some forgetful people tend to claim delivery, express, and freight expenses twice by adding the charges for delivery, express, and freight to the cost of their goods and then claiming them again as a separate expense. Don't do this!

Watch for mislaid and unaccounted-for receipts because they can add up to a substantial sum. I mentioned this to a business friend who used to drop off parcels at the bus depot on his way home and pay for the shipping with loose change. For five years he had been putting these receipts in a box and his accountant had never enquired. The receipts for these years amounted to $4,000!

If your accountant or tax advisor does not dig into your affairs, run to the nearest exit. He or she is not doing an adequate job for you.

Another observation I would make here is that people tend to want the same individual to do the mechanical part of their tax returns and bookkeeping. This is not always the best idea. Having another person start from scratch every couple of years should give a deeper review into both the current return and your prior returns. Bookkeepers and accountants tend to get lazy, and they copy details from one year to the next.

3.11 Interest, exchange, and bank charges

Interest is self-explanatory. It is the rent you pay for money borrowed or for the outstanding balance on stock, equipment, and fixtures. The general rule is that interest paid on borrowed money to earn business or investment income is deductible. The only problem is when real estate is involved. If this is your situation, you will need professional help because the rules are complicated. What is often missed is mortgage interest on the family home, which can often be claimed as a business expense because the mortgage was arranged to put capital into the business, or for other investment purposes.

Exchange refers to foreign exchange between countries. An organization with a poor accounting system will usually miss this very important item.

As for bank charges, I find that most businesses spend more than $500 in various bank charges in a year. (I am talking about the small one- or two-person business that encounters the occasional overdraft.) The charges are usually $40 per month and, if the bank statements are not adequately reconciled, you are paying an extra $15 to $20 per month in tax to save half an hour's work.

3.12 Maintenance and repairs

What is maintenance? What are repairs? When do repairs turn into an *addition?*

Maintenance is the general upkeep of an asset. It refers to routine painting, oiling, or replacing filters or rubber hoses.

Repairs refers to a breakdown. If something won't work or is unsuitable because of its mechanical condition, it should be considered a repair. The problem starts when the "repair" becomes materially better than the original was or ever could be.

If a store roof is leaking and the owner patches it with some asphalt, it is a repair. If the roof leaks and the owner prices out the repair and decides that for a bit or even a lot more he or she can raise the roof and put in another mezzanine floor, then it is an addition, even though it was prompted by the need for a repair.

The difference is that a repair may be listed as an expense in the current year. An addition must be added to the capital cost of the asset and depreciated over a number of years. Also, if the addition is depreciated and then sold for more than the depreciated value, there would be a "recapture" of depreciation and tax would have to be paid on the recapture.

It is easy to see that it is to the advantage of the taxpayer to try to "expense" the item. (The tax office will always check into large "repair" items.)

3.13 Office expenses, petty cash, postage, and stationery

Every time you spend $2 for postage and don't record the expenditure, you have just thrown a dollar in tax savings out the window.

I suggest that if you make it a habit to always take the money from petty cash to buy a small item, your balancing of the petty cash will force you to remember the receipt. Petty cash should be balanced on a regular basis for this reason.

It is becoming increasing popular for small businesses to supply their personnel with charge cards rather than paying out petty cash allowances in advance.

The advantage of this arrangement is that not only does the company gain from 15 to 45 days to pay, but the use of credit cards also results in precise, honest records of transactions, which improve operating controls. The amounts involved may seem small in isolation, but the overall effect can be very important to the small firm.

3.14 Medical and dental expenses

Once your business has its head above water, you should investigate instituting medical, dental, and possibly group term life insurance plans for you and your employees.

Unfortunately, you can't institute policies just for yourself (and your family) where the business pays the premiums and claims an expense. It must be open to all full-time employees for the expense to be deductible. The deduction can be the entire premium as long as it does not discriminate against some employees and employees are charged a taxable benefit.

Even with these restrictions, if you operate a very small business (two or three people) the expense is justified because, if you want, you can have the employees (including yourself) pay half, the company the other half, and you have complete health protection at a very reasonable rate. Besides, it is a nice fringe benefit for the employees. (See Chapter 17 for more details.)

3.15 Office expenses (in the home)

Any space used in the home for purposes of the business can be charged against business income as an expense. Under Canadian law, mortgage payments are not tax deductible for private residences, so anything you can do to make them so will result in significant tax benefits to yourself.

You are entitled to deduct a portion of the mortgage interest (the largest part of your mortgage payment), taxes, utilities, and maintenance payments for your home office. Note that if you make this claim, you will lose the principal residence status on the portion of the house you are using for business. Also, if you try to claim capital cost allowance (depreciation) on any portion of the house, you will lose the principal residence for the whole house. Watch out for this one.

Because of this, many accountants have been telling their clients that they should cease to claim offices in their homes. Personally, I have not yet worked out a case where I feel it is to the taxpayer's advantage to postpone a claim for an expense today in the hopes of an expected gain some time in the future.

Note: Recent amendments to the Income Tax Act will deny deductions in the home unless it is the only office from which an individual or corporation operates its business. This will have its largest impact on staff who "telecommute" to work most days in the month, but spend certain, mandated days in the office — watch out for this if you have workers in this situation.

3.16 Property taxes

Property taxes carry an interest figure if not paid in time. Often there is also a penalty. I usually tell the average small-business person that it is cheaper to pay the interest and penalty than it is to borrow the equivalent amount of money elsewhere. But check it out first because some cities have recently adjusted their penalties upwards.

Another point that comes to mind applies only to those people who are using the business premises as a personal residence in those provinces with home owner grants. In this case, make sure that you do not split the home owner's grant evenly between the business and the residence. The grant applies only to your residence and you do not need to split it with your business premises for tax calculation purposes.

3.17 Rent

Make sure that you remember all the figures for rent. Business people frequently trade off for rent. If you traded a personal car for a month's rent, remember to claim the value paid.

3.18 Salaries, wages, allowances, and bonuses

Remember when claiming the salaries of employees to claim the gross amount before deductions for taxes, EI, or CPP. If you have been claiming after-deductions amounts, you could be losing a considerable amount of money. The taxes you have deducted from salaries are not your taxes but the employees' taxes.

Also be careful about agreeing not to deduct taxes from an employee's salary; the *Income Tax Act* very clearly says that such an agreement is void. This means that even if you have a signed written agreement with your employee, you are still the one liable for penalties if you fail to withhold.

An interesting aspect of bonuses is that, through a limited company, you can judicially time bonuses to key employees to gain some nice tax deferrals. For example, a company with a year-end of July 31 could declare a bonus payable on January 31 following and gain a write-off, and the employee would not have to pay tax on it personally until April in the following year.

Wages paid to a spouse can be deducted. As with "other salaries," remember to deduct the gross amount of salary. Don't forget to issue a T4 slip and, of course, be sure to submit payments for CPP.

Contributions to CPP are particularly important because at age 65 they allow both you and your spouse to draw a full pension.

3.19 Supplies and materials

I do not like to see supplies and materials listed under "cost of goods sold." Ideally, this area refers to supplies such as bags, wrapping papers, and labels.

Of course, when you carry an inventory of any size, it is necessary to prepare a balance sheet. Ideally, that balance sheet should be a continuation of the year before.

In practice, most one-person businesses just do not carry accurate enough figures for proper balancing. In this case, the deficiency is usually "plugged" into the proprietor's equity.

3.20 Telephone, light, heat, and water

A problem arises over telephone, light, heat, and water when you operate out of your home. If you have only one telephone line and use it for both business and pleasure, the monthly rental is not deductible no matter how much time you spend on it for business purposes.

However, all long distance calls made for business purposes are deductible. Also deductible would be the cost of an extension line if you could show it was hooked into an office in the home.

If you operate a business out of the home and have both a private and a business telephone (and thus, separate numbers), you can deduct the monthly rent on the business telephone only, plus any long distance calls.

A similar principle applies to light, heat, and water expenses.

3.21 Travel expenses

If you travel out of the trade area of the business, it is doubtful if the expense would be allowed at a tax audit. Although business people have been doing their travelling at the taxpayer's expense for a long time, with the sophistication of current audit systems it is no longer acceptable to make a yearly trip to Hawaii to investigate new accounts.

Meals are also important, but people are embarrassed to ask for receipts. However, if there are no receipts, the auditor does not have to allow your claim for meal expenses. How does he or she know that you didn't eat every day with Aunt Hilda? Ask for the receipt. Get it. Keep it. Every $2 receipt is worth up to a dollar in your pocket and you don't usually throw away dollar coins.

3.22 New product development

CRA, through its Scientific Research and Experimental Development Program (SR & ED), will allow your company a 20 percent to 35 percent tax credit on all funds allocated for new product development. If this program is one that you could benefit from, you'll need to be well organized in advance to ensure that your financial reporting system accurately records all expenses related to the research and development costs you'd be claiming. Like any claim, you must have accurate backup documentation. Consult your tax advisor. CRA runs seminars on a regular basis to outline the requirements and benefits of this program. For an up-to-date schedule, contact your regional CRA office.

4. WHERE DOES THE MONEY AT THE BOTTOM LINE GO?

Another area of tax savings is splitting the take at the bottom line. You probably have been taking some draw on a regular basis and that is to be your salary, or perhaps you are lucky and have some left over.

Now comes one of the biggest advantages of being in business for yourself — because now (unlike your wage-earning neighbour) you can arrange your affairs to get the maximum benefit of the tax laws.

4.1 Incorporate to save tax dollars

If your business is earning a reasonable return over and above paying you a living wage (e.g., $40,000 to $50,000 per year), incorporating can pay benefits. You'll notice I have stressed the word "if." There is a very good reason for this and it is simply that many people start a business part time and continue to work for salary or working wages while running the business on weekends. Usually the business ends up losing money for the first six months to two years. If you incorporate too soon you will lose the deductibility of the business losses against your other income as these losses can only be carried forward on the company books.

Provided you remain as a proprietor or partner, however, you are entitled to fully offset the business losses against your salary income. This can result in considerable tax savings for you in the first few years and these years are usually the most crucial to your survival. It's something to keep in mind.

Anyway, assume your business is making money and you are wondering whether or not to incorporate. The first thing you should know is that the federal government has decided that small Canadian-owned, private corporations are entitled to a special tax rate.

In order to qualify for the small-business rate there are several tests to meet.

First, the company has to be Canadian controlled. This means 50.001 percent of the voting shares must be owned by Canadian residents or, looking at it from the other side, non-residents may own up to 49.999 percent of the voting shares without losing the small-business rate. If you have a problem here, see a lawyer about "qualifying" your company.

Second, your company must be a "private" company. In other words, public companies such as those that trade on stock exchanges are not eligible. (See Chapter 4 for further information on what a private company is.)

4.2 Splitting your income

Because you and your company are legally two different entities, you can use a company to effectively "split" your income. This is accomplished by causing the company to pay you a salary that puts you in the same (or nearly the same) tax bracket as the small-business corporate tax rate (say, for example, 25 percent). The balance of your "profit" would remain in the company and be used to finance future growth.

That way you keep your effective tax to the lowest possible level. (In actual fact, you would adjust your salary upward somewhat because of the opportunity to maximize your contributions to a Registered Retirement Savings Plan (RRSP) to which contributions are tax deductible from your personal income.)

Also depending on the tax situation of your spouse and children, a further split is possible. After paying the small-business corporate rate you can also choose to pay other family members a salary, or if they're shareholders, a dividend. For example, if your spouse is not working or earning very little, you can effectively split your income by paying him or her a salary from your business and deduct it as an expense to the business. You can also do the same with your kids. The only restrictions are that the "employees" actually do some work and the amount paid, under the circumstances, is reasonable. Check with your accountant to see what current tax policy will allow for an annual salary to a child and to a spouse without raising red flags.

Another idea is that if your children are too young to work, you could make them shareholders and pay dividends on a yearly basis. In fact, you can work any combination of salary and dividends that places you in the most advantageous tax position. One critical point about dividends to keep in mind is that dividend income does not qualify as "earned income" for purposes of making a deductible contribution to an RRSP. Thus, if your entire income consisted of dividends, you could not get a deduction for any contribution to your RRSP.

4.3　Set up tax shelters

It doesn't take much imagination to see how you can gain some significant tax benefits in situations where you are paying expenses for your children (such as tuition fees) out of after-tax money which can be converted into before-tax expenditures by simply paying them a salary and letting them pay their own expenses.

4.4　Delay tax payments for a year — or how to choose a fiscal year-end (Corporations only)

You are probably aware that most businesses — and even governments — do not operate on the basis of a calendar year. Instead, they elect to base their operations on a different timetable — either because of the fluctuation of business or for tax reasons — or both.

By choosing a proper fiscal year for your business, you can delay paying taxes for a year or more. For example, suppose you started your business on December 1. If you were operating through a company using a calendar year as your business year as well, you would have to file your first tax return within six months after December 31 and pay taxes accordingly. If you were operating a proprietorship or partnership, you would file your tax return by April 30 and include in your income the earnings from the business for the month of December and pay tax accordingly.

If, however, you chose as a year-end November 30 of the following year, you would not have to pay taxes until three months following your year-end or by February 28 of the next again year.

4.5　Estate planning benefits

With a company, you have substantial estate planning advantages. As this is a technical area and beyond the scope of this book, it will not be discussed at any length. Suffice it to say that the existence of a company enables you to own a widely diversified portfolio of assets (including all kinds of property) under the ownership of a single entity.

This can be a great advantage both from a tax and administrative point of view, especially if the company is located in a non-taxing jurisdiction (e.g., Alberta) and the assets are located in a taxing jurisdiction (e.g., Washington state).

4.6　Use salary and bonus accruals to save taxes

Through a company, you can declare yourself a bonus that is deductible from the company's income but need not be declared by you as income until it is actually paid. However, the tax department has rules about how long you can delay declaring the payment as income to you.

The bonus has to be taken within 180 days and declared in your return for that year. For example, if your company's year-end was January and you declared yourself a bonus of $10,000 on December 30, 2007, the company would deduct it as a salary expense for the 2007 year and you would have until June 2008 to have the income taken into your own hands.

You can see that this gives you a fair amount of flexibility. To be deductible, these bonuses must be reasonable (in relation to services rendered to the company) and represent a legal liability of the company (passing a directors' resolution is adequate).

In addition, there are a number of other tax wrinkles and elections relating to the salary/dividend/bonus route that any competent tax advisor can tell you about. The important thing to remember is that you must be careful in planning bonuses to look at the overall tax liability of your company and yourself.

If you want to reduce your company's earnings so that it can take advantage of the small-business rate, you might want to declare a bonus payable to yourself, and then wait before paying it to yourself. In this way you can "even out" the earnings and so pay less total tax over a period of years.

For example, if you can foresee that your company's earnings for the fiscal year will exceed the amount eligible for the small-business tax rate, declare a bonus for yourself as it may reduce the earnings sufficiently to enable the company to be taxed at the lower small-business rate, or mean less money is taxable at a higher rate.

You see how bonuses can be used to defer taxes and, in certain cases, even out the earnings of a small business over the years.

Furthermore, by reducing your corporate profits, you reduce the size of the tax installment payments payable by the corporation and, therefore, improve your cash flow position.

If you declare dividends payable to yourself, there is no time limit on when they can be paid to you. Once the corporation has paid tax on its profits, dividends can be distributed at any time. This might be beneficial from the point of view of liability for personal income tax.

Remember, whichever method you choose to distribute your corporate earnings, it must be designed to meet the monetary needs and tax liability of both the company and you.

4.7 Planning for your retirement

An employee whose company has a deferred profit sharing plan may contribute to an RRSP up to a maximum amount calculated annually by the CRA. So, if you are an owner/employer, your maximum RRSP contribution will be based on $13,500 or 18 percent of your prior year earned income, whichever is less, minus the value of the pension benefit earned in your company's Deferred Profit Sharing Plan (DPSP). If the company does not have a DPSP, your maximum contribution is $13,500, or 18 percent of your prior year earned income, whichever is less.

Since the company cannot deduct DPSP contributions, there is no incentive to have such a plan, which limits your retirement savings.

4.8 Interest-free and low-interest loans to employees and shareholders

Regarding loans made to employees to purchase shares in their employer company, the rules are that these loans will attract interest income to the employee if made interest-free or below the "prescribed" loan rate set by the government. This rate is adjusted quarterly based on the prime lending rate.

However, the employee will be able to deduct the interest expense against all other employment income or income from property and dividends provided —

(a) the employer is a "qualified private corporation" (a public company does not qualify), and

(b) the employee is a "significant shareholder."

Simply defined, a qualified private corporation means a private Canadian-owned active company, which includes most private companies doing business in Canada. Significant shareholder means you have to own 10 percent or more of the voting shares. An employee who does not meet the 10 percent share requirement can still deduct the interest expense if such interest does not exceed his or her income and dividends.

An employee who borrows money to purchase shares in a Canadian public company (even if it's his or her employer) will be allowed a deduction of up to $10,000 interest expense only.

A better way to help your employees purchase shares in your company is by using a stock option plan (see Chapter 17).

5. WHAT IF YOU HAVE BUSINESS LOSSES?

If you anticipate your business losing money for a few years and you have outside sources of income (another job, property income, etc.) you can use the losses of your unincorporated business to reduce your personal income taxes. Remember, once you incorporate, your business losses belong to the business, so don't incorporate until profits are reasonably assured.

If your business lost $100,000 this year, for example, and you made $20,000 from outside sources, you can apply the remaining $80,000 against income earned in the previous three years and apply what's left against income earned in the following seven years.

If you are in a partnership, you can divide the firm's losses among the partners. However, be forewarned that CRA frowns on partners who play games with business losses if the principal objective is to postpone or reduce your income taxes.

Another way of using losses to offset taxes is to transfer the operations of a profitable company to a second company (if you own one) that has losses. You might also choose to pay yourself dividends rather than a salary. Depending on your marital status, other sources of income, and the province you live in, you can avoid a significant amount of tax this way.

For more details on how you can benefit from business losses consult your accountant, as most of the tax rules in this area are complicated.

15
INSURING YOUR BUSINESS (AND YOURSELF)

1. INTRODUCTION

Insurance can be a problem for the small-business person, especially to the uninformed. Like anything else, you can pay a lot more for it than you would if you knew what you were doing. It helps to understand a few of the basics about the insurance industry.

Insurance companies are all the giants you have heard about who brag about how much money they have. There are many kinds of insurance companies ranging all the way from Lloyds of London, which likes to advertise that it will underwrite any risk, to those companies that offer only one type of insurance, for example, small life insurance companies. Insurance companies market their wares chiefly through the following methods.

1.1 Agencies

These are normally the smaller, individualized operations that place car, home, and other common types of insurance with several insurance companies to which they are contracted.

Warning: Watch small agencies because in order to earn their commission, they are under an obligation to place a certain volume of insurance with each company they deal with. Therefore, they are likely to try to sell you policies offered by these companies that may not suit your needs, and they will not necessarily place the insurance on a competitive basis.

1.2 Direct salespeople

The larger insurance companies employ their own salespeople to sell other kinds of insurance besides life insurance, such as fire, liability, and business interruption. The smaller ones use independent brokers or agents.

1.3 Clubs and associations

If you belong to a trade association, such as the Retail Council of Canada, for instance, you may want to investigate insurance packages they offer to their members. Sometimes they can negotiate lower premiums that may save you some money.

1.4 Insurance brokers or consultants

Insurance brokers or consultants are people and companies who advertise complete independence from any insurance company and more flexibility than the common agency. For my money, these people are your best bet for the following reasons:

- You usually get someone who is more knowledgeable than you would in an agency.

- They are more flexible and can offer a far greater variety of policies and coverage than the average agency.

- They have no vested interest in placing insurance with any particular company and so will go after the best price and the best coverage for you.

Warning: This is true only if the broker is large enough not to be "tied in" with certain insurance companies.

Insurance agents and brokers operate like travel bureaus. Their commissions come from the insurance companies, so are not directly paid by you. Therefore, the lesson here is to find someone who will work for you — not the insurance company. Independent brokers offer you the best chance for this.

You are now running a successful business. Your insurance needs are sure to grow and change as time rolls along. You need someone you can confide in and rely on to handle all your insurance problems.

You need someone who will do his or her best to get you the coverage you want at the best price. Begin immediately to find a professional insurance broker/consultant who works for a medium-sized firm.

How do you find one? Try the Yellow Pages under Insurance Agents and Brokers (other than life). There is no separation between agents and brokers in the Yellow Pages, so you must ask a couple of preliminary questions to determine who it is you are talking to.

Ask what companies the firm places its business with. If you are told two or three companies, then this is not a firm for you. If you do not get an answer or are told that the firm places business with all companies, then ask whether it has any branch offices. (All of the larger broker consultants do, agencies usually do not.)

2. WATCH THOSE LOOPHOLES

Remember — read your insurance policies carefully and make sure you are well protected.

One of the most common mistakes small-business people make is not insuring for *replacement value*. In the event of a loss under a normal policy, you will be compensated for depreciated value only and not replacement value. You may not be able to replace your equipment for the depreciated value, and this loss could put you out of business.

It is not uncommon for business people to neglect the report of a loss promptly. That kind of error can be costly.

It is equally important to remember to report any new property you have acquired, an expansion of your operations, or the expiration of a policy.

3. WHAT COVERAGE DOES YOUR FIRM NEED?

It is often tempting to buy insurance from the first salesperson who walks in your door when you open your business. However, it is important to remember that these people are trained in sales, not in insurance.

Carefully research various insurance plans and decide which is best for your business. Then you can approach the company that seems the best.

Insurance basically falls into three categories: essential, optional, and frill. Essential insurance covers fire and extended liability. (**Note:** Workers' compensation is usually covered through your provincial government.) Don't forget to get fidelity bonds as insurance against any employee who might embezzle from or defraud you.

Optional insurance means business interruption, crime coverage, and auto property damage. **Note:** Business interruption covers you for loss of profits (or earnings) during the period you are out of circulation.

An example of frills insurance is special coverage for artwork in one of your offices.

Following is a summary of the coverage you need to consider.

3.1 Loss of physical assets

Loss of physical assets includes loss from fire, explosion, earthquakes, theft, water damage, machinery accidents, and other similar perils including the following:

(a) Direct damage to premises by any cause whatsoever. Many policies exclude things like flooding and earthquakes. If this concerns you, be sure to raise it with your agent

(b) Loss of earnings as a result of damage to premises or vehicles

(c) Crime (employee theft or embezzlement, burglary, robbery, and theft)

(d) Damage to vehicles and other mobile equipment

3.2 Liability to third parties

During the course of your business operations, you are faced with the possibility of lawsuits. These may result from acts or omissions for which you are responsible.

For example, a customer may slip on the floor, be injured, and sue; or a customer may be injured by the failure of a product sold to him or her, and sue; or an employee may injure a third party while driving a company car and be sued. The type of liability insurance you need covers the following:

(a) Company vehicles

(b) Vehicles owned by employees but used on company business

(c) Premises (customer injury)

(d) Business operations (an employee causing injury to a third party during the course of business activity)

(e) Products sold by the business that result in an injury to the buyer

3.3 Business interruption

You will want insurance to cover your business losses in case, for example, your warehouse burns down and you're out of business for six months. Before collecting, you will have to prove that your business was actually making money. Therefore, don't forget to keep duplicate sets of your financial statements at home or in some other safe place away from the business.

3.4 Loss or sickness of key people

What happens to your business if you suddenly get run over by a truck and are killed or if you have gangrene of the left foot and can't work for six months? Disability and life insurance coverage for key people in your business can be crucial — especially if you totally depend on your business earnings to pay the bills.

In this area especially, a good broker or agent can be of immense value as coverage and plans (and prices) vary greatly, particularly when combined with fringe benefit insurance such as medical and dental plans. (See section **3.6b** following for further details on key person insurance.)

3.5 You can afford some self-insurance

The key to insurance is to cover yourself against catastrophes. It would be too expensive to try to cover your business for every possible loss. If you are just starting out in business, you will want to be well insured because mistakes will be common and costly.

As you learn the ropes, however, mistakes will be less common and you will have more capital to cover losses that might occur. At that time, you might want to consider reducing some of your insurance policies.

Insurance only makes sense when it is purchased with this in mind. Even the smallest business can get along without insurance against minor losses. If you have to make choices about what to insure, choose first to insure the most important things. Then, as your budget permits, insure less important aspects of your business.

Once you decide what the maximum is you can afford to lose, you should buy blanket coverage at very low cost for everything over that. You can change this limit as your company is able to afford more.

3.6 All about business life insurance

Life insurance can be very important to you if your family depends on your earnings. This type of life insurance policy provides that, when you die, the disposition of your business will be handled according to your wishes, with the funds being used to finance these wishes. Therefore, business life insurance is one of the best ways to guarantee the control and continued value of the business if you should die.

Often, upon the death of a business person, the creditors may become concerned about the money that is owed to them and sue the estate of the deceased. In other words, a sole proprietor and partners in a partnership put their personal assets "on the line" to support the debts of the business. If creditors bring suit against the estate, this may force the widow or widower to sell the home and other personal assets in order to satisfy the claims of creditors.

In a business, cash may be needed upon the death of the owner to liquidate the business or to continue the business operation until a buyer can be found. In addition, cash is needed to take care of any losses or shrinkage the business may suffer.

Often what happens is that as long as a business is actively operating, some of its assets, such as accounts receivable, retain their full value. However, upon the death of the owner, the value of the accounts receivable may decrease as much as 50 percent.

Debtors of the business, realizing that the owner has passed away, may take this opportunity to default or prolong payments on their debts.

3.6a Personal life insurance

Personal life insurance protects your family and personal estate in case of death. Personal life insurance can assure your children of a college education, pay off the house mortgage, pay off personal obligations, and provide funds for your family's living expenses.

3.6b Key person life insurance

In most businesses, particularly small ones, there is usually one individual (sometimes more) who makes things go for the business. In many cases, this person is the president, who actually does most of the work in the business such as selling, marketing, managing, and negotiating bank loans.

It is the president's imagination, innovations, and ingenuity that contribute largely to the success of the business. If something were to happen to this individual, the business would probably suffer a large financial loss or go out of business.

The company may take out a "key person" life insurance policy on such a person's life. The company pays the premiums and is the owner and beneficiary. If, while still in business, the key person dies, the cash from the insurance policy can be used to indemnify the company and keep the business in operation until a replacement is found for the key person.

The very fact that the business had the foresight to insure against the hazard of financial loss in case of the death of its key person indicates that it is serious about its future and has made long-range plans for meeting contingencies.

Banks, under these conditions, may be more inclined to give extended consideration for the business's credit requests. The cash from the life insurance on the key person can also be used to keep the business in operation and save the jobs of employees until the business is reorganized or sold.

3.7 Taxes and insurance

If you have a bank loan for the business, you should consider having the loan life insured. This protects your family against foreclosure if you die before the loan is paid off. The premiums are tax deductible.

Note: Premiums for key person insurance or under buy-sell agreements are *not* tax deductible even if the company is the beneficiary unless these rules are followed:

(a) The insurance must be purchased as a result of a specific request by your banker or other lender for collateral security on a business loan because your business might not be viable if something happened to you. Your lender should write you a letter requesting that you obtain life insurance and name the lender as the first loss payable up to the amount of the loan. If you operate on a fluctuating line of credit, the amount should cover the full amount of the line of credit.

(b) The insurance must be term insurance and not whole life insurance.

(c) The amount of the insurance purchased must be reasonable in relation to the loan amount.

If you are ever in the unfortunate position of having to claim on such insurance, the proceeds are tax-free.

16
WHAT TO DO WHEN YOU ARE SHORT OF CASH*

One of the most common questions of the small-business person is, "Why am I always short of cash?" In my experience, there are basically two reasons.

The first revolves around our own expectations of business growth (especially in an inflationary period). Because we need to be positive about the future of the business and all its aspects, we all tend to be overly optimistic about how much money is coming in and how much we need from outside sources.

Your projection of reaching the break-even point in a year can easily stretch to 18 months or 2 years. During this time, you may need to refinance or look for additional help (see Chapter 6 on how to find money) or squeeze every dime you can out of the business.

The second reason is that the average small-business person does not have time to pay proper attention to the state of his or her accounts and to the handling of payables. Many business people are too busy trying to close that big sale or simply meet next week's payroll to be bothered by these details.

The problem is that the people who owe you money know this and tend to delay paying your account as opposed to your bigger, better-organized competitor. Individually, the various points in this chapter on maximizing internal cash flow may not seem to be earth-shattering.

---

*Parts of this chapter are adapted from the article "How to Build Up Your Cash Position," which appeared in *CGA Magazine*, with thanks to the author, Claude A. Thomas and *CGA Magazine*.

Put together, however, the suggestions can make the difference between a cash-strapped firm and one that rolls along smoothly on cash-greased wheels.

1. HAVE SUPPLIERS BILL YOU ON YOUR BEST DAY

There are probably only a couple of days each month when much of your revenue is physically received. Depending on your business and your location often this is on or immediately following major local paydays.

Instruct your regular suppliers to invoice you on those days. This will mean that you pay your bills after you receive large amounts of cash from your customers or clients.

A few suppliers may balk at your request, saying it is impossible to change their existing billing routine. Stick with it. After all, you're the customer in this case, and there's no reason why a simple request like this can't be accommodated.

To save everyone's time, have a form letter printed on your company letterhead. State clearly the monthly billing day you prefer and send it to all your suppliers. Most will make the change as you have requested.

2. USE DISCOUNT DAY PAYMENT

To make their jobs easier, many bookkeepers prefer to pay bills just once or twice a month. As invoices come in, they are set aside into one or two groups for the next payment date.

But that means most often that at least some bills are paid in advance of the final discount date. For example, an incoming bill is received on the 12th with a discount date of the 22nd. But because your bookkeeper likes to pay bills just twice a month, on the 15th and 30th, the bill goes into the 15th group.

When it is paid on the 15th, it means that you have lost the use of that cash for seven days — until the 22nd when it was actually due — simply because your bookkeeper likes that simple system.

What to do: Instruct your bookkeeper to pay bills on the date they are actually due. If this means paying one or two bills every day, the cost of the extra time is still more than offset by the free use of those funds. And make sure that all discounts are taken. Not doing so is costly. For instance, if an invoice is marked "2 percent — ten days, net 30 days," and you do not take the discount, you are, in effect, paying interest at the annual rate of 36 percent-plus for those extra 20 days. Even finance company funds would be a lot cheaper than that. (Table 1 shows what it costs you not to take the discount.)

TABLE 1
EFFECTIVE ANNUAL INTEREST RATE

Terms	Effective Annual Interest Rate
1% ten days, net 30	18%
2% thirty days, net 60	24%
2% ten days, net 30	36%
3% ten days, net 60	21%

3. REFINANCE FIXED OBLIGATIONS

You may have a mortgage on your office or warehouse building or an instalment note on delivery of office equipment. Consider rewriting those obligations over a longer period.

This will immediately reduce your current payments and free some cash for other needs. Even if the interest rate on the longer term is higher than your present rate, don't automatically discard the idea.

Remember that with inflation — and you can expect it to continue at its current rate for some time — dollars paid in the future will be "cheaper" than present dollars.

It's quite possible that with a new interest rate that is higher by about 2 percent or 3 percent, coupled with a continuing inflation factor, your net savings will be significant in addition to the easing of cash payments now.

What to do: Have your bookkeeper send a letter to all creditors who hold long-term obligations from you. Instruct them to specify the exact terms and conditions under which they would rewrite the obligation over a longer term.

When their replies come in, you can quickly inspect them to see which should be rewritten in terms of present interest rates and probable future inflation rates.

4. SPREAD OUT MAJOR PURCHASES

Some managers and executives have a thing about cash and credit: they like to use the former to avoid the latter. This is commendable, but today it is unrealistic.

Many suppliers now offer reasonable extended payment terms at no interest cost. If you purchase a photocopying unit, for example, the supplier may offer you the option of paying the balance over three or even six months at the cash price.

Paying cash in this situation is foolish. Take whatever extended terms your suppliers will offer. Even if an interest cost is quoted, negotiate. On major purchases, this term will often be waived, or sometimes it makes sense to pay interest charged by suppliers.

If a supplier charges an effective annual rate of 12 percent or 15 percent, while other sources of funds use an 18 percent or 24 percent rate, you may actually save money by stretching out payments on the purchase and at the same time paying off some other higher-interest cost indebtedness.

How to do it: On all major purchases, ask your supplier if the cash price can be paid over several months. More often than not, he or she will acquiesce, and you will have interest-free use of those funds for a couple of months.

5. MAKE EVERY DAY A BILLING DAY

As with paying bills only once or twice a month, some bookkeepers prefer to issue bills or statements to customers just a few times each month because it's "easier." That it is. It's also costly for you.

There is no reason why bills and statements cannot be sent out every day. This is also sounder psychologically, because customers tend to pay bills faster when the reason for the bill is still fresh in their minds. Wait until the end of the month and they forget how important the product or service they bought was to them.

How to do it: Have your bookkeeper keep the last hour of each working day solely for sending out statements and bills. Even if there are only two or three bills to go, don't put them off until "there's enough to make it worthwhile."

6. PLUG LOOPHOLES

Sometimes customers will use confusion as a reason for not promptly paying their accounts. For example, your bookkeeper might show a credit adjustment for a payment received from some third party on the customer's behalf.

In short, the statement or bill should stand on its own feet with no further clarification needed. This will mean faster payments by customers and clients.

What to do: Tell your bookkeeper to keep accounting shorthand off statements. Make sure that bills and statements are clearly understandable to all customers. If you use a computer for statement preparation, make sure it is programmed to deliver understandable documents, not accounting jargon.

7. KEEP AWARE OF PAST DUE ACCOUNTS

Some owners have no system for following up past due accounts. They wait until the accounts are a year or so old, then either turn them over to a collection agency (generally with poor results at that late date) or simply write them off as bad debts. Neither approach is sensible.

Have your bookkeeper flag or physically segregate accounts by 30-day periods. At the end of the first 30 days, send out a friendly but firm form letter. Do the same at the end of 60

and 90 days, with each letter getting increasingly firm. Don't be embarrassed about this. Tell your customers the truth: that you also have bills to pay and that you expect them to pay theirs.

The majority of people are honest and well intentioned. But if you treat their past due accounts as unimportant, you can hardly expect them to do otherwise.

How to do it: Instruct your bookkeeper to set up and use a 30-, 60-, and 90-day follow-up system for all accounts. In practice, form letters have proven just as effective as more costly and time-consuming personal letters; so have the bookkeeper write and use printed letters for each time period. For examples of past due letters, see *Business Letters Kit*, another title from Self-Counsel Press.

8. CUT OFF THE DEADBEATS

Unfortunately, there will always be a few people who make a career of ignoring their debts. You have to decide at just what point you will draw the line, but there should be a line somewhere.

When a customer reaches that point, send out a short letter explaining why you can no longer treat him or her on a credit basis. All future services will have to be on a cash basis. And don't try to draw the matter out; as with all separations, a clean break is preferable to all concerned.

What to do: When a customer passes the credit cut-off point — which you have established in advance — instruct your bookkeeper to turn the account over to you. You then have to decide whether the customer is a deadbeat or an honest debtor in hard times.

Follow your own feelings in the latter case. If the former, send out your "cash only" letter, and, if it's worth the effort, place the account with a collection agency. But take positive action; then forget about the matter.

9. DEVELOP SHORT-TERM CREDIT TERMS

Many businesses go broke because they get caught in a short-term financial squeeze and have nowhere to turn. It's the old story of no one wanting to take a chance when you are in trouble.

So, you should develop and use various credit sources from the beginning. Table 2 lists the various sources of short-term credit along with my assessment of their popularity and accessibility.

Refer back to Chapter 6 for more detailed information on these sources of cash.

TABLE 2
SHORT-TERM CREDIT POSSIBILITIES

Kind of credit	Ease of obtaining	Interest rate	Popularity
Accounts/notes receivable factoring	Easy	High	Low
Bank credit	Easy	Low	High
Commercial paper	Difficult	Low	Low
Deposits and advances	Easy	Low	Low
Government-granted loans	Difficult	Low-medium	Low
Industrial banks	Difficult	High	Low
Insurance policies	Easy	Low-medium	Low
Inventory loans	Easy	Medium-high	Low
Loans from friends or relatives	Difficult	Low	Low
Personal loans	Difficult	High	Low
Promissory notes	Easy	Medium	High
Trade credit	Easy	Medium-high	High

17
HOW TO FIND AND KEEP GOOD EMPLOYEES

While I have stressed the value of try- ing to run your business *yourself*, without employing unnecessary help, sooner or later (as you expand) you will have to hire people.

Selecting and supervising employees will be your toughest job. My experience tells me that 90 percent of your mistakes will be mistakes re- garding people, not business.

No one who has ever run a business ques- tions the value of getting and keeping good em- ployees. Much has been written on the subject. Theories abound but conclusive answers are scarce. There are as many examples of compa- nies that are successful with the "theory X" tech- nique (authoritative management) as of those

who are successful with "theory Y" (participatory management).

There are also, in each case, as many failures. I am going to stay out of that controversy. You must operate in your own way, using your own style. This chapter stresses those things that will work, whether you are a tough boss or a persua- sive one.

1. HIRE OR CONTRACT OUT?

When your business needs the help of another person to get all the work done, you need to make a decision. Should you hire an employee or to contract the work out?

Consider the following issues before making your decision.

1.1 Costs

Independent contractors are running a business, with all the overhead costs that entails, so they will usually charge a higher hourly rate than you would pay employees. But you will not be providing the contractor benefits such as paid sick leave and vacation days, and you will save some bookkeeping time and money by not having to make and record tax and other deductions.

1.2 Space

If a contractor works off-site, you will usually not need to provide work space or equipment.

Note: If a contractor works at your office, using your equipment, she (or CRA) could argue that you are her only client and a court could decide she is actually a legal employee and make you liable for all the benefits the law provides employees. If a contractor will be working a significant number of hours a month for you, and/or if a contractor will be working in your office, be sure to have a written agreement that stipulates the contractor is an independent contractor and not an employee.

1.3 Replacement

In some areas the law makes it very difficult to terminate an employee without facing some penalty or even a lawsuit. If a contractor is not satisfactory, he or she is much easier to replace.

1.4 Availability

Assuming good health, an employee's availability is guaranteed. Most contractors will have other clients and so may not always be available when you need them. You can address this through your contract, mutually guaranteeing a certain number of hours of work per month and having the contractor guarantee availability within a certain period of time after you request it, but you can expect the contractor to seek a premium for such guarantees.

1.5 Cross-Promotion

In some circumstances, contracting can help promote your business. Let's say your business is making custom wooden furniture. Instead of hiring an employee to do the upholstery work, you contract it out. You are now able to offer a more complete service, and at the same time your business and the upholstery business can promote each other to new clients.

2. HOW TO FIND EMPLOYEES

Somewhere out there in the world is a man or woman who is perfect for the job opening in your business. Can you flush out that person? Probably not.

There are too many obstacles. The number of people, their wide geographic distribution, and the probability that the right person will not be interested all work against you in the search.

Moreover, it is unlikely that you would recognize the person if you met him or her. The applicant's personality might displease you. His or her nervousness at the interview might discourage you. After all, you hire people to whom you relate. Yet your best choice probably is a person with whom you would clash. What you will do is pick people who sell themselves at the interview, provided their background and references are adequate.

As you pick people you like, you will find it more difficult to fire them if they are unsuitable. This is a dilemma all business people face. My own experience has shown that it is best to hire someone you have worked with in the past. Although perhaps not the best person for the job, he or she will probably be your best choice.

If you do not know such a person, ask a business associate whose judgment you respect. Personal references seem to provide the most suitable employees. You can see, of course, that this method eliminates from consideration all but a small fraction of the potential applicants.

If you must hire an unknown, do it systematically. Write down the job description, the characteristics you think appropriate for a person holding that job, and the minimum requirements of experience and education. If possible, have two or three other people within your company participate with you in the search. Have them go over the list for omissions or errors. Tell them you want the applicant checked on every point.

Divide the task of checking references among your associates. Use the reference list provided by the applicant, but try to come up with at least as many on your own. Try, particularly, to find people who worked for the applicant. They will have excellent knowledge of his or her shortcomings and may be more candid than a former supervisor.

Have each of your associates interview the prospect privately, then record his or her opinion before he or she discusses it with anyone else. After each of you has had a turn at an interview, get together for the final evaluation. Listen to whatever is said and then make up your own mind.

(**Remember:** Each of the interviewers, including you, will have prejudices. Each will view the applicant in the light of his or her own job. There will be a tendency to downgrade anyone who appears to be a threat.)

No formal personnel department or battery of psychological tests will work any better than this technique. Yet, both what the applicant said and what you heard will differ from the facts. That is why you will make many mistakes.

There are many adequate ways of turning up applicants with suitable backgrounds. Just remember that advertising in the local newspaper or in your trade publication may result in more résumés than you can process.

For more information on hiring, see *Employee Management for Small Business*, another title in the Self-Counsel Business Series, written to address the needs of small-business managers.

3. HOW TO KEEP EMPLOYEES

Volumes have been written on motivation. There are many theories on behaviour, some very astute and all with some element of truth. This book is intended to be practical, however, and it is a fact that most small-business people have neither the time nor the inclination to shape their companies to suit their employees' hierarchy of needs.

So I am going to focus on five simple points:

(a) Build pride.

(b) Be consistent.

(c) Listen and communicate.

(d) Cull marginal performers.

(e) Pay fairly.

3.1 Pride

You know about pride. It is what coaches strive for. It makes winners out of losers. Your employees must have it if their work is to be good.

Your product or service is the source of your employees' pride, but it is not enough just to have a good product. Your employees must know it is good and must feel that they have contributed to it.

The way to get this across is through praise — not only your praise for a job well done but the customer's praise for a fine product.

Get the word around. Ask your customers to say something to your employees when they are in the shop. Show people how their work contributes to the whole.

3.2 Consistency

Unless you have turned them off, your employees will try to please you. If you are consistent, they will know what you want. When you set goals, you must measure progress according to those goals.

If you set standards, you must insist they be met. If you can force yourself to be consistent, you will make it easy for them to work for you, even though your standards are high.

However, lip service is not enough. Actions foster belief. The best time to start is when you hire people. Before you make them any offers, lay out what they must do and the rules they must follow. This should be written down.

Even small companies can prepare personnel manuals. If employees know what to expect, they will not resent what might otherwise appear to be demeaning.

A large Toronto restaurant has a separate locker room with an outside entrance for employees. They must deposit bags and purses in their lockers before entering the workplace. Nothing can be taken from the restaurant, not even table scraps for dogs. There is no exception to this rule.

Employees accept it because it is written in the personnel manual and was made known before they were hired. Had it been imposed after hiring, the employees would have taken it as a slur. Although theft is a major cause for dismissal in the restaurant business, this firm has a low turnover.

If you want to curb personal telephone calls, absenteeism, smoking, horseplay among employees, and accepting gratuities, make your rules known in the hiring process.

Actions are more important than what you say. If you promote people who agree with you, you will have a business full of yes-people. If you treat poor work as natural and unavoidable, you will have a poor-quality product. If you accept excuses, you will get them. Your employees will give you what your actions say you want.

As head of the company, you want profit and perhaps growth. That is all. Do not get caught in the trap of counting secondary objectives. If you count shipments only, quality will suffer. If you call for cost reductions, shipments may suffer. Your people will score according to your rules.

Your people must know that profits are what you want, not just efficient departments. They must co-operate to meet the team goal and some departments must spend effort bolstering others.

3.3 Listen and communicate

Communication is a two-way deal. Whether you are a manager who hands down decisions from the top or are one who builds from the roots, what matters most is whether your people listen to one another.

You must build an atmosphere in which people feel free to speak up and know they will be heard. If you do this, the company will have good communications.

Every question deserves an answer, and every suggestion should be received with gratitude. People who ask questions and make suggestions are trying to help, even if their motives are self-serving. If allowed to develop, this becomes a source of added power. As the sports writers like to say, it gives you an added dimension.

It should be obvious that you should treat every employee with fairness, even if it is not possible to treat them all alike.

3.4 What about the person who does not fit in?

The most common managerial error is retaining people who cannot do their jobs. Large companies go to the extreme of institutionalizing this mistake by moving the square pegs around to see whether there are holes they will fit.

A small business absolutely cannot afford this luxury. If you have such a person, take a deep breath, and tell him or her goodbye. The sooner the better, for both of you.

One final word on this. Never hang on to people because they appear to be essential. You cannot afford to have such employees or such a business. If you do, sell it to them and start something else.

3.5 Compensation

Relative compensation is more important than actual remuneration, provided the wages you pay are adequate and reasonably competitive. Your salespeople may be making 50 percent less than the national average and be perfectly happy, but let them discover that the production manager makes $2,000 a year more and all hell breaks loose.

Good young people are never satisfied with their rate of pay for very long, regardless of the circumstances. So you have to keep things in balance, and you have to give periodic increases. Still, everyone will not be happy. It is a juggling act without a handy set of instructions.

4. HOW TO EVALUATE EMPLOYEES

Annual evaluations will help you measure an employee's contribution to your business. But don't let it become the time for a pep talk or a "shape up or ship out" interview. Evaluations should be used only to determine what further training your employees need to be able to contribute more to the job.

It is important that both you and the employee fill out the same evaluation form and compare ratings so that you can see clearly where you differ in identifying areas of strengths and weaknesses. Your discussion should concentrate first on coming to some agreement about this and second on what can be done to bolster the weak spots.

An evaluation should be a positive experience. Allow ample time for discussion, check any tendency on your part to be critical, deal with facts, not opinions or impressions, and, above all, try to come up with specific suggestions for courses or further training and encourage positive anticipation of the good results these will bring.

The rewards of evaluations can be enormous. Handled right, they allow you to assess each person's performance, plan the development each requires, exchange opinions, establish a working agreement, and generally build better relationships.

5. HANDLING CREATIVE PEOPLE

Employee relations is your toughest job and handling creative people the toughest part of it. If you are concerned that you have not been able to solve this problem, concern yourself no longer.

You will always have it and there is no permanent solution, only a series of day-to-day temporizing measures. A majority of the highly creative individuals who make up the fields of fashion, entertainment, and advertising, and even a large portion of research scientists have personalities that cannot be placated for very long.

You put up with creative people for one reason: they make your product superior. If you are in such a situation, you probably recognize this fact and are willing to go out of your way to satisfy these people. Unfortunately, they have a way of destroying the morale of your sane employees. There are times when you must choose between keeping a valuable and talented individual and keeping the rest of your organization. Try to avoid this kind of showdown at all costs.

Some broad humour with a touch of deference is a device that has worked well for several managers I have observed. If the rest of the company goes along with it, there is an all-around slacking off of tension. Unfortunately, some talented people are too sensitive to be joshed. So, this technique has its limitations.

6. WHAT ABOUT A HEALTH BENEFITS PACKAGE?

One way of helping your staff is by installing a group benefit plan. Typically, such a plan provides coverage for dental work and for life and disability insurance. If you pay half the cost and have the employees pay the other half, it will be perceived as a real benefit and a valuable tool for holding on to your key people. As well, it gives you and your family inexpensive insurance.

Plans and coverage vary greatly depending on the number of employees and extent of the coverage.

Remember, even more important than the generosity of the program is how well you describe it to your employees.

Your best source of information about benefit plans is from an independent insurance broker. If you don't know any, ask your lawyer or accountant to recommend someone. The Chamber of Commerce has an excellent program, or check with your trade association to see if it offers a plan.

7. USE SHARE OPTION PLANS

A share option plan is simply an agreement between you and your employees whereby you give your employees the right to purchase shares in your company for a certain price (usually at a discount). The option is held open for a certain length of time. Such plans provide financial inducements for your employees to become shareholders.

An employee of a private company is permitted to buy shares at any price from $1 to fair market value. As long as the employee holds the shares in his or her own name for at least two years, it is not considered a taxable benefit. When the shares are then sold, the difference between the purchase price and the selling price will be taxed as a capital gain. Another condition to this plan is that the employee must deal at arm's length with the Canadian-controlled private corporation.

18
MORE SUCCESS TIPS

1. CONSTANTLY REVIEW YOUR FINANCIAL GOAL

To get what you want from your business, you should set a financial goal and work consistently toward it. Think seriously about this — it's smart and it's practical, especially for the first two or three years that you are in business for yourself.

If you've been working all your life for someone else, then you probably have had to get by on an equal amount, or even less, per year. By setting your financial goal for the first one or two years of business operation, you give yourself a goal that should be easily within your reach, once you know the patterns of success that you must follow in running your own business.

In other words, set your financial goal at the outset, and stick to it, keeping the amount of money you want to earn fixed clearly in your mind's eye. (Pasting the amount, in large figures, on the wall above your desk will keep you in the money-making groove.)

You must, in order to be a successful business person, set yourself a goal that is practical, fits in with your life's needs, suits your special skills, and, above all, fires up your imagination, zeal, and enthusiasm.

2. NEVER STOP LEARNING

The professional business person is always experimenting with new ideas. You cannot stand still; you must forge ahead in line with your financial goal. Ideas are part and parcel of progress.

True, you will have many ideas that are unworkable, or just not suited to your business needs, but it is extremely important to make a habit of trying to dream up new ways and means of increasing your business profits.

2.1 Use your public library

Your local public library is a storehouse of free knowledge, money-making facts, and ideas that you should use. The librarians will be only too happy to help. Again, asking for what you want is important. Before you go to the library for information, make notes of what you are looking for. This will save you valuable time.

Besides using your public library for information, start now to compile your own business library. On many occasions you will need to refer only to one particular section or chapter of a publication for some advice on a certain problem area. It will save you time and effort if you have these sources on hand rather than having to make a special trip to the library.

2.2 Know how to read books

Most people read books for entertainment, but as a business person anxious to learn ways and means of saving money and making more money, you should read books with a dual purpose in mind: for entertainment first, and then, for profit.

I suggest that you get in the habit of underlining passages you want to remember with a colored pen or pencil (if they are your own books). This is a fast way of pegging down special information that you may need later.

That is why building your own library of self-help books is so important for you — you must underline and mark areas in each book that provide you with money-making ideas.

Any books or business periodicals that you buy for the sole purpose of using in your business are a part of your business library and you can deduct the cost from taxes payable. Thus, you can save money and make money by building a business library that will help you run your own business more efficiently.

The mere trick of writing something down on paper may trigger a worthwhile idea in your own mind. This happens to me all the time. It will happen for you, too, if you start now to keep notes.

Making notes, jotting ideas down on paper (or, if you can afford it, dictating into a pocket recorder) is the only way to save ideas that might otherwise be lost forever. Don't trust your memory because things happen too fast. You can't remember everything. Better to write it down than to lose it.

2.3 Use the Internet

The Internet is unparalleled as a business resource. It can provide valuable information on government services, professional associations, and business issues. It is also an excellent source of financial information and can put you in touch with other business professionals who can be of benefit to your business.

3. YOUR COMPETITION CAN HELP

How can this be, you ask? Other than providing you with a little extra incentive to work harder, you will find, as you progress in running your own business, that opportunities for increasing your profits (doing more in less time) are all around you.

Now and then, take time out to look around you to see how your competition is doing and to see how other people in businesses not linked to your industry operate. You may learn something that can increase your profits. Profitable ideas are not restricted to any one kind of business. What works well for someone else may work even better for you, provided that you take the idea or method, twist it around, and bend it until it fits in with your needs.

Do not underestimate your competitors. They need their businesses as much as you need yours. They want to succeed just as much as you do. They may be as smart as you. Just hope they make the mistake of underestimating you, but do not return the favour.

There are three common ways of underestimating your competitors:

- Thinking you see a market no one else sees

- Basing your plans on what competitors are doing now

- Thinking you have them hopelessly out-maneuvered

The semiconductor industry is an excellent example of enticing new markets that attracted capital assets and capacity at a rate that far outpaced the rapid rate of market growth. Each producer thought he or she could get a stranglehold on the new, virgin territory. The result was rapid development and price competition beyond anyone's wildest expectations.

At the beginning of the 1980s, the Swiss watch industry dominated the watch business, selling manual and self-winding mechanical watches through jewellery stores and similar outlets. Five years later, the Swiss industry was being kept afloat and restructured by its government and the timepieces business was dominated by companies in Southeast Asia. The Swiss lost their market dominance for three reasons:

(a) They believed the watch market was a jewellery market, so they sold through jewellery stores where wholesale-to-retail markups were 100 percent. Asian producers introduced digital electronic watches and sold them through discount stores.

(b) The Swiss made plans based on Asian makers' production of mechanical watches and ignored the trend to electronics.

(c) The Swiss were convinced that watches would always use mechanical movements made by skilled workers because "that was the way it had always been"; the Asians dreamed of using automation to make "disposable" watches with few or no moving parts which they could sell at supermarket check-out counters.

The lesson? New technologies open up new opportunities and sometimes these changes can change an entire industry. You and your competitors may be selling through traditional channels today, but will those channels be appropriate a year from now, or will the Internet (today's "hot" technology) change all that next week, or next year?

Also remember, your competitors will always react to attacks on their business. Their reactions may be more violent than you anticipate. They may also be illogical. But react they will, so be ready.

4. MAKE YOUR OWN DECISIONS

It is your life, your business, your future. Get all the help you need from financial experts, accountants, lawyers, and bankers, but make all your own decisions.

You should always know more about your business than anyone else. This is most important because other people don't know or care as much about your business as you do. So you must, for your future's sake, always make your own decisions.

Sometimes large fees are paid unnecessarily to so-called "experts" who don't know any more than you do about your business and often do not know one-eighth as much! An outside expert whom you call in will not be as concerned over your business problems as you are, despite obvious knowledge or apparent concern. The outsider is usually much more interested in his or her own business affairs than in yours.

When you know as much as your accountant, you can always check and double check to make sure that what is being done is right for you.

Be wary of hiring someone who claims to be an expert. Check credentials before you sign any agreement. In fact, one of the best ways to ensure performance is to base the rate of pay on results, though this is often easier said than done when dealing with people.

Example 1:

Is your accountant prepared to back his or her claim that, based on information you give, you will pay the least amount of taxes you need to? If so, will he or she waive the bill if you are able to find someone who can show you where you could have paid less in taxes?

Example 2:

Is your lawyer prepared to collect an account on a contingency basis? Collection agencies do. You will soon find out how much the particular "expert" wants your business by asking him or her to work on the basis of performance.

There are bungling lawyers, inefficient accountants, and incompetent mechanics, just as there are inefficient operators in every profession. Don't let anyone persuade you to hire him or her before you have had a chance to check credentials. Always ask for "proof of ability" before saying yes.

5. USE TIME EFFECTIVELY

Never get into the trap of taking time off from your normal occupation, in which you might have made $50 or $60 for each hour, just to do a task that you could pay someone else much less to do. For example, I discovered a good friend of mine, a well-known writer, painting his house. As a writer he made $50 an hour, while a painter would only have cost $30 an hour.

There was a professional writer wasting his time and losing money, just because he didn't think. Besides that, he was doing another professional — a house painter — out of a job.

Doesn't make sense, does it? Make a rule now to use your business time only to "do your thing" professionally, and that is to run your business.

6. KEEP EXPENSES DOWN

It is especially important to keep your expenses down when you are first getting started. When making purchases, always secure at least three estimates. Never accept the first price offered;

shop around. Better still, try to develop a string of low-cost suppliers. This can be done no matter how humble your purchasing power.

Furthermore, never stop soliciting competing quotes even after your business is operating successfully. You will be amazed at how low you can get your costs if you are persistent.

Develop the habit of asking questions. Never accept anything at face value. Check everything out and be sure of what you are getting.

In managing your business, you must make a habit of doing as much as you possibly can yourself before you think of hiring help. I mentioned this in an earlier chapter, and I repeat it here because you must keep expenses down in order to drive profits up!

Your business is your life and your future, so you must wrap your life around your business and be willing to do anything honest to advance yourself. Doing things yourself cuts costs, helps you to know everything that's happening to your business, and gets the job done on time better, usually, than a hired hand would do it. Remember, when you do things yourself, especially early in your ownership career, you are learning, gaining experience, saving money, and paving the way to a secure financial future.

Some people hate minor details. They feel that success depends on big decisions and big, fancy moves only. How untrue! It is how you handle the small things in business that determines the longevity and size of your success. So, the lesson here is that you are not some big-time executive who has a thousand gnomes about to take care of all the little details.

You must pay attention to every detail, at least at the start, to ensure success. Do not hire help until you are so overwhelmed with orders that hiring a person will actually *make* you money, not cost you money.

Whenever possible, always buy used office furniture and machines — things like desks, chairs, photocopiers, filing cabinets, etc.

You will need a telephone and can use a private number, an answering service, or voice mail to cut expenses, but if you do, you cannot get a business listing in the telephone book or the Yellow Pages. Business rates for a telephone are about double those for a private line.

Many businesses have telephones all over the place, and they are never used. Even worse, there are usually not enough incoming lines so callers frequently receive busy signals.

Rarely advertised by telephone companies are their measured service lines, which provide you with cheap service (about half price) provided that you restrict your *outgoing* calls. Some smart business people use a measured line for all *incoming* calls and make outgoing calls on another line — usually a private one. (For more information on telephone service, see section 14. of this chapter.)

7. IF YOU WANT SOMETHING, ASK FOR IT

Many people are afraid to ask when they need help or a service, or even when they want to buy something. People can't read your mind, so speak up. Ask for what you want.

Moreover, if you ask for a favour, you may be pleasantly surprised. Most people, even hard-nosed business people, like to be asked a favour now and then. It makes them feel needed. Laugh if you like, but this is a fact! Ask a person for advice and you've made a friend!

If you don't ask for anything, how can anyone say yes? Make asking for what you want a habit in your business life!

8. DOES THE WEATHER AFFECT YOUR BUSINESS?

Now, your business may depend a certain amount on the weather. For example, if you operate a marina, then the weather will play an important part in your ultimate success.

If your business is seasonal, try to make it a year-round operation. For bigger profits, you must, if possible, turn a seasonal business into a 12-month profit-making affair. And it can be done!

If weather is an important, money-robbing factor in your business, then keep a record of the weather so that you can make daily and weekly comparisons of how the weather affects your profits. Better still, do some serious thinking and you may be able to come up with a method of making even the most adverse weather work for you instead of against you. Try it and see what happens.

9. KNOW HOW TO PROTECT YOUR PRODUCT

You should protect your product ideas from appropriation by others as well as you can, but you shouldn't make a fetish of it. As a rule, your competitors will have a low regard for any ideas that are not theirs, but there is no point in taking chances.

If your product is unique, it may be patentable. Whether you apply for a patent should depend on the long-range potential of the product and your ability to police and enforce the patent. Often, it is better to keep your product secret than to patent it. Unfortunately, almost any product can be reverse engineered, that is, examined and dissected by knowledgeable persons to determine its working secrets.

Reverse engineering is legal, provided the product has not been obtained under false pretenses. Anyone has the right to buy a product, reverse engineer it, and sell a duplicate unless the product is patented.

Although it is hard to keep the makeup of devices secret, it is possible to keep formulas and process techniques out of circulation. You can protect proprietary ideas from disclosure by treating them as secrets and by requiring employees and other parties to sign nondisclosure agreements. This is a precaution that costs little and may save much.

Your lawyer can draft an agreement for you, but it is easier and less expensive to get a sample that you can copy from the personnel office of a nearby large corporation. Have each of your employees sign one of these agreement forms before starting work or when receiving a raise.

10. KNOW HOW MUCH PAST-DUE ACCOUNTS REALLY COST YOU

In most cases, it is much easier to charge an item to a customer than it is to collect it. Many accounts could and should be avoided.

First of all, 75 percent of the bookkeeper's time is spent on the accounts receivable, so for every charge item that is entered on the books, three cash items could be entered.

Many jobbers, because of increased inventories, accounts receivable, increased salaries, and expenses, have to borrow money on which to operate. Current accounts are the only ones on which to make a profit. To illustrate —

Sales	$100
All selling costs	$ 97
Profit	$ 3

If this is a cash sale, you are all right. The income tax people will get their share and leave you with a profit. But suppose this is not a cash sale, yet you must pay your bills on time, so you have to borrow money to pay for this $100 sale.

You must borrow $97 to pay all selling costs, and if you are lucky, in today's money market you may borrow it at 7 percent —

$97 at 7 percent for 1 month —
Interest $0.57   Profit $2.43

$97 at 7 percent for 2 months —
Interest $1.14   Profit $1.86

$97 at 7 percent for 3 months —
Interest $1.71   Profit $1.29

$97 at 7 percent for 4 months —
Interest $2.28   Profit $0.72

$97 at 7 percent for 5 months —
Interest $2.85   Profit $0.15

$97 at 7 percent for 6 months —
Interest $3.42   Loss

And so on. After five months, all the profit is gone — just from interest charges. This doesn't take into account all the other costs of trying to collect the money. Actually, you would have been better off had you not sold the item in the first place.

11. LOOK BEFORE YOU CUT PRICES

If you cut your prices, you will have to increase your unit sales in order to break even. Table 3 shows how much you will have to increase your sales to make the same gross profit.

Find the percentage of your price cut, then follow it across the page to the column under your present gross profit. The figure where the two lines meet is the percentage you will have to increase your sales.

For example, if you cut your price 15 percent and your present gross profit is 30 percent, you will have to increase sales by 100 percent to net the same as before the price cut. (Amazing, but true!)

12. USE PARETO'S LAW TO ADVANTAGE

We are all aware of the maxims of business that sound catchy and cute and that contain a certain element of truth. Some of the more famous are these three:

- Parkinson's Law: Work expands to fill the time available for its completion.

- The Peter Principle: In a hierarchy every employee tends to rise to his level of incompetence.

- Murphy's Law: If anything can possibly go wrong, it will.

But, let's face it — they are more appropriate when placed in the context of a bureaucracy (large business) rather than a small enterprise, and, even then, they are not particularly helpful in showing you what to do or not to do.

TABLE 3
SALES INCREASE NEEDED WHEN PRICES CUT

Price cut	Present gross profit (%)							
	5%	10%	15%	20%	25%	30%	35%	40%
1	25.0	11.1	7.1	5.3	4.2	3.4	2.9	2.9
2	66.6	25.0	15.4	11.1	8.7	7.1	6.1	5.3
3	150.0	42.8	25.0	17.6	13.6	1.1	9.4	8.1
4	400.0	66.6	36.4	25.0	19.0	15.4	12.9	11.1
5		100.0	50.0	33.3	25.0	20.0	16.7	14.3
6		150.0	66.7	42.9	31.6	25.0	20.7	17.6
7		233.3	87.5	53.8	38.9	30.4	25.0	21.2
8		400.0	114.3	66.7	47.1	36.4	29.6	25.0
9		1000.0	150.0	81.8	56.3	42.9	34.6	29.0
10			200.0	100.0	66.7	50.0	40.0	33.3
11			275.0	122.2	78.6	57.9	45.8	37.9
12			400.0	150.0	92.3	66.7	52.2	42.9
13			650.0	185.7	108.3	76.5	59.1	48.1
14			1400.0	233.3	127.3	87.5	66.7	53.8
15				300.0	150.0	100.0	75.0	60.0
16				400.0	177.8	114.3	84.2	66.7
17				566.7	212.5	130.8	94.4	73.9
18				900.0	257.1	150.0	105.9	81.8
19				1900.0	316.7	172.7	118.8	90.5
20					400.0	200.0	133.3	100.0
21					525.0	233.3	150.0	110.5
22					733.3	275.0	169.2	122.2
23					1115.0	328.6	191.7	135.3
24					2400.0	400.0	218.2	150.0
25						500.0	250.0	166.7

Yet, there is one demonstrably useful law that most business people are unaware of, even though it has been around far longer than Parkinson or Peter. It's called Pareto's Law, after the Italian economist Vilfredo Pareto (1848–1923), and it has a hard core of enthusiastic exponents among corporate heavyweights. To those who are aware of it, it can be a fundamental guide to the way your business is run.

In the abstract form, Pareto's law says, "The significant items in a given group normally constitute a small portion of the total; the majority of items will be, in the aggregate, of minor significance."

If that sounds less than relevant to the problems your business faces in manufacturing and marketing widgets, think of it as the 80-20 rule. Specifically, it looks like this:

80 percent of my maintenance problems are incurred by 20 percent of the machines;

or

80 percent of the turnover of inventory occurs among 20 percent of the items in stock;

or

80 percent of the sales potential exists among 20 percent of my customers.

The 80-20 figures, of course, aren't to be taken literally. The ratio may be 70-30 or 60-40, or whatever. And they won't necessarily total 100 percent. Maybe in your business, 60 percent of sales are made by 30 percent of the sales force.

But the principle remains. Whether you're looking at strengths or weaknesses in a business operation, you'll find that the significant items — products, work hours, costs, or whatever — make up a small proportion of the total.

Pareto's Law won't *solve* any problems, mind you — at least not all by itself. What it will do, however, is enable you to pinpoint, rather quickly, either a trouble spot or an area of strength. Having done that, you'll be in a position to start asking the right questions — a knack which, as many business people know only too well, is often the hardest part of the exercise.

With those questions asked and answered, you probably won't find it all that hard to decide what action to take.

13. KNOW WHERE TO GO FOR OUTSIDE HELP

Are you puzzled by the fact that you seem to be paying 50 percent more wages than your competitor down the street? Can't figure out why sales of your new improved super widget have been lagging despite a 20 percent increase in your advertising budget? Are you bugged by the seemingly persistent and annoying high turnover in your sales staff? Or have you got an idea for a new product but need some market research to determine its viability?

All these questions and more can be answered by using outside resources available to you.

Business owners often don't realize how much free advice they can get with very little effort. You can help increase profits if you listen to the great number of experts who are a wealth of knowledge. The average business person who has owned a business for a reasonable period of time feels he or she knows it inside out and doesn't need help from anyone else. Unless an instant solution is offered to an immediate dilemma, business owners aren't often interested.

13.1 Government programs

Besides lending money, various government agencies offer other types of assistance such as seminars, courses, management training, information, and consulting services.

13.1a Business Development Bank of Canada

The Business Development Bank of Canada (BDC) offers a wide range of management training, counselling, and mentoring services designed to meet the needs of entrepreneurs at each stage of a business's development — from start-up through to expansion, diversification, and succession.

BDC takes a practical, problem-solving approach to helping entrepreneurs develop and improve their management skills. BDC offers Counselling Assistance to Small Enterprises (CASE), International Standards Organization (ISO) registration assistance, seminars and workshops on numerous business topics, as well as educational publications and do-it-yourself kits.

BDC has programs specially designed to meet the needs of high-technology companies, exporters, women entrepreneurs, aboriginal businesses, and other emerging sectors of the economy.

One common misconception is that you have to be the recipient of a BDC loan to participate in these programs. That's not true. BDC's management services can be offered alone or as part of one of the bank's many financing programs, and they are available to any proprietorship, partnership, or limited company conducting virtually any type of business in Canada.

For more information, or to apply for counselling or other programs, contact the BDC office nearest you (see the listing in your telephone book or call 1-888-INFO-BDC or check the BDC website at www.bdc.ca).

13.1b Canada Business Service Centres

The Business Service Centres (BSC) set up by Industry Canada in conjunction with provincial governments are good sources of information on government services and programs, both local and national. Their website features numerous documents on business start-up and management, marketing, training, and a variety of specific industries. The centres themselves offer a library of videos, publications, directories, CD-ROMS, and computer databases of business and government program information. BSCs are listed in the white pages, or you can look them up at www.canadabusiness.ca.

13.2 Suppliers can help you

Never underestimate the worth of salespeople. These salespeople, representing the various companies that supply you with equipment, will be glad to give you free consultation on any facet of your business. After all, it will probably mean that they will be able to sell you something as a result of your discussions. Large corporations often have internal consulting staff just to help their customers.

Your relationship with salespeople will be more effective if you remain friendly. It costs you nothing but it can give you information about your competitors' businesses that you would never be able to find out yourself. They know the market better than anyone. However, if you don't make the effort to be friendly to your suppliers, they will not respond well to you and will save their inside knowledge for another customer.

It is also good business sense to let salespeople know the general plans for your business. When salespeople hear you talk about future expansion, marketing changes, and increased orders, they will let their credit department know that you are a good risk. This way your credit terms might be eased up, which in turn will ease your working capital.

13.3 Join organizations that can help

It isn't necessary to join every trade club and association there is, but it can help to look around and choose one that can give you a boost in business.

Some trade groups collect and hand out important information on wages, sales, and prices. Others offer training courses for owners, managers, and employees. Almost all of them keep credit reports that can save you time and money.

If you find that you want to get hold of some technical information to study, you will want to consider trade clubs. Their banks of information are more affordable than any individual effort by you to try to get the same information.

Trade associations are also important sources of prospective customers. You will be able to introduce your product or service to many business people. You still have to do the selling, of course, but the club can open the doors.

13.4 Use your banker for credit information

You probably can't afford to subscribe to Dun & Bradstreet or any other large credit reporting service. Don't let this stop you from doing a credit check on your customers and suppliers.

One bad credit loss is enough to seriously harm, or completely destroy, your entire business.

Don't wait until your suspicions are aroused before you do the check. If the news is bad, it will be too late for you to regain any losses. Check customers before you agree to deal with them, no matter how secure you think they are.

Credit reporting services are available from every bank. As part of their service they will either give you a report at no charge or at their cost. You can arrange with your bank's vice-president to use the Dun & Bradstreet service for all your customers and suppliers. This will also assure the bank that you are a careful business person and follow sound credit policies.

13.5 Free student aid

Maybe your business isn't thriving and you wonder why. Try calling your nearest university or college business administration faculty and plug into a class on case study problems. Every college has these courses in which students get valuable knowledge by applying classroom techniques to actual business problems.

The instructor in charge will be glad to set you up with one or more students who will come and analyze your situation. Best of all, it's free.

14. DISCOVER HOW TO GET BETTER TELEPHONE SERVICE

One of the first services you will probably get for your small business is a business telephone line. A business line costs more than a second household line, and you may be tempted to add another line to your home telephone instead of getting one for your company. But besides being against telephone company regulations, you will not be able to get a listing for your business in directory assistance. In addition, you will not be establishing any kind of credit record for your company, and a telephone company credit approval can be worth a lot to a small-business person.

14.1 Ask your telephone company to help you save money

Your telephone system is something that should be re-evaluated as your business grows and your needs change. The telephone company can do a "traffic survey" for you that will show how many calls to your office are blocked by busy signals. If more than 3 percent of your total calls are being blocked, you should consider getting more trunk lines. You don't want customers going to the competition because they couldn't get through to your switchboard.

If the study shows that there is no busy signal problem, perhaps you should eliminate some of your lines and save some money.

The traffic survey will also tell you if your switchboard is working at maximum efficiency. Someone will watch your operators and let you know if you should hire another operator if volume demands.

You might also ask for a complete audit of your telephone system. The telephone company will itemize what you are paying for services and equipment. This is an important service when you often change your equipment. You don't want to be paying for services that were discontinued months ago.

You can also get the telephone company to provide you with an analysis of all outgoing long-distance calls. This examination will take three months to complete, but it will let you find out whether it is worth your while installing a WATS or tie line to save you money (see the next section).

You can get free repairs from the telephone company whenever your system needs service. But if you live in a big city, you may be unsatisfied with the speed of the service. Don't be afraid to call a local division manager or vice-president to ask for quicker service. Tell him or her that your company is losing money every minute the telephones aren't working. That should be enough to get the repair representative out.

14.2 Telephone options

The range of services you can obtain from the telephone company is constantly growing, and many of them can be of use to you.

14.2a Call waiting

Call waiting allows you to hear when someone is trying to get through when you are already on the telephone. It also allows you to put the first caller on hold to answer the second call.

14.2b Multiple lines to one telephone

The telephone company can put another line through to a single telephone. The two lines will usually ring differently so that you know which number is being called. With this option together with call waiting, it is theoretically possible that you could be carrying on four conversations on one line. (Good luck!)

14.2c Call forwarding

With the call-forwarding option, you can "tell" your telephone that you can be reached at another number. When someone calls your office, the call will be automatically transferred to the new number you select without the caller being aware of the change.

14.2d Remote call forwarding

Remote call forwarding (RCF) lets a company in Toronto, for example, have a local telephone number listed in the directory in Vancouver. Calls to the Vancouver number are automatically connected to the company office in Toronto. This provides an option to opening a branch office. Bear in mind, you will want to have an operator in Toronto working Vancouver office hours if you want to benefit from this service.

14.2e WATS lines and toll-free service

The installation of a wide-area telephone service (WATS) means you have rented a block of time from the telephone company for outgoing long-distance calls for a certain area and for a set price. A toll-free service works the same way for incoming calls; your customers can call you for free, and you pay a set price.

You pay a flat monthly rate according to the number of hours for which the service is used, the number of telephones that can call the number, and the average distance of the calls.

These services can be great money savers if your business has a large number of long distance calls. A WATS line can be expensive, however, because employees will do more long-distance calling. To them, the call is free, and the system can be abused.

However, a toll-free service alone is often enough to encourage customers to call in. It won't cost them anything, and your employees are unable to exploit the system by calling out.

14.2f Tie lines

Tie lines are useful for businesses that spend a lot of money on telephone calls between branch offices in different cities. For a flat monthly rate, depending on the distance between offices, a company can carry on as many conversations of any duration between the head office and the branches as it wishes.

14.2g Credit card

Your telephone company will issue you credit cards for use by you and/or selected employees that allow calls to be billed to your business number no matter where calls are made from. These cards are usually available free of charge and each contains a coded number unique to your business. A telephone credit card is valuable if you (or other people in your company) are away from the office on a regular basis and need to make business calls. Detailed records of credit card usage is another benefit. In many cases hotels don't charge extra for calls made using a credit card.

14.2h Long distance discounts

Long distance carriers have discount plans for extensive long distance usage; they don't always remember to tell you about them. Check with your carrier for available discount plans. Most plans have a minimum and take effect only after a specific dollar amount is billed, but they can offer discounts of 20 percent to 50 percent depending on your long distance usage.

Also be aware of the rapidly changing nature of the long distance carrier business. Deregulation of this part of the telephone business has brought about a lot of competition and those competing carriers are all interested in "making a deal" for commercial traffic. The best advice I can give you is to avoid long-term contracts and regularly re-evaluate your options in this fast-changing field.

14.2i Voice messaging

You've heard it in action in almost every large, and not so large, business you've called in the past decade. Certainly you have encountered it when you have called a government office or Crown corporation. Some people hate it; some love it. It seems to depend on what side of the telephone you're on.

Voice messaging is a sophisticated retrieval system intended to give you control over your calls. Not only does it take calls on your telephone line when you're out of the office or otherwise engaged, but it also serves the caller by giving him or her touch-tone initiated information or rerouting the call to someone else who can assist them.

How effective a voice messaging system is will be up to you. Your telephone company will provide details and options of how such a system can work for your company. But remember, your telephone is often your first, and sometimes your only, contact with your customer, so be certain that your voice messaging system reflects the importance of that contact.

14.3 Consider Interconnect

In Canada you now have a choice of renting your telephone from the telephone company or buying it from a private Interconnect company. This is a great boon to the small-business person because it gives you some options.

This industry is growing and changing so rapidly that any specific comments I make here will likely be outdated soon. However, I can safely tell you the following:

(a) If your telephone needs are simple and unlikely to change over a long time period, give Interconnect serious consideration. You can lease Interconnect equipment for about the same amount of money you pay the telephone company and you end up owning the system after five years.

(b) If your needs are changing rapidly, continuing contact with the telephone company is inevitable because it still controls the incoming service or trunk lines. In this case, you are probably better off staying with the telephone company because, by renting the equipment, you don't make any long-term commitment, and if you experience problems you avoid the "blame the other guy" syndrome.

(c) Telephone companies themselves are setting up subsidiaries to sell equipment, and if their products are priced competitively, you may get the best of both worlds.

Even if you decide to use the equipment or services of an outside company for your telephone system, you should consider having at least one telephone that is rented from the telephone company. If you have none of its equipment and you encounter a problem with your telephone lines, the telephone company will usually charge for a service call. On the other hand, if a telephone belongs to them, the service call will be free.

14.4 Consider VOIP

Voice Over Internet Protocol (VOIP) is an emerging alternative to Plain Old Telephone Service (POTS). In simple terms, VOIP uses the Internet to carry your telephone call, instead of telephone lines.

VOIP systems connect your telephone to the Internet using a fast ("broadband") connection such as a cable or DSL connection. A VOIP telephone can be used to place a call to or receive a call from any other telephone, anywhere in the world.

As mentioned, this is a technology that is still emerging, so rates and terms of service can and usually do vary widely from one service provider to another.

Companies such as Skype (bought by eBay for an enormous amount of money) allow free or nearly free Skype-to-Skype telephone calls anywhere in the world.

Some Internet service providers have started to offer VOIP services (sometimes promoted as "digital telephones"), with rates that vary from very expensive to very inexpensive.

For the home office, a minimal VOIP installation will involve some software and a sound card for your computer, and a set of headphones with a microphone. For most people, such a setup will prove too restrictive.

Subscription services will provide a special router, a box that connects to your Internet connection. You can then connect a conventional telephone or telephones to the VOIP router. Or you can get quite fancy and add a software-based digital exchange to your network, allowing each telephone in the office to have its own extension.

I recommend working with a consultant if you want to install such an exchange.

An interesting benefit of VOIP services is that you can "locate" your telephone number almost anywhere in the world. I know a small West Coast company that does a lot of business in Hong Kong. The owner signed up for a VOIP service and asked for a Hong Kong telephone number to be assigned to that service. That company is now a *local* call for any of its Hong Kong clients, and calling Hong Kong telephone numbers from the West Coast office is also treated as a local call. Calls to anywhere in North America were billing at 3 cents a minute. In mid-2007 this business was paying less than $10 a month for the base service.

If you choose to use VOIP for a small office, include these things in your evaluation:

- Does the service include 911 or similar emergency calls?

- If you have a DSL or ADSL connection to the Internet and a building security alarm service, will the VOIP installation conflict with the alarm service system's use of the telephone line?

- Will the VOIP vendor allow you to have multiple telephone numbers, each in a or country where you do a lot of busi

- Will the VOIP vendor sign a c that is renewable monthly or an

The last point is important. This of is moving fast and today's inexpensi on a VOIP services may not be your year from now.

15. DO YOU NEED A BUY-SELL AGREEMENT?

Starting a business with a partner is easy compared to figuring out in advance how you're going to get out of it if some unforeseen event happens.

Consider this picture: you are a partner in a successful business without a buy-sell agreement. In fact, your life for the past ten years has been tied up with the majority of your assets in the business. You are married and have two children in high school. Suddenly you suffer a severe heart attack and your doctor says retirement is a must. Your partner isn't happy because she now has to carry the full load. Your income ceases because the business cannot afford to pay your salary for no work.

What happens now? Your spouse cannot run the business. Your partner could buy you out but in your position you have little room for ne-
gotiation. Even selling your interest to an out-
side party is risky because your partner would
have to approve anyone coming in, which puts
him in the position of being able to control any
deal you may come up with. In the meantime,
your family needs a certain monthly income to

answer to these problems is a buy-sell
buy. The heart of an agreement is the
purchase that provides the rules for the
business sale of each partner's interest in the
whatever there is a parting of the ways, for
partner and (In this discussion, the terms
but in proholder are used interchangeably,
involve incorporation buy-sell agreements in-
businesses.)

The purpose of the agreement is to enable the existing shareholders to retain control of the company while providing a fair price and payout of the departing or deceased partner's interest. The death of a shareholder in a small business creates a serious situation both for the estate of the deceased shareholder and the remaining shareholders.

From the point of view of the departing shareholder, the shares of the company held by the shareholder may have no market as outsiders will seldom buy such shares unless the business is an established one and they are able to purchase the majority interest in the company. The only persons who may be interested in buying shares may be the remaining shareholders. But, if the departing shareholder had a minority interest in the company, the remaining shareholders would retain control anyway. Thus they would have no real interest in buying the shares and, therefore, have the power to force the departing shareholder to sell the shares at bargain prices.

From the point of view of the company, it may be very important to prevent the sale of the shares to a stranger or to someone with whom the remaining shareholders do not get along, or to prevent the shares from being held by the beneficiaries of the deceased shareholder. The death or departure of a shareholder in a close corporation with no prior agreement on the disposition of the shares may also adversely affect the credit position of the company because of the uncertainty as to the future of the business.

Buy-sell agreements present two major problems:

(a) The funding of the purchase of the shares

(b) The valuation of the shares of the deceased

Usually, the purchase of the shares is funded by business life insurance policies under which each shareholder insures the lives of his or her fellow shareholders, naming himself or herself as beneficiary of each policy.

The idea is that the surviving shareholders will use the insurance proceeds to purchase the shares of the deceased shareholder from the estate of the deceased shareholder.

There are, of course, different types of life insurance and the decision as to which type should be obtained by the parties, the amount, and other related matters should be made only after consulting with an experienced life insurance underwriter. (See Chapter 15.)

The price setting problem may be dealt with in a number of ways as no single method of valuation is appropriate to all types of business operation or circumstances. The important thing is that it must be a fair method of valuation.

There are five general methods by which shares can be valued:

- By using the valuation imposed by the estate tax authorities

- By some form of fixed formula (book value, capitalization of earnings, etc., or a combination of two or more of these methods)

- By some form of appraisal or arbitration

- By a fixed dollar amount by agreement among the parties, with or without a provision for periodic revision

- By a combination of two or more of these methods

In situations in which the partners are not sure whether or not the surviving shareholders or beneficiaries will want to sell or buy the remaining interest a put/call clause can be used.

With a put/call clause, the shares pass on to the beneficiaries, and they can "put" or require the surviving shareholder to buy the shares at any time. On the other hand, the shareholder can "call" or require the beneficiaries to sell the shares.

When partners can't agree, a shotgun clause is often effective. A shotgun clause is often used in husband-wife businesses when one or the other wants to get out of the business because of an impending divorce. One partner indicates in writing that he wants out of the business and sets a price at which he is willing to sell his shares or buy his partner's shares, and the other partner can then decide whether she wants to sell or purchase at the proposed price.

Whatever the terms of the agreement, it is a good idea to have this matter settled before a marriage breaks up. Many people have made the unfortunate discovery that it is extremely difficult to make maintenance payments to someone out of earnings derived from the company that is disrupted by disagreements between its directors. Too often, if no agreement is reached, the company is wound up and both parties experience unnecessary economic loss. By adopting a buy-sell agreement, the parties are bound to resolve a messy situation according to a predetermined formula — one that can be enforced in the courts if need be.

The buy-sell agreement shown in Sample 8 is very simple and is provided only as an example of what might be included in one. I suggest obtaining competent legal advice if you wish to enter into a buy-sell agreement unless you are certain about what you are doing.

16. WHY NOT EXPORT?

Even the smallest company can find profits in export markets. Before you pursue overseas customers, however, you must answer a few hard questions about the condition of your business. Then, with the help of government programs, trade associations, and the Chamber of Commerce, you have to learn as much as you can about your intended market. As with any business decision, sound preparation spells the difference between success and failure.

Once you've identified your market and sized up the competition, you have to determine how you should begin. Exporting must take into account the business practices of foreign markets, keeping in mind that what is proper in one country may be improper in another.

The best place to start looking for information advice is at the regional offices of Industry Canada. They represent Foreign Affairs and International Trade and can provide you with that department's studies of export markets by product and by region.

Another source of help is Canada's trade commissioner service. Trade commissioners have immediate access to export markets and are knowledgeable about business practices in various regions.

To varying degrees, trade associations and chambers of commerce can also help you if you want to do business abroad. Contact your local chamber to see what particular services it offers.

If you want to establish a direct relationship with foreign clients, you should contact one of the chartered banks; each has an international division with connections in every country in which Canada does business. The staff can advise you in all areas of exporting, run credit checks on potential foreign clients, etc.

To export successfully, you need to be persistent and methodical and consider all the angles and costs before making a move. You can never do enough research before entering the export market. For a further discussion of the export business, see *Exporting from Canada*, another title from Self-Counsel Press.

SAMPLE 8
BUY-SELL AGREEMENT

BUY-SELL AGREEMENT made the _____ day of _____, 20___,

between_____ of the _____ of _____

in the _____ of _____(herein called _____),

and _____ of the _____ of _____

(herein called _____).

WHEREAS:

(1) The parties own or control all the issued and outstanding shares in

_____

Corporation Limited (herein called "the Corporation") as follows:

[Set out shareholdings]

(2) The parties desire to provide for their mutual protection if either dies or wishes to withdraw from the Corporation:

THIS AGREEMENT WITNESSES that the parties covenant and agree as follows:

1. The parties shall not transfer, encumber, or in any way deal with any of their shares in the Corporation except as provided for in this agreement.

During the lifetime of the parties

2. If either_____ or_____ wishes to dispose of his or her shares in the Corporation, he or she (herein called "the Offeror") shall first offer in writing to sell all his or her shares to the other party (herein called "the Offeree") on the following terms and conditions:

3. The offer shall contain:

(a) an offer to sell all the shares of the Corporation owned or controlled by the Offeror (herein called "all his or her shares" or "the shares") at the arbitrary price stipulated in the offer;

(b) an offer to purchase all the shares of the Corporation owned or controlled by the Offeree (herein called "all his or her shares" or "the shares") at the same price;

(c) an undertaking to close the purchase or sale on a date fixed not less than [eighty(80)] days and not more than [one hundred (100)] days from the service of the offer on the Offeree at the time and place fixed in the offer;

4. If the Offeree accepts the offer to sell under paragraph 3, the Offeror (herein called "the Vendor") shall sell and transfer all his/her shares to the Offeree (herein called "the Purchaser") who shall purchase and pay for them on the date and at the place stated in the offer for the arbitrary price stipulated in the offer.

5.   If the Offeree accepts the offer to purchase under paragraph 3(b), the Offeror (herein called "the Vendor") shall sell all his/her shares to the Offeree (herein called "the Purchaser") who shall purchase and pay for them on the date and at the place stated in the offer for the arbitrary price stipulated in the offer.

6.   If the Offeree does not accept either of the alternative offers in accordance with the provisions, he or she shall be deemed to have accepted the Offeror's offer to sell all his or her shares to the Offeree, and the Offeree (herein called "the Purchaser") shall purchase and pay for them on the date and at the place stated in the offer for the arbitrary price stipulated in the offer.

7.   At the time set for closing, the Vendor shall deliver to the Purchaser in exchange for the items set out in paragraph 8:

(a) certificates for all his or her shares duly endorsed in blank for transfer;

(b) his or her resignation from the board and that of his or her spouse and nominees, if applicable;

(c) his or her resignation as an employee and that of his or her spouse and members of his or her family who may be in the employ of the Corporation;

(d) an assignment to the Purchaser of all debts, if any, owing by the Corporation to the Vendor;

(e) a release of all claims the Vendor has or may have against the Corporation and the Purchaser;

(f) assignment of all insurance policies on the life of the purchaser as set out in Appendix A;

(g) a certified cheque payable to the Purchaser for an amount equal to the aggregate of the cash surrender value of all policies on the life of the Vendor as set out in Appendix A;

(h) all other documents necessary or desirable in order to carry out the true intent of this agreement.

8.   At the time set for closing, the Purchaser shall deliver to the Vendor in exchange for the items set out in paragraph 7 above:

(a) a certified cheque payable to the Vendor for the full amount of the arbitrary purchase price of the shares;

(b) a certified cheque payable to the Vendor for the full amount of any indebtedness owing by the Corporation to the Vendor as recorded on the books of the Corporation and verified by the Corporation's accountant;

(c) a certified cheque payable to the Vendor for an amount equal to the aggregate of the cash surrender value of all policies on the life of the Purchaser as set out in Appendix A;

(d) a release by the Corporation of all debts, if any, owing by the Vendor to the Corporation;

(e) a release of all claims the Corporation and the Purchaser have or may have against the Vendor;

(f) a release of all guarantees given by the Vendor on behalf of the Corporation;

(g) all securities, free and clear of all claims, which belong to the Vendor and are lodged with any person (including the Corporation's banks) to secure any indebtedness or credit of the corporation;

(h) assignments of all insurance policies on the life of the Vendor as set out in Appendix A;

(i)   all other documents necessary or desirable in order to carry out the true intent of this agreement.

9.   If on the closing date the Vendor neglects or refuses to complete the transaction or does not comply with the procedures herein set out, the Purchaser has the right upon such default (without prejudice to any other rights that he or she may have), upon payment by him or her of the purchase price (plus or minus any adjustments herein provided) to the credit of the Vendor in any chartered bank in the [city] of _____ (or to the solicitor for the Corporation in trust for, on behalf of and in the name of the Vendor), to complete the transaction as above. The Vendor hereby irrevocably constitutes the Purchaser his or her true and lawful attorney to complete the said transaction and execute on behalf of the Vendor every document necessary or desirable in that behalf. [If there is more than one vendor, this power of attorney shall apply to all vendors.]

10.   If on the closing date the Purchaser neglects or refuses to complete the transaction, or does not comply with the procedures herein set out, the Vendor has the right upon such default (without prejudice to any other rights that he or she may have) to give to the Purchaser, within ten (10) days after such default, notice that on the twenty-first day after the original closing date, he or she (herein called "the New Purchaser") will purchase from the Purchaser (herein called "the New Vendor") all the shares of the Corporation owned or controlled by the New Vendor, for an amount equal to seventy-five percent (75%) of the purchase price set out in paragraph 8(a) and at the same time fix a new date within thirty (30) days and a time and place for closing; whereupon, on the new date for closing, the New Vendor shall sell all his or her shares to the New Purchaser who shall purchase the same for the new purchase price, and it is expressly agreed that all the terms of this agreement applicable to the closing of the sale and purchase of shares and to the adjustment of purchase price, if any, shall be applicable to the said closing. The New Vendor hereby constitutes the New Purchaser his or her true and lawful attorney to complete the said transaction and execute on behalf of the New Vendor every document necessary or desirable in that behalf. [If there is more than one vendor, this power of attorney shall apply to all vendors.]

11.   No offer hereunder shall be given while another offer is outstanding or a sale pending or until [one hundred (100)] days after any sale is aborted.

After the death of a party

12.   Within [one hundred (100)] days of the death of either _____ or _____ (provided the survivor is alive on the thirtieth day after the death of the first deceased) the survivor (Purchaser) shall purchase and the estate of the deceased (Vendor) shall sell to the survivor all shares owned or controlled by the deceased at the time of his or her death for the most recent price stipulated in the offer.

13.   The legal representatives of the deceased shall in writing fix a date not more than [one hundred (100)] days from the date of death and a time and place for the closing of the sale of its shares.

14.   At the same time set for closing, the Purchaser shall deliver to the Vendor/Estate in exchange for the items set out in paragraph 15:

(a)   a certified cheque payable to the Vendor/Estate for the full amount of the purchase price as set out in the offer;

(b)   a certified cheque payable to the Vendor/Estate for the full amount of any indebtedness owing by the Corporation to the deceased;

(c) a certified cheque payable to the Vendor/Estate for the amount of the cash surrender value on all insurance policies on the life of the Purchaser listed in Appendix A;

(d) a certified cheque payable to the Vendor/Estate for the amount, if any, by which the aggregate net proceeds received by the Purchaser from the insurers in Appendix A exceeds the aggregate of (a), (b), and (c), above;

(e) a release by the Corporation and the Purchaser of all debts and other claims that they have or may have against the Vendor/Estate;

(f) a release of all guarantees given by the deceased Vendor on behalf of the Corporation;

(g) all securities, free and clear of all claims, belonging to the deceased Vendor which are lodged with any person (including the Corporation's banks) to secure any indebtedness or credit of the Corporation;

(h) all other documents necessary or desirable in order to carry out the true intent of this agreement.

15. At the time set for closing, the Vendor/Estate shall deliver to the Purchaser in exchange for the items set out in paragraph 14:

(a) certificates for all the Vendor's shares duly endorsed for transfer in blank with signature guaranteed by a bank or trust company;

(b) evidence of authority of executors to sign;

(c) succession duty release for the shares if applicable;

(d) resignations from the board and employment of all members of the deceased's family and nominees;

(e) an assignment to the Purchaser of all debts, if any, owing by the Corporation to the Vendor;

(f) a release of all claims the deceased Vendor or his/her estate has or may have against the Corporation or the Purchaser;

(g) an assignment to the Purchaser of all insurance policies on the life of the Purchaser listed in Appendix A;

(h) all other documents necessary or desirable in order to carry out the true intent of this agreement.

Insurance

16. In order to ensure that all or a substantial part of the purchase price for the shares of the deceased party will be available immediately in cash upon his or her death, each of the parties hereto has procured insurance on the other's life as set out in Appendix A. Additional policies may be taken out for the purposes of this agreement and they shall be added to Appendix A.

17. Each of the parties hereto agrees, throughout the term of this agreement, to maintain and pay the premiums as they fall due on the life insurance policies listed in Appendix A owned by him or her.

18. The insurers set out in Appendix A are hereby authorized and directed to give any party hereto, upon written request, all information concerning the status of the said policies.

19. If any premium on any insurance policy is not paid within [twenty(20)] days after its due date, the party insured shall have the right to pay such premium and be reimbursed therefor by the owner thereof together with interest at the rate of [two (2)] percent per month on the amount so paid in respect of such premium from the overdue payment until the date of reimbursement.

20. Immediately upon the death of one of the parties hereto the survivor shall proceed as expeditiously as possible to collect the proceeds of the policies on the deceased party, and the legal representatives of the estate of the deceased party shall apply and expedite the application for letters of administration or letters probate, as may be required.

21. The parties shall not assign, encumber, borrow upon, or otherwise deal with any of the insurance policies set out in Appendix A.

General

22. The parties shall not throughout the term of this agreement and until a valid sale of the shares is completed under this agreement do or cause or permit to be done anything out of the normal course of business of the Corporation.

23. Time shall be of the essence of this agreement and everything that relates thereto.

24. The parties agree to execute and deliver any documents necessary or desirable to carry out the true purpose and intent of this agreement.

25. This agreement shall be binding upon and enure to the benefit of the parties hereto and their respective heirs, executors, administrators, and assigns.

IN WITNESS, etc.

SIGNED, SEALED, AND DELIVERED, etc.   [Signatures and seals]

APPENDIX A

_____CORPORATION LIMITED

BUY-SELL AGREEMENT

APPENDIX A

Life insurance policies on the life of _____owned by_____
       Insurer   *Number*   *Amount*

Life insurance policies on the life of _____owned by_____
       Insurer   *Number*   *Amount*

ALTERNATIVE VALUATION CLAUSES

Valuation by auditor: Book value at fixed date

The survivor and the executors or administrators of the deceased shall cause a valuation of all other shares of common and preferred stock of the Corporation to be made by the auditors of the Corporation based on the book value of the Corporation on the first day of the month immediately preceding the deceased's death. If within thirty days the survivor and the executors or administrators of the deceased have not signified their approval of the valuation of the shares of the Corporation as determined by the auditors, the value of such shares shall be fixed by a board of three arbitrators selected as follows: the survivor shall select one arbitrator, the executors or administrators of the deceased shall select one arbitrator, and the two so selected shall select the third arbitrator, and the decision of a majority of the said arbitrators as to such valuation shall be final.

Book value: Capitalization of fixed assets

To the book value of the shares of the Corporation shall be added an amount equal to [six (6)] times the difference between the average net profit of the Corporation, after payment of all taxes and dividends for [three (3)] complete fiscal years of the corporation immediately preceding the deceased's death and [ten (10)] percent of the adjusted net asset value of the Corporation as above determined at the date of the death of the deceased.

APPENDIX — PREPARING A BUSINESS PLAN

Writing a plan for your business is a good idea and something I strongly recommend you should do.

Your business plan will help you in various ways. It will —

- help you better understand the business you are getting into;

- show you the potential strengths and weaknesses of the business you are planning;

- give you a good understanding of your business objectives;

- give you goals to work towards;

- provide a list of financial and other milestones which you can use to measure your actual results; and

- be a document you can give potential investors to help them decide if your business is a good investment for them.

The last point — using the business plan to raise funds — is usually the focus of books about writing your own plan. While raising funds is important at various times in the life of a business, I think being able to use a business plan as a road map so you can keep on course during start-up and all the stages afterwards is the most valuable reason for writing one.

Note that many owners of small businesses do use a credit card to cover early expenses. Although this may not be an ideal means of funding a business (the interest rate is terrible!), it can be sufficient to cover the occasional shortfall in a business that does not require a lot of invested capital.

THE SKELETON

Here are some basic elements of a business plan:

- Introduction and executive summary
- The team members
- The product/service, the market, and the competition
- The business environment and the operations plan
- Financial data
- Appendix

In the pages that follow, I will be putting meat to this skeleton, describing each of the parts listed above. I intend to be brief — this is an appendix, not a book — and whenever possible I will use bullet points to identify the things you need to do.

Do have a look at the CD that came with this book. There is some additional information about business plans, and also some basic spreadsheets to help with the financial aspects of the plan.

COVER PAGE AND TABLE OF CONTENTS

Create an attention-grabbing cover page. Ideally, it should include your company logo and if appropriate a picture of your product.

If your business is offering a service, you could also provide an image, or perhaps use bullet points to highlight your service and what you see as opportunities. (See the cover of this book as an example!)

Choose a design and colours that reflect how you want your business to be seen: bright and

energetic, cool and conservative, or somewhere in between.

The cover page should include the following:

- Legal name of the business
- The date you prepared the document (updated whenever you update the plan)
- Your name, address, and telephone number(s)
- A notice that the contents of the plan are confidential

Make sure your table of contents is organized and easy to follow. For design ideas, look at the table of contents of books you come across, including this one.

THE INTRODUCTION

This part of your plan is very important.

Whenever you are preparing to give your plan to someone, such as an investor or a bank, the introduction should be structured as a letter. It should say why you are submitting your plan, and you should highlight important information.

If you will be sending the proposal to a specific person, be *very* sure to spell their name, company name, and address correctly!

EXECUTIVE SUMMARY

You will not write this until you need to present your plan to someone. Definitely do not write it until you have completed the rest of the plan!

If you will be submitting your business plan to people who might invest in your business, this section will either encourage them to read the rest of the plan, or to say no very quickly. In other words, think of this as a selling tool.

I would write this in the form of a letter — a professional letter, not one to my Aunt Matilda! Include the following:

- Who is this plan about? Is this a sole proprietorship, a partnership, or a corporation?

- What is the opportunity? Briefly describe the business venture or product being proposed, and the magnitude of the business and the expected growth rate.

- What is the total financial requirement and where will most of the money be applied (for equipment, facilities, etc.)?

- What sources of funds do you have for the venture (such as owner's contribution, term loans)?

- What is the expected return on investment? (More information on this is on the CD.)

- If you are seeking a loan, how and when do you plan to repay the loan?

- Vision statement: This should be a brief description of where you see the business in five to ten years.

- Environmental statement: Provide a short description of environmental issues associated with the project, and emphasize your efforts at minimizing environmental liabilities and maximizing potential opportunities. (More information on this is on the CD.)

THE BUSINESS
Description

Describe what type of business it is (such as services, retail, manufacturing), the form of business (sole proprietorship, partnership, or corporation), its status (start-up, expansion, acquisition), and its size (sales volume, number and size of facilities, and number of employees).

Management

Next, describe the owners and the management team — who they are and what strengths, expertise, and experience they bring to the business. Keep this brief and put résumés in the appendix.

List each management position with the name of the individual, and indicate for each person if this will be their only employment (if not, indicate their other employment too).

Also list your professional advisors including accountants, bankers, consultants, and lawyers.

Succession

Describe your plans for succession — do you plan to sell, or who do you expect to take over after you retire?

If you are young, talking about succession may seem odd, and it probably is. You might instead describe briefly your intention to make a lifetime career from this business.

If you have ambitions to grow the business and take it public through a financial offering, say so, and describe your timetable.

THE OPPORTUNITY

This is the core of any business plan. This is where you demonstrate that you have a "unique selling proposition" — a competitive edge or a distinct niche that your new business will bring to the marketplace.

If someone reading this section of your plan sees you are proposing something like an electric typewriter business in the age of personal computers, obviously there is little chance they will read further, or respond favourably. In other words, here is where you sell the reader on how unique, exciting, special, and profitable your business will be!

When you are buying a car, even a very standard subcompact, the salesperson will tell you why you should buy *this* model, and what makes it so much better and different than all those other ones you have been considering. Your task here is to make what you are offering similarly attractive.

Gather as much useful information for this section as you can. Research is key. Don't avoid this step, because you will get invaluable insights into the market you intend to enter.

The Internet is obviously a useful place to start your research. Most of your competitors will probably have a presence on the Internet, either through their own website or through the websites of vendors who sell their products or services. And a lot of valuable resources are now being made available online. The CD that accompanies this book contains useful resource links, including Statistics Canada, which you can use in your research.

Another excellent source of information is trade magazines — magazines that are aimed at business readers and which report on the industry sector your new business will be in. Check your local library to see what they carry. Look for issues that list the current "Top 50" or "Top 100" leaders in the industry, because those issues often also provide useful industry facts and figures.

It is a good idea to write this section of the business plan twice. First, compare yourself with the competition with as little bias as possible, being as truthful as you can about where and why they might be better. Think long and hard about what you plan to do, and how you can eliminate or reduce those weaknesses in order to stay competitive. Then do the exercise a second time, updating the original and putting emphasis on the positive.

In this section you need to cover the detail under a number of headings.

The product or service

In this section you should include the following:

- What it is you are offering, and what it is used for or when.

- Whether this is a new idea, and if it has been protected by patent, copyright, or other legal means.

- Any unique or innovative features and why customers will love them.

- How soon it could be expected to become obsolete, and whether you plan to modify or update it in the future.

- Any negative environmental impacts of the product or service, including those associated with production, use, and disposal, and how these can be minimized.

- Unique and innovative features, including efforts at promoting eco-efficiency.

The market

In defining the market you should include the following:

- Who your potential customers are and where they are.

- How your product or service satisfies the needs of these customers.

- Whether your product or service can tap into the growing environmental awareness of consumers.

- The size of the market, supported by market research data, statistics, etc.

- The potential for market growth, also supported by factual data. Look at local, national, and international markets.

- Your market share and the share you hope to obtain in the first year (more information on this is on the CD).

- How your pricing strategy will let you make a profit and remain competitive.

- Three versions — pessimistic, optimistic, and expected — of a sales forecast for the next five years. This can be done as a graph which shows the "expected sales" line with an "optimistic" line above and a "pessimistic" line below. Set the optimistic and pessimistic forecasts realistically — 10 or 15 percent above and below would be good.

Competition

Identify your competition and provide some analysis. Obviously, the analysis should be in your favour — if it is not, now is the time to re-think your business.

You need to research and provide the following information:

- Names and known or estimated market shares of your major competitors.

- Whether competitor sales are increasing, decreasing, or steady, and why. The *why* will usually be your expert opinion, though you should try to support it with evidence from the media or elsewhere.

- Comparison of your company with the competition (in terms of size, reputation, location, distribution channels, etc.) to highlight your strengths and weaknesses. Don't be afraid to indicate what you see as your weaknesses.

- Comparison of your product/service with the competition's (warranty, quality, price, image, etc.). Again, don't be afraid to point out any weaknesses.

- What you have learned from watching the competition operate.

Sales and marketing

Describe how your service or product will be sold. Will you use a website, mail-order, a sales team, or some other approach or approaches?

How will you get the word out about what you are selling? Will you use advertising or other promotional tools?

PRODUCTION

Whether you are proposing to start a company in the manufacturing or service sector, it is essential that you demonstrate a thorough grasp of how to manage business operations in a cost-effective manner.

Location

What makes your location suitable (proximity to markets, suppliers, transportation, labour, etc.)?

Facilities

Are your facilities owned or leased? State the terms.

Briefly describe your facilities. You may wish to include sketches or floor plans. Do say if renovations will be required and indicate the cost and how long this would take.

Describe your current level of usage of the plant and the equipment, and estimate how long these facilities will be sufficient.

Describe the potential environmental liabilities arising as a result of your business activities at the facilities. (The CD has a link to the Environment Canada website to help you with this.)

Materials/Supplies

If your business requires materials or supplies (very few businesses do not), you need to describe any risks associated with your materials/supplies. Can any supplies be obtained from only one source? Are your supplies perishable? Do you have adequate storage facilities? Can supplies/materials be substituted so as to minimize environmental risk and reduce operating costs?

Describe any regulations, permits, and/or approvals needed as a result of materials/supplies used in production.

Personnel

Describe your current personnel needs. If the staff will be large, include an organizational chart in the appendix.

What skills and training are required, including those related to health and safety? How much will training cost? Are any local, provincial, or federal funds or programs available to help reduce the cost?

List the compensation and benefits that will be provided for each position. Include salaries, wages, overtime, and fringe benefits.

Setup

How long will it take to acquire facilities, equipment, personnel, etc. and to set up operations?

For manufacturing companies: How long after the operation has been set up will the first production run be completed?

What special municipal or other government approvals may be required? Can any environmental requirements be met by simply adopting pollution prevention approaches? (See the CD for more on environmental issues.)

Operations

Are you meeting the standards of maximum safety? Are your facilities utilizing the best available techniques and technologies in all stages of your operations?

What hazardous materials and environmental risks are associated with the production, use, and disposal of the product or service?

FINANCIAL DATA

No matter how interesting your business proposition may appear to you, the only way you will persuade a potential investor is with a convincing analysis of financial data.

Required investment

Come right to the point and indicate the total amount of funding required.

Next, list applications of the funds, such as equipment, renovation, inventory, working capital, etc. A detailed expense breakdown is not required.

List existing sources of funds, such as the owners' investment, mortgage loans, term loans, and so on.

Every investor will want to know, when can investors expect repayment? Do not be overly optimistic here — you will be asked to justify your claim. If you say repayment will happen in six months, you run the risk of being seen as unrealistic and that is a trait that investors *do not* want to see!

Finally, identify the liability limits and insurance coverage necessary to handle environmental and other risks.

Break-even analysis

The break-even point for a business is when the total revenues received for the products of the business equal the total cost of producing (or acquiring) and selling those products. If the product can be sold in a larger quantity than occurs at the break-even point, then the firm will make a profit; below this point, it will make a loss.

So a break-even analysis simply determines the sales volume at which your firm will start making money.

The break-even formula is: *fixed costs* divided by (*revenue per unit* minus *variable costs per unit*).

Your fixed costs are the ones that must be paid even if you sell nothing, while your variable costs are the ones that vary directly with the number of products produced (or purchased for resale).

This is a complicated topic and one I am not convinced you need to deal with if you are starting a typical small business from home or on a part-time basis. If you want a deeper understanding of how to make these calculations, there is a link to a good Internet resource on the CD.

Pro forma balance sheet

You should include a pro forma balance sheet in your plan. A balance sheet is a "snapshot" of what you own and what you owe on a specific date. A pro forma balance sheet looks forward and is a "guesstimate" of how things will be under given conditions rather than how they are.

A business plan to show to potential lenders will usually contain an opening balance sheet, which shows the details of what you own and owe at the start of the business, as well as projected monthly balance sheets for year one. Some borrowers may also ask to see monthly or quarterly balance sheets for years two and three.

If you are self-funding the launch of your business, I suggest you prepare a pro forma balance sheet at least for the first 12 months of operations. Doing this will make you think carefully about income and expenditures, and if you are realistic in your estimates, the balance sheet will help identify points in the year when you may need extra funds to keep operating.

Once the business is launched, update your balance sheet for each new month, and compare your current numbers with what you put in the original, pro forma balance sheet for the year.

(See the CD for an example of a pro forma balance sheet that you can use.)

Pro forma income statement

An income statement is also known as a "profit and loss statement" or an "operating statement." It is a tool to show whether a business has earned a profit or has suffered a loss after a period of time.

A "Pro Forma Income Statement" is used for forecasting, to show how things will be under given conditions rather than how they are at present.

As with the pro forma balance sheet, lenders will usually want to see a monthly pro forma income statement for the first year of the business, as well as for years two and three.

(The CD also contains a blank pro forma income statement for your use.)

Cash flow forecast

A cash flow statement identifies cash flowing into and out of the business each month and whether a company will have enough money to meet its needs on a monthly basis.

You will normally prepare a cash flow statement for each month, at the end of the month. When the time comes to present a business plan

to lenders, they will want to see the latest year's worth of monthly cash flow statements. Cash receipts for each month will normally be included with the statements.

Also, you should prepare at least a quarterly cash flow forecast to cover the next two years. This will provide your lenders with a picture of how you see the business developing.

For more information, see the instructions and sample worksheets on the CD.

Historical financial reports

Finally, lenders will want to see the following:

- An income statement for the past year, together with monthly cash receipts

- Income statements for the past three to five years (or less if you haven't been in business for that long)

- Balance sheets for the past three to five years

APPENDIX

Finally, add an appendix to your business plan, putting in the résumés of all key personnel (owners and management) and an organizational chart, if appropriate. Lenders are usually very interested in the experience and qualifications of the people operating the business. This does not mean you need a team of MBA graduates working for you, but practical experience always counts.

SUMMARY

At the start of this appendix I recommended you use the elements of a business plan to provide yourself with targets and a road map for your business. You do not have to be a skilled accountant to do this — most of the key spreadsheets are quite easy to understand and work with, and the few that are complicated are ones you do not need to worry about at the start. All it takes is the discipline to set aside some time at the end of each month to bring your numbers up to date.

Once your business has grown a little, you may decide to seek financing, from a bank or some other lender. That is when you will need to prepare a "formal" business plan, and by then you should be in a position to retain the services of an accountant to make sure it is done exactly the way it should be.

The following is included on the enclosed CD-ROM. The worksheets are in PDF, MS Word, and/or MS Excel formats.

Self-Assessment Workbook

- Analyzing your entrepreneurial strengths and weaknesses
- From mission to goals
- What are my present living expenses?
- What is my present income?
- When does the cash come and go?
- What is my vision?
- What experience do I have?
- What am I good at?
- What is the best business for me?
- What business structure is right for me?
- What effect will my business have on my income and expenses?
- Summing it up
- Where can I get money to start my business?
- Checking out the sources
- Is a franchise the right kind of business for me?
- What am I getting for my money?
- Should I buy this business?
- What are the legal requirements of running my business at home?
- What effect will my business have on my home and life?
- What could I sell?
- To whom could I sell?

- Who are my competitors?
- What are my competitors' strengths and weaknesses?
- What are the strengths and weaknesses of my business?
- How do I market my product or service?
- How will I persuade people to buy from me?
- What would a computer do for me?
- Do I need to hire staff?
- How do I decide what kind of staff I need?
- How do I write a job description?
- How do I choose the best applicant?
- How well am I doing?

Online Resources

- Incorporating in Canada
- Websites of organizations mentioned in the book
- Calculating the break-even point
- Links to free, open-source software

Your Business Plan

- Calculating your market position
- Financial spreadsheets, including a balance sheet, income statement, and cash flow forecast
- Environmental issues associated with your business